THE
CIVIL RIGHTS
MOVEMENT

THE
CIVIL RIGHTS
MOVEMENT

Peter B. Levy

Greenwood Press Guides to
Historic Events of the Twentieth Century
Randall M. Miller, Series Editor

Greenwood Press
Westport, Connecticut • London

323
Lev

Library of Congress Cataloging-in-Publication Data

Levy, Peter B.
    The civil rights movement / Peter B. Levy.
       p. cm.—(Greenwood Press guides to historic events of
  the twentieth century, ISSN 1092-177X)
    Includes bibliographical references and index.
    ISBN 0–313–29854–8 (alk. paper)
    1. Civil rights movements—United States—History—20th century.
 2. Afro-Americans—Civil rights—History—20th century. 3. Civil
 rights movements—United States—History—20th century—Sources.
 4. Afro-Americans—Civil rights—History—20th century—Sources.
 5. Civil rights workers—United States—Biography. 6. United
 States—Race relations. I. Title. II. Series.
 E185.61.L519 1998
 323′.0973—dc21   97–22553   *12801*

British Library Cataloguing in Publication Data is available.

Copyright © 1998 by Peter B. Levy

Library of Congress Catalog Card Number: 97–22553
ISBN: 0–313–29854–8
ISSN: 1092–177X

First published in 1998

Greenwood Press, 88 Post Road West, Westport, CT 06881
An imprint of Greenwood Publishing Group, Inc.

Printed in the United States of America

The paper used in this book complies with the
Permanent Paper Standard issued by the National
Information Standards Organization (Z39.48–1984).

10 9 8 7 6 5 4 3

Front cover photo: Rev. Martin Luther King, Jr. shown waving to participants
in the March on Washington. UPI/CORBIS-BETTMANN.

Back cover photo: Martin Luther King, Jr. at March on Washington, 1963. National Archives.

Contents

A photo essay follows page 78

Series Foreword

As the twenty-first century approaches, it is time to take stock of the political, social, economic, intellectual, and cultural forces and factors that have made the twentieth century the most dramatic period of change in history. To that end, the Greenwood Press Guides to Historic Events of the Twentieth Century presents interpretive histories of the most significant events of the century. Each book in the series combines narrative history and analysis with primary documents and biographical sketches, with an eye to providing both a reference guide to the principal persons, ideas, and experiences defining each historic event, and a reliable, readable overview of that event. Each book further provides analyses and discussions, grounded in both primary and secondary sources, of the causes and consequences, in thought and action, that give meaning to the historic event under review. By assuming a historical perspective, drawing on the latest and best writing on each subject, and offering fresh insights, each book promises to explain how and why a particular event defined the twentieth century. No consensus about the meaning of the twentieth century emerges from the series, but, collectively, the books identify the most salient concerns of the century. In so doing, the series reminds us of the many ways those historic events continue to affect our lives.

Each book follows a similar format designed to encourage readers to consult it both as a reference and a history in its own right. Each volume opens with a chronology of the historic event, followed by a narrative overview, which also serves to introduce and examine briefly the main themes and issues related to that event. The next set of chapters is composed of topical essays, each analyzing closely an issue or problem of interpretation introduced in the opening chapter. A concluding chapter suggesting the long-term implications and meanings of the historic event brings the strands of the preceding chapters together while placing the event in the larger historical context. Each book also includes a section of short biographies of the principal persons related to the event, followed by a section introducing and reprinting key historical documents illustrative of and pertinent to the event. A glossary of selected terms adds to the utility of each book. An annotated bibliography—of significant books, films, and CD-ROMs—and an index conclude each volume.

The editors made no attempt to impose any theoretical model or historical perspective on the individual authors. Rather, in developing the series, an advisory board of noted historians and informed high school history teachers and public and school librarians identified the topics needful of exploration and the scholars eminently qualified to examine those events with intelligence and sensitivity. The common commitment throughout the series is to provide accurate, informative, and readable books, free of jargon and up to date in evidence and analysis.

Each book stands as a complete historical analysis and reference guide to a particular historic event. Each book also has many uses, from understanding contemporary perspectives on critical historical issues, to providing biographical treatments of key figures related to each event, to offering excerpts and complete texts of essential documents about the event, to suggesting and describing books and media materials for further study and presentation of the event, and more. The combination of historical narrative and individual topical chapters addressing significant issues and problems encourages students and teachers to approach each historic event from multiple perspectives and with a critical eye. The arrangement and content of each book thus invite students and teachers, through classroom discussions and position papers, to debate the character and significance of great historic events and to discover for themselves how and why history matters.

The series emphasizes the main currents that have shaped the modern world. Much of that focus necessarily looks at the West, especially Europe and the United States. The political, commercial, and cultural expansion of the West wrought largely, though not wholly, the most fundamental changes of the century. Taken together, however, books in the series reveal the interactions between Western and non-Western peoples and society, and also the tensions between modern and traditional cultures. They also point to the ways in which non-Western peoples have adapted Western ideas and technology and, in turn, influenced Western life and thought. Several books examine such increasingly powerful global forces as the rise of Islamic fundamentalism, the emergence of modern Japan, the Communist revolution in China, and the collapse of communism in eastern Europe and the former Soviet Union. American interests and experiences receive special attention in the series, not only in deference to the primary readership of the books but also in recognition that the United States emerged as the dominant political, economic, social, and cultural force during the twentieth century. By looking at the century through the lens of American events and experiences, it is possible to see why the age has come to be known as "The American Century."

Assessing the history of the twentieth century is a formidable prospect. It has been a period of remarkable transformation. The world broadened and narrowed at the same time. Frontiers shifted from the interiors of Africa and Latin America to the moon and beyond; communication spread from mass circulation newspapers and magazines to radio, television, and now the Internet; skyscrapers reached upward and suburbs stretched outward; energy switched from steam, to electric, to atomic power. Many changes did not lead to a complete abandonment of established patterns and practices so much as a synthesis of old and new, as, for example, the increased use of (even reliance on) the telephone in the age of the computer. The automobile and the truck, the airplane, and telecommunications closed distances, and people in unprecedented numbers migrated from rural to urban, industrial, and ever more ethnically diverse areas. Tractors and chemical fertilizers made it possible for fewer people to grow more, but the environmental and demographic costs of an exploding global population threatened to outstrip natural resources and human innovation. Disparities in wealth increased, with developed nations prospering and underdeveloped nations starving. Amid the crumbling of former European colonial empires, Western technology, goods, and culture increasingly enveloped the globe, seeping into, and undermining, non-Western cultures—a process that contributed to a surge of religious fundamentalism and ethno-nationalism in the Middle East, Asia, and Africa. As people became more alike, they also became more aware of their differences. Ethnic and religious rivalries grew in intensity everywhere as the century closed.

The political changes during the twentieth century have been no less profound than the social, economic, and cultural ones. Many of the books in the series focus on political events, broadly defined, but no books are confined to politics alone. Political ideas and events have social effects, just as they spring from a complex interplay of non-political forces in culture, society, and economy. Thus, for example, the modern civil rights and women's rights movements were at once social and political events in cause and consequence.

Likewise, the Cold War created the geopolitical framework for dealing with competing ideologies and nations abroad and served as the touchstone for political and cultural identities at home. The books treating political events do so within their social, cultural, and economic contexts.

Several books in the series examine particular wars in depth. Wars are defining moments for people and eras. During the twentieth century war became more widespread and terrible than ever before, encouraging new efforts to end war through strategies and organizations of international cooperation and disarmament while also fueling new ideologies and instruments of mass persuasion that fostered distrust and festered old national rivalries. Two world wars during the century redrew the political map, slaughtered or uprooted two generations of people, and introduced and hastened the development of new technologies and weapons of mass destruction. The First World War spelled the end of the old European order and spurred communist revolution in Russia and fascism in Italy, Germany, and elsewhere. The Second World War killed fascism and inspired the final push for freedom from European colonial rule in Asia and Africa. It also led to the Cold War that suffocated much of the world for almost half a century. Large wars begat small ones, and brutal totalitarian regimes cropped up across the globe. After (and in some ways because of) the fall of communism in eastern Europe and the former Soviet Union, wars of competing cultures, national interests, and political systems persisted in the struggle to make a new world order. Continuing, too, has been the belief that military technology can achieve political ends, whether in the superior American firepower that failed to "win" in Vietnam or in the American "smart bombs" and other military wizardry that "won" in the Persian Gulf.

Another theme evident in the series is that throughout the century nationalism has continued to drive events. Whether in the Balkans in 1914 triggering World War I or in the Balkans in the 1990s threatening the post–Cold War peace—or in many other places—nationalist ambitions and forces would not die. The persistence of nationalism is yet another reminder of the many ways that the past becomes prologue.

We thus offer the series as a modern guide to and interpretation of the historic events of the twentieth century and as an invitation to consider how and why those events have defined not only the past and present but also charted the political, social, intellectual, cultural, and economic routes into the next century.

Randall M. Miller
Saint Joseph's University, Philadelphia

Preface

The twentieth century has witnessed numerous historic events, from the Russian and Chinese revolutions to World War I and World War II. These wars and revolutions, along with the space program, the collapse of communism, and the Holocaust, have had a dramatic impact on the historical terrain. Likewise, the modern civil rights movement has been one of the century's historic events. Emerging in the 1950s and reaching a peak in the 1960s, the civil rights movement prompted the federal government to enact sweeping reforms that toppled Jim Crow, virtually eliminated public assertions of white supremacy, a mainstay of the American cultural and intellectual tradition, and boosted black pride. In addition to altering race relations in the United States, especially in the South, the civil rights movement sparked other liberation struggles in America and abroad, from the women's liberation movement to the drive to overcome apartheid in South Africa. Indeed, even though the civil rights movement did not achieve all of its goals, nearly a half-century after Rosa Parks refused to give up her seat on a segregated bus in Montgomery, Alabama, it continues to have an impact on the course of history, serving as an agent and as a model of the quest for human rights.

While many fine works on the civil rights movement already have been written, ranging from two voluminous Pulitzer Prize–winning biographies of Martin Luther King, Jr. (one of which covers only up to 1963), to award-winning examinations of the Student Nonviolent Coordinating Committee and the movement in Mississippi, readers seeking a concise work that combines description, analysis, and primary sources are at a loss. By presenting analytical chapters on specific aspects of the movement, brief biographies of key figures, and selections of seminal documents, this book aims to fill this void. It seeks to reach the general audience and the budding specialist, to meet the needs of both students involved in researching specific aspects of the movement and those seeking an overview of the period.

The book opens with a succinct but comprehensive overview of the modern civil rights movement. Chapter 1 examines the status of African Americans on the eve of the movement and discusses the most important struggles for freedom, from the Montgomery bus boycott and the Little Rock, Arkansas, school crisis, to the sit-ins, freedom rides, and protests across the South. Chapters 2 through 6 focus on specific aspects of the movement. "Freedom's Coming and It Won't Be Long" analyzes the origins of the modern civil rights movement. "Is This America?" focuses on the movement in Mississippi. "With All Deliberate Speed" discusses the fight for legal equality that took place over the course of a century in the courts, Congress, and the White House. "Sisterhood Is Powerful" examines the often underappreciated role that women played in the struggle for racial equality. "A Second Redemption?" considers the impact and legacy of the movement.

Also included are a chronology of important events, brief biographies of twenty civil rights activists, fifteen seminal documents, ranging from the *Brown* v. *Board of Education* decision to Martin Luther King's "I Have a Dream" speech, and a glossary of key terms. The book concludes with an annotated bibliography and a general subject index.

Acknowledgments

I owe a tremendous debt to numerous individuals who assisted me in making this a much better book. Foremost, let me thank Randall Miller, the series editor. Put simply, all writers should be so lucky to work with an editor as helpful and constructive as Randall. Second, let me thank the editors at Greenwood Press, Barbara Rader, Maureen Melino, Barbara Goodhouse, and Liz Leiba, who helped me with everything from obtaining proper permissions to republish material to catching careless grammatical errors. Third, let me express gratitude to my students at York College, especially to those in my History of the Civil Rights Movement class, who read and commented on drafts of several chapters of this book. Along the same lines, I owe special thanks to Eric Roth, Adam Doutrich, and Cathy Holt, who served as research assistants for me at various stages of my work. My colleagues in the Department of History and Political Science, especially my chairperson Phil Avillo, and my department secretary, Rosemary Wivagg, provided continual support and important distractions. My Dean at York College, Jean Wyld, the Faculty Enhancement Committee, and Research and Publication Committee granted me the funds and the time that made it possible to complete this book and I thank them for both. I have received invaluable assistance from too many librarians, archivists, work study students, and friends to name, but I thank them all nonetheless. Last, let me express my greatest gratitude to my family, my wife, Diane Krejsa, and my two children, Jessica and Brian, for making what I do possible and worthwhile.

Chronology of Events

1857	*Dred Scott* v. *Sandford*
1863	Emancipation Proclamation goes into force
1865	Thirteenth Amendment ratified
1866	Congress passes the Civil Rights Act
1868	Fourteenth Amendment ratified
1870	Fifteenth Amendment ratified
1873	*Slaughterhouse* cases undermine Civil Rights Act of 1866
1875	Congress passes Civil Rights Act of 1875
1877	Compromise of 1877; end of Reconstruction
1883	Supreme Court further narrows reach of acts of Reconstruction
1895	Booker T. Washington gives Atlanta Compromise speech
1896	*Plessy* v. *Ferguson*
1896	National Association of Colored Women organized
1905	W.E.B. Du Bois publishes *Souls of Black Folk*
1909	National Association for the Advancement of Colored People (NAACP) established
1911	National Urban League founded

1919	Race riots erupt in Chicago and East St. Louis
1920	Marcus Garvey establishes United Negro Improvement Association
1920s	Harlem Renaissance
1936	Jesse Owens wins Olympic gold medals in Berlin
1938	Joe Louis crowned heavyweight champion of the world
1938	*Missouri ex rel. Gaines* v. *Canada*
1941	A. Philip Randolph organizes March on Washington Movement; President Franklin D. Roosevelt desegregates defense industries
1942	Congress of Racial Equality (CORE) founded
1943	Massive race riot in Detroit, Michigan

1946

| December 5 | President Truman appoints Committee on Civil Rights |

1947

April 9	CORE initiates Journey of Reconciliation
April 10	Jackie Robinson breaks color line in major league baseball
October 29	Committee on Civil Rights issues report, *To Secure These Rights*

1948

| July 26 | President Truman orders desegregation of military |

1950

| June 5 | United States Supreme Court hands down series of victories for NAACP in *Sweatt* v. *Painter*, *McLaurin* v. *Oklahoma State Regents*, and *Henderson* v. *United States* |

1954

| May 17 | Supreme Court rules segregation in public education unconstitutional in *Brown* v. *Board of Education of Topeka, Kansas* |
| July 11 | First White Citizens' Council formed in Indianola, Mississippi |

1955

May 31	Supreme Court issues *Brown II* (Enforcement Decree)
August 28	Emmett Till murdered in Money, Mississippi
December 1	Rosa Parks arrested, sparking Montgomery bus boycott

1956

March 12	Southern congressmen and senators release "Southern Manifesto"
December 21	Blacks ride desegregated buses in Montgomery, Alabama

1957

January 10	Southern Christian Leadership Conference (SCLC) organized
May 17	25,000 join Prayer Pilgrimage in Washington, D.C.
August 29	Congress passes Civil Rights Act of 1957
September 25	President Dwight Eisenhower sends federal troops to Little Rock, Arkansas, to resolve school crisis

1960

February 1	First sit-ins take place in Greensboro, North Carolina; sit-ins spread across the South
February 27	Nashville student movement begins
April 15	Student Nonviolent Coordinating Committee (SNCC) formed
October 19	Martin Luther King, Jr., arrested during sit-ins in Atlanta, Georgia

1961

May 4	Freedom rides begin in Washington, D.C.
May 14	Freedom riders attacked outside Anniston and in Birmingham, Alabama
July	Robert Moses establishes voter education drive in McComb, Mississippi
December 11–14	SNCC initiates campaign in Albany, Georgia; joined by Martin Luther King, Jr.

1962

| September 30–October 1 | Riots erupt at University of Mississippi aimed at preventing James Meredith from enrolling at Ole Miss |

1963

April–May	SCLC organizes protests in Birmingham, Alabama
March–June	Protests sweep across the South, from St. Augustine, Florida, to Cambridge, Maryland
June 11	Governor George Wallace attempts to block integration of University of Alabama
June 11	President Kennedy delivers major address on civil rights
June 11	Medgar Evers assassinated in Jackson, Mississippi
August 28	200,000–250,000 participate in March on Washington; King delivers "I Have a Dream" address
September 15	Sixteenth Street Baptist Church, Birmingham, Alabama, bombed; four young girls killed
November 22	President John F. Kennedy assassinated

1964

March 12	Malcolm X leaves Nation of Islam, establishes Organization of Afro-American Unity
June–August	Mississippi or Freedom Summer
June 21	Michael Schwerner, James Chaney, and Andrew Goodman disappear in Mississippi; later found dead
July–August	Riots in Harlem and Rochester, New York
July 2	Congress passes Civil Rights Act of 1964
August	MFDP challenge rebuffed at Democratic national convention, Atlantic City, New Jersey
December 10	Martin Luther King, Jr., awarded Nobel Peace Prize

1965

| January 18 | SCLC initiates demonstrations in Selma, Alabama |
| February 21 | Malcolm X assassinated |

March 7	"Bloody Sunday," state troopers beat demonstrators as they attempt to cross Edmund Pettus Bridge, Selma, Alabama
March 9	King turns back second march in Selma; James Reeb murdered
March 15	President Lyndon Johnson delivers major address on voting rights
March 21–25	Civil rights activists march from Selma to Montgomery, Alabama
August 6	President Johnson signs Voting Rights Act of 1965
August 11–16	Rioting erupts in Watts, Los Angeles

1966

January 6	SNCC publicly condemns Vietnam War
January 22	Martin Luther King, Jr., initiates antipoverty campaign in Chicago
June 6–26	James Meredith shot during his March Against Fear; SNCC leader Stokely Carmichael coins slogan "Black Power"
July 12–15	Chicago shaken by race riots
August 5	King begins open housing marches in Chicago
October	Black Panther Party for Self-Defense (BPP) founded in Oakland, California

1967

April 28	Muhammad Ali stripped of his heavyweight boxing crown for refusing to be inducted into the army
June 12	In *Loving* v. *Virginia* Supreme Court rules that laws banning interracial marriage are unconstitutional
July 12–30	Worst wave of urban rioting in American history, beginning in Newark, New Jersey, and culminating in Detroit, Michigan
July 20	Black Power Conference held in Newark, New Jersey
August 25	FBI Director J. Edgar Hoover expands COINTELPRO program

September 1   Thurgood Marshall sworn in as first black Supreme Court
                     justice

1968

February 29   National Advisory Commission on Civil Disorders
                     (Kerner Commission) releases report

April 4   Martin Luther King, Jr., assassinated in Memphis,
                     Tennessee; race riots erupt across the nation

February–May   Black students protest at Columbia and Howard
                     universities

April 11   President Johnson signs Open (Fair) Housing Act

April–May   Ralph Abernathy leads Poor People's Campaign in
                     Washington, D.C.

1969

April–May   Black students protest at Cornell, North Carolina A & T,
                     and elsewhere

June 27   Nixon administration issues Philadelphia Plan

December 4   Black Panther leader Fred Hampton shot to death by
                     police in Chicago

1970

May 14   Two black students killed by police at Jackson State
                     University, Mississippi

1971

April 20   In *Swann* v. *Charlotte-Mecklenburg Board of Education*,
                     Supreme Court upholds constitutionality of busing

May 2   In *Griggs* v. *Duke Power Co.*, Supreme Court rules that
                     employment practices having discriminatory impact are
                     illegal

September 9–13   Hostage-taking at Attica Prison in New York culminates
                     in crackdown on black prisoners

1972

March   National Black Political (Power) Convention held in
                     Gary, Indiana

March 16	President Nixon calls for a moratorium on court-ordered busing

1974

December 11	Violent clashes over busing take place in South Boston, Massachusetts

1978

June 28	In *University of California Regents* v. *Bakke*, Supreme Court upholds affirmative action in principle, but rules against the program in place at the university's Davis campus

1979

June 24	Supreme Court upholds affirmative action in *United Steelworkers of America* v. *Weber*

1981

May 23	Attorney General William French Smith announces federal government's opposition to racial quotas and busing

1983

April 13	Harold Washington elected as first black mayor of Chicago
October 20	President Reagan signs bill making Martin Luther King, Jr.'s birthday a national holiday

1986

February 21	Killing of black man by white youths in Howard Beach neighborhood of New York City sets off unrest and national debate on race
July 2	In *Local 93 International Association of Firefighters AFL-CIO* v. *Cleveland*, Supreme Court upholds voluntary affirmative action plan

1989

January 16	Riots erupt in Overton section of Miami, Florida
January 23	In *City of Richmond* v. *J. R. Croson Co.*, Supreme Court disallows "set-aside" plan

June 5   In *Wards Cove Packing Co.* v. *Antonio*, Supreme Court narrows reach of affirmative action

June 26   President Bush signs Americans with Disabilities Act

October 22   President Bush vetoes Civil Rights Act, calling it a "quota bill"

1991

October 6–15   Confirmation hearings for Supreme Court nominee Clarence Thomas capture the nation's attention when Anita Hill accuses Thomas of sexual harassment; Thomas narrowly confirmed

November 21   President Bush signs modified civil rights bill

1992

April 29   Riots erupt in south-central Los Angeles

1994

February 2   Byron de la Beckwith convicted of the murder of Medgar Evers

June 20   O. J. Simpson, former football star, arrested for murdering his wife, Nicole Simpson, and her friend, Ronald Goldman, setting in motion "trial of the century"

1995

June 12   In *Adarand Constructors* v. *Peña*, Supreme Court further narrows affirmative action

June 29   In *Ruth O. Shaw* v. *Janet Reno*, Supreme Court rules against using race as the predominant factor in drawing election districts

October 10   Nation of Islam leader Louis Farrakhan organizes "Million Man March"

1996

June 13   Supreme Court invalidates four minority-majority congressional districts, two in North Carolina and two in Texas

November 5   California voters pass Proposition 209, barring affirmative action in public hiring, contracting, and college admissions

THE CIVIL RIGHTS MOVEMENT EXPLAINED

I

The Modern Civil Rights Movement: An Overview

THE DUSK BEFORE THE DAWN

Throughout the 1936 Summer Olympics, Nazi führer Adolf Hitler cast a watchful eye, hoping that the competition held in Berlin, Germany's capital, would lend prestige and legitimacy to the Third Reich and his philosophy of Aryan supremacy. German athletes performed admirably; yet, much to Hitler's dismay, the games belonged to Jesse Owens, an African American track and field star from Oakville, Alabama, who ran and jumped to four gold medals, three individual and one team. Two years later, Joe Louis, another Alabama native, the first African American heavyweight champion since Jack Johnson, successfully defended his title by knocking out Max Schmelling, a German, in the first round of a scheduled ten-round bout before a capacity crowd at Yankee Stadium in New York City. In both cases, white Americans cheered on the victors, suggesting that at least in the international sports arena color mattered less than nationality. African Americans, however, cheered even louder. For them, Owens and Louis were more than champion athletes; they stood as symbols of the cause of racial equality. As the Reverend Jesse Louis Jackson, onetime presidential candidate and protégé of Martin Luther King, Jr., stated in his eulogy for Louis in Las Vegas on April 17, 1981, "With Joe Louis we had made it from the guttermost to the uttermost, from slave ship to championship. . . . He was the answer to the sincere prayers of the disinherited and the dispossessed. Joe made everybody somebody. . . . Something on the inside said we ought to be free; something on the outside said we can be free."[1]

The accomplishments of Louis and Owens notwithstanding, at mid-century African Americans, or "colored people" as they were then called, still constituted a separate caste and class in the United States. As late as 1940, three-fourths of the African American population resided in the South, disproportionately in rural, economically marginal areas. In the work force they occupied the bottom rungs of the ladder. Nationwide, blacks earned less, had higher rates of poverty, and by all objective measurements suffered from a far worse standard of living than whites. In political life, they had been disenfranchised or, in instances where they enjoyed the vote, remained vastly underrepresented. In society, they were separated from whites through de jure segregation in the South and through semi-explicit codes of behavior and racial covenants in the North. (See Table 1.1.)

Table 1.1
Social and Economic Status of African Americans on the Eve of World War II

	Whites	**Blacks**
Population (Total in 1,000s)	118,000	11,700
Population by Residence:		
Urban (in 1,000s)	68,000	5,200
Rural (in 1,000s)	50,000	6,500
Median Family Income	$1,325	$489
Median School Years for Persons 25 Yrs. and Older:		
Male	8.4	5.4
Female	8.7	6.1
Illiteracy Rate for Persons 14 Yrs. and Older	2.0%	11.5%
Life Expectancy (Years)	64.2	53.1
Infant Mortality Rate per 1,000 Live Births	43.2	73.8
% of Households in Living Units Lacking Some or All Plumbing	41.0	79.5
Rate of Home Ownership	47.0%	23.5%

Sources: Historical Statistics of the United States (1976); Statistical Abstract of the United States (1950).

While African Americans who migrated north found greater political, social, and economic opportunities than they had in the South, the North did not fulfill its potential as a "promised land." Blacks remained the last hired and first fired, disproportionately relegated to low-skilled and poorly paying jobs. Jackie Robinson's breaking of the color line in major league baseball proved the exception, not the rule, as most blacks found blatant barriers to entry in numerous segments of the labor market. Residential segregation prevailed, confining blacks to poor neighborhoods, and since schools were located in the neighborhood in which one lived, African American migrants had less of a chance to move up the economic and social ladder than their white counterparts. When African Americans pushed the limits of this informal system of apartheid, seeking housing in all-white neighborhoods, they were physically turned out. In Detroit, in 1943, for example, conflicts over housing climaxed in one of the worst race riots in American history. By the time the riots subsided, seventeen blacks lay dead—no whites were killed—and the federal government had reneged on an agreement to allow African Americans to move into the Sojourner Truth Homes, a new federal public housing project in a Polish American section of the city. Similarly, in the immediate post–World War II years, blacks in Chicago found themselves routed out of all-white neighborhoods and relegated to overcrowded and underserviced slums.

Despite such violence, the great migration of African Americans from the rural South to the urban North continued apace, because the situation in the South remained even worse. In early February 1946, Isaac Woodward, of Aiken, South Carolina, was fatally beaten by a white policeman only hours after he was honorably discharged from the military. Woodward had spent over fourteen months in the Philippines fighting the Japanese and was wearing his uniform when he was assaulted. The policeman who killed Woodward was acquitted of all charges against him. Less than two weeks after Woodward's murder, following an altercation in Columbia, Tennessee, between a white radio repairman and a black female customer and her son who came to her defense, whites went on a rampage against blacks, who did their best to defend themselves. Even though whites precipitated the violence, the police arrested seventy blacks, charging over twenty of them with capital crimes. Two black prisoners died in police custody. On July 25, 1946, Roger Malcolm was lynched near Monroe, Georgia, by members of the local Ku Klux Klan who feared that black World War II veterans "were getting out of their place." Nearby, four white men lynched Macio Snipes, the only black man who dared vote in his district.

Protests by the National Association for the Advancement of Colored People (NAACP) about these atrocities prodded President Harry Truman to form a special Committee on Civil Rights. While the committee was preparing its report, the Congress of Racial Equality (CORE) staged a Journey of Reconciliation in several upper South states. Like the better-known freedom rides of the early 1960s, which CORE also organized, the Journey of Reconciliation sought to desegregate public facilities and raise public awareness of the racial problem in America. Perhaps because of its concern about the harm that lynchings in the South were doing to America's reputation in the international arena, in 1947 the Committee on Civil Rights issued a surprisingly strong pro–civil rights report, entitled *To Secure These Rights*. Among the rights the committee argued needed to be addressed were the right to vote, the ability to serve in a nonsegregated military, and the opportunity to be treated equally in the fields of education and employment.

Nonetheless, very little changed for blacks in the South. None of the reforms endorsed by the committee or by the Democratic Party in 1948 made headway in Congress. Indeed, Truman's push for civil rights split his party, as southern "Dixiecrats" bolted from the Democrats in 1948 to support their own presidential candidate. Even though Truman won in 1948, the threat of political disunion over civil rights discouraged bold actions by presidents or Congress for about fifteen years. Not until 1964 did the federal government enact significant civil rights legislation. On the contrary, in the wake of the lynching of black World War II veterans, Congress killed the only major racial reform of the war years, the Fair Employment Practice Committee, which had been established to oversee the desegregation of the defense industry.

Moreover, in the decade after the end of World War II, the fear of communism, abroad and at home, made it next to impossible to enact new reforms and led to the rolling back of reforms passed while Franklin Roosevelt occupied the White House. Several well-known black spokespersons, from Paul Robeson to W.E.B. Du Bois, were hounded by anticommunist politicians and forsaken by moderate civil rights groups like the NAACP, which sought (largely unsuccessfully) to avoid the wrath of Senator Joe McCarthy of Wisconsin and other purveyors of the "red scare." White and interracial allies of the burgeoning civil rights movement, from the Southern Conference of Human Welfare, founded in 1938 by several southern moderates with the support of First Lady Eleanor Roosevelt, to the Civil Rights Congress, were red-baited out of existence or reduced to irrelevancy. As a result, even before the 1954 *Brown* decision by the Supreme Court, which unleashed a massive wave of resistance to desegregation, the voice of moderation in the South, which favored gradual racial reform, lay near extinction. True, some southern white moderates, most notably Lillian Smith, Hodding Carter, Ralph McGill, and Harry Ashmore, continued to brave the current of repression, speaking in favor of racial reforms, but to little avail.

Meanwhile, millions of African Americans continued to languish in poverty as the nation celebrated its affluence. At a time when the government was developing numerous programs that benefitted the predominantly white middle class (from tax deductions for home owners to massive spending on superhighways), blacks, who were trapped in segments of the economy that were rapidly shedding surplus workers, lacked the political and economic power to demand federal help. The only significant racial reform enacted by the federal government in the decade after the end of World War II was the desegregation of the armed forces, ordered by President Truman in 1948. To some blacks, even this represented a Pyrrhic victory. To wit, if a black leader dared declare that African Americans would or should not "go to war on behalf of those who have oppressed us for generations," as Paul Robeson did in 1949, they were branded as traitors, attacked by mobs, and told to get out of America. As Congressman John Rankin of Mississippi put it from the floor of the House of Representatives, "If that N—— Robeson does not like this country, let him go to Russia." (House Speaker Sam Rayburn, Lyndon Johnson's mentor, defended Rankin's use of the word "nigger.") Meanwhile, many blacks who enlisted in the military encountered blatant discrimination while in the service and then, after risking their lives for the preservation of the free world, returned to a society that continued to deem them second-class citizens.[2]

THE *BROWN* DECISION AND SOUTHERN RESISTANCE

Only in the federal courts did the future look better, as NAACP lawyers, led by Thurgood Marshall, whittled away at Jim Crow. The NAACP looked to the federal courts for relief because local and state courts as well as local and state legislative and executive bodies in the South remained closed to them. In the late 1940s and early 1950s, the NAACP filed a series of federal lawsuits against segregation, which culminated with the momentous Supreme Court decision in the case of *Brown* v. *Board of Education*. In these suits the NAACP aimed not simply at showing that southern and border states had not lived up to the legal standard of providing "separate but equal" facilities but that the 1896 *Plessy* v. *Ferguson* decision, which had set this legal standard in the first place, was unconstitutional.

The Supreme Court first heard oral arguments in *Brown* in December 1952. The death of Chief Justice Fred Vinson and the Court's call for more information on the intent of the framers of the Fourteenth Amendment, however, delayed its decision. Finally, on May 17, 1954, the Supreme Court ruled 9–0 that "separate educational facilities are inherently unequal," with Chief Justice Earl Warren's opinion making it clear that *Plessy* v. *Ferguson* (1896), the case that had upheld segregation, had been overturned.

Not surprisingly, the NAACP and many others celebrated the Court's ruling. Thurgood Marshall and NAACP president Roy Wilkins wrote that "compliance without legal action will be the rule," and that the NAACP "looked confidently to the future." The *Washington Post* predicted "a new birth of freedom." Even more glowingly, the Cincinnati *Enquirer* claimed that the justices had "acted as a conscience of the American nation," that the days of stepping on the black man had come to an end.[3] Yet, while *Brown* stood as a key moment in the history of the civil rights movement, putting the law of the land on the side of those who sought to eradicate racial inequality, the decision signaled only the beginning of the modern civil rights movement, not its culmination. It gave blacks new hope, setting much of the agenda for the following years. It did not end Jim Crow. Nor did it touch upon the problem of de facto segregation or economic inequality.

Somewhat lost in the celebration over *Brown* was the fact that the Court delayed issuing a remedy or plan for desegregating public schools. On May 31, 1955, in *Brown II*, the Court called for desegregation to take place "with all deliberate speed"; it also ordered lower federal courts to oversee this process. Warren felt that this deliberate response, coupled with the Court's unanimous verdict, would guarantee compliance. Much to his chagrin, it did not, to a large extent because state and local authorities remained dead set against desegregation. Indeed, those with political aspirations in the South often stood in the forefront of the battle to maintain the southern way of life, championing the strategy of massive resistance to desegregation as the most effective means for getting around *Brown*.

Even before the Supreme Court issued *Brown II*, whites in Mississippi had formed the White Citizens' Councils. The councils quickly enlisted hundreds of thousands of members determined to maintain Jim Crow. As one pamphlet put it, "The Citizens' Council is the South's answer to the mongrelizers. *We will not be integrated!* . . . The white people of the South will again stand fast and preserve an unsullied race as our forefathers did eighty years ago. We will not be integrated, either suddenly or gradually."[4]

The Ku Klux Klan (KKK) enjoyed a revival as well, ironically lending legitimacy to the Citizens' Councils, which, at least officially, foreswore vigilantism. Further proof of the South's commitment to maintaining Jim Crow came with the publication of "The Southern Manifesto." Signed by nineteen Senators and one hundred congressman from eleven states of the old Confederacy, the "Manifesto" termed the *Brown* decision an "abuse of judicial power," contrary to the words of the Constitution, and endorsed resistance to its implementation by "any lawful means."

THE MONTGOMERY BUS BOYCOTT

On December 1, 1955, after a day's work at the Montgomery Fair department store, Rosa Parks, a middle-aged black seamstress, boarded a Montgomery, Alabama, bus to take her home. Several stops later, the bus driver requested that she give up her seat to a white passenger. Montgomery law required black passengers to occupy seats in the back of the bus and to cede an entire row of seats to whites once a white person occupied a seat in a given row. When Parks refused to comply with the law, the bus driver informed her that he was going to have to call the police. Still Parks refused to comply. Parks recalled: "They [two policemen] asked if the driver had asked me to stand up, and I said yes, and they wanted to know why I didn't. I told them I didn't think I should have to stand up. After I had paid my fare and occupied a seat, I didn't think I should have to give it up."5

Rosa Parks's action was to the civil rights movement what the Battle of Lexington and Concord was to the American Revolution: a shot—in this case a nonviolent one—heard round the world. It set in motion a series of acts of defiance aimed at gaining full equality that grew in intensity over the course of the next ten to fifteen years. After being booked, Parks called E. D. Nixon, an officer with the all-black Brotherhood of Sleeping Car Porters and local head of the NAACP, with whom she had worked. Nixon, who had fought for years for gradual racial reforms, quickly bailed Parks out of jail. He also asked her if he could use her arrest as an opportunity to mount a broader challenge against segregation, in particular by calling for a one-day bus boycott. Parks gave her permission, and over the course of a few days a core of activists mobilized the black community behind the idea.

On the day of the boycott, Nixon asked Dr. Martin Luther King, Jr., to present the keynote address at the mass meeting of the Montgomery Improvement Association (MIA), the name given to the body officially in charge of the protest. Up until this point in his life, King, the son of a prominent Atlanta minister and a newcomer to Montgomery, had displayed little inclination toward political activism. King had many reasons not to accept Nixon's offer, especially his responsibilities to his congregation and to his young wife, Coretta, who had recently given birth to their first child. Nonetheless, he accepted Nixon's invitation.

Speaking before an overflow audience at the Holt Street Baptist Church, which, like many other black churches, especially in the South, played an instrumental role in the civil rights movement, both as a site and source of leadership and mass participation, King delivered one of the most memorable and moving orations of his life. In a sense, King had been preparing himself for this moment all his life. His training as a preacher, particularly as a preacher within the African American community, heightened his appreciation for and mastery of the spoken word. His message that night and thereafter was rooted in his Christian faith, which had been nurtured since his birth by his parents and grandparents and by his formal education.

After reviewing the long history of abuses that African Americans had suffered, King declared, "We . . . are tired—tired of being segregated and humiliated; tired of being kicked about by the brutal feet of oppression." Black Montgomerians, King added, had no alternative "but to protest." Warming to the audience, King contrasted the actions of the boycotters to those of the Citizens' Councils and the KKK. The latter organizations, King said, "are protesting for the perpetuation of injustice . . . we are protesting for the birth of justice. . . . Their methods lead to violence and lawlessness. . . . our actions must be guided by the deepest principles of our Christian faith." In the future, King prophetically concluded, "when the history books are written . . . the historians will have to pause and say, 'There lived a great people—black people—who injected new meaning and dignity into the veins of civilization.' "[6]

With King as their leader, the black community in Montgomery extended their one-day boycott into a one-week, then a one-month, and eventually a one-year protest. Initially, the MIA demanded only a more humane form of segregation. Ultimately, with the help of a Supreme Court decision that invalidated Montgomery's segregationist bus ordinance, they won much more. They did so in spite of arrests, bomb threats, KKK marches and cross burnings, and the everyday difficulties of getting to work. In addition to desegregating the buses, black Montgomerians gained a much fuller appreciation of themselves as first-class citizens, uncovered a strategy for further protests, and, in King, introduced the world to an extraordinary leader. The Montgomery bus boycott also captured the attention of the national news media, which presented sympathetic coverage of King and the protest. To a degree, civil rights activists learned from this experience how to use the media effectively to gain attention across America and around the globe. In contrast, southern whites were much slower in learning how to couch their opposition to racial reforms in ways that played well on the nightly news.

THE LITTLE ROCK SCHOOL CRISIS

Not all southern communities put forth as united a defense of Jim Crow as Montgomery. By the mid-1950s, Little Rock, Arkansas, had desegregated its buses, libraries, and public parks. One-third of all eligible blacks in the community were registered to vote. A few blacks belonged to the police force and lived in integrated neighborhoods. Furthermore, in the wake of *Brown*, the school board developed a plan to desegregate Little Rock's schools gradually, beginning with the enrollment of nine black students at Central High School in the fall of 1957. (This decision to comply with *Brown* grew out of the desire to attract business to the city, which moderates believed could be done only by putting forth a progressive image.)

Before the school year began, however, support for the plan began to unravel. Fearful of losing the pro-segregationist vote in his bid for reelection, Arkansas governor Orval Faubus, heretofore considered a moderate, announced his disapproval of "any attempt to force acceptance of change to which the people are so overwhelmingly opposed."[7] The Arkansas Senate declared its opposition to desegregation of public schools. Nonetheless, Daisy Bates, local leader of the NAACP, along with the national office of the NAACP, insisted that local blacks had already compromised enough. Bates and the NAACP's lawyers obtained a court order that compelled Little Rock to live up to its plan.

On the first day of classes, Elizabeth Eckford, one of the nine black students who had been admitted to Central High (termed the Little Rock Nine) arrived at school. She was alone, and she encountered a mob of whites and National Guardsmen, sent by Orval Faubus, bent on stopping her from entering the school. After the National Guard stopped Eckford, she heard someone in the mob yell, "Lynch her! Lynch her!" Another individual added, "No nigger bitch is going to get in our school! Get out of here!" Still another declared, "Drag her over to this tree! Let's take care of that nigger." Fortunately for Eckford, a lone sympathetic white woman, Grace Lorch, whisked her away to safety on a city bus.[8]

Up until this moment, President Dwight Eisenhower had avoided the civil rights fray. While he had declared his support for the *Brown* decision, privately he had misgivings about the Warren Court. Eisenhower believed that desegregation could come only gradually to the South, that the federal government could not force racial reform on the region. Several months earlier Eisenhower had stated that he could not foresee the "circumstances that would ever induce me to send federal troops" to the South.[9] Faubus's defiance of the law and the mob's action, however, presented Eisenhower with a dilemma. As president, he had sworn to enforce the law of the land, which meant sending troops to Little Rock. Yet, politically and personally, he opposed such a solution.

On September 14, 1957, Eisenhower convened a private meeting with Governor Faubus. The president left the meeting believing that Faubus had agreed to follow the court's orders, which meant the former could avoid intervening further in local affairs. However, when Faubus reneged on this agreement by pulling state troops from Little Rock, thus leaving the Little Rock Nine at the mercy of the white mob, Eisenhower felt compelled to do more. On September 25, 1957, the day after white mobs again hounded the Little Rock Nine, Eisenhower mobilized the Arkansas National Guard—under federal command—and sent a thousand U.S. soldiers, members of the 101st Airborne Division, to Little Rock. As he informed the American public in a nationally televised address, he had a duty to preserve the "peace and order of the community." "Our enemies are gloating over this incident and using it everywhere to misrepresent our whole nation," Eisenhower explained. "We are portrayed as a violator of those standards of conduct which the people of the world united to proclaim in the Charter of the United Nations." The dispatch of troops to Little Rock would help restore "the image of America and all its parts as one nation, indivisible, with liberty and justice for all."

Troops (in reduced numbers) remained in Little Rock for the rest of the school year, escorting the Little Rock Nine to and from school and providing protection during the school day. On May 29, 1958, Ernest Green, the only senior of the nine, received his diploma. His graduation demonstrated that decisive action on the part of the federal government could overcome mob violence and promote the cause of civil rights. Yet, as with the *Brown* decision, the victory proved much smaller than first appeared. Rather than accept broader desegregation, Little Rock closed its schools in the fall of 1958. As part of a strategy of massive resistance, some school districts, such as that of Prince Edward County, Virginia, followed Little Rock's example and closed their school doors. Others adopted "school choice" programs, knowing that few blacks would enroll their children at white schools lest they lose their jobs or face eviction from their homes. In many instances, whites transferred to private academies, which at the time were not covered by *Brown*. Often states or localities made enrollment at these private academies affordable by paying for textbooks and other school materials with public dollars.

As a result, even though the Supreme Court and other federal courts repeatedly ordered such schools to reopen, in 1964, ten years after *Brown*, only 2.3 percent of all southern black children attended desegregated public schools. Due to higher birth rates among blacks than whites, more black youths went to segregated schools in 1964 than had in 1954. In the same time period, Congress managed to pass only two watered-down civil rights bills. Even though the Civil Rights Acts of 1957 and 1960 represented the first legislation of their kind since Reconstruction, neither had a significant impact on everyday life in the South. In addition, convinced that changes would have to come gradually, without decisive federal intervention, Eisenhower remained on the sidelines. He kept federal forces out of other communities that evaded the law and provided no forthright moral support to civil rights forces. Only through his appointment to the courts of judges who ultimately issued numerous pro–civil rights decisions did Eisenhower promote the struggle for racial equality.

THE SIT-INS AND FREEDOM RIDES

If Rosa Parks's refusal to give up her seat on a bus in Montgomery, Alabama, symbolized a modern-day version of the "shot heard round the world" at Lexington and Concord, the decision of four North Carolina Agricultural and Technical College students to demand service at the lunch counter at Woolworth's in Greensboro, North Carolina, on February 1, 1960, represented an updated Battle of Bunker Hill. On this day, Joseph McNeill, Ezell Blair, Jr., David Richmond, and Franklin McCain sat down at the lunch counter and ordered coffee and doughnuts. "As anticipated," McCain recalls, "the reply was, 'I'm sorry, we don't serve you here.' " Rather than leave, however, McCain and the three others remained seated until closing time. When they finally returned to campus, they were welcomed as heroes for doing what many had contemplated but few had done, standing up (or in this case sitting down) for their rights as human beings.[10]

The sit-ins at Woolworth's in Greensboro continued throughout the spring, sparking a wave of sit-ins and similar protests, from wade-ins at public beaches to read-ins at public libraries across the South. By the fall of 1960 over seventy thousand individuals had participated in sit-ins in over one hundred communities. Still more donated money, wrote letters of support, or took part in sympathy demonstrations in the North, where lunch counters were not officially segregated.

The sit-ins displayed the birth of a new militancy, especially among young blacks. They took place against a backdrop of heightened but unfulfilled expectations. The *Brown* decision led young blacks to believe that Jim Crow was on its deathbed. The Montgomery bus boycott and the Little Rock crisis reinforced this feeling. Yet as the 1960s dawned, young blacks still found segregation pervasive. The four students who took part in the first sit-ins decided that the time for waiting for the courts to bring about change had passed. Without the prodding or planning of any national leader or organization, thousands of youths put America on notice that they wanted "freedom now!"

On Easter weekend, 1960 (April 15–17), close to 175 students from thirty states, mostly southern, gathered at Shaw University in Raleigh, North Carolina, seeking to maintain the momentum of the sit-ins and to coordinate future actions. The NAACP and the Southern Christian Leadership Conference (SCLC), founded by Martin Luther King, Jr., in the wake of the Montgomery bus boycott, hoped to convince the students to join their organizations, as student branches or auxiliaries. Largely on the advice of Ella Baker, a middle-aged onetime assistant field secretary of the NAACP, and, as of 1960, the acting executive director of the SCLC, however, the students chose to remain independent, establishing the Student Nonviolent Coordinating Committee (SNCC).

Over the course of the 1960s, SNCC attracted hundreds of young men and women from across the country who were willing to risk their lives for freedom. As James Lawson observed at SNCC's founding convention in his keynote address, "From a lunch-counter stool" SNCC sought more than integration and legal reforms. It sought to "raise the moral issue," to point out the "viciousness of racial segregation and prejudice," to compel the nation to accept the "sinful nature of racism." SNCC often ventured where other established civil rights organizations dared not go, into rural regions of the deep South. SNCC also prodded King and the NAACP to adopt more militant positions. Initially dominated by students from Nashville, Tennessee, who were deeply committed to nonviolence, SNCC's membership and philosophy changed over time. By the late 1960s it no longer advocated nonviolence or stood under the emblem of black and white working together. Instead, it called for black power. While some perceived this shift as a dramatic rejection of its core principles, others contend that the call for black power was consistent with the vanguard role that SNCC had played since it birth and its insistence that the nation speed up the pace of change.

An incident that took place not long after its formation shows how SNCC served as the cutting edge of the movement. After a period of deferring to the wishes of their elders, who preferred quiet negotiations with the business elite to direct-action protests, Lonnie King (no relation to Martin Luther King) and Julian Bond, two of SNCC's earliest members, determined to stage sit-ins at Rich's, a prestigious department store in Atlanta. Before starting these protests, they enlisted the support of Martin Luther King, Jr., who had moved back to his native Atlanta from Montgomery to serve as a minister in his father's church. On October 19, 1960, after attempting to obtain service at the Magnolia Room, Rich's most elegant restaurant, Dr. King, along with numerous students from the Atlanta University complex, was arrested and sent to jail. A little short of a week later, city authorities and sit-in leaders signed a truce, ending the protests. While most of the demonstrators were freed, Dr. King was not because a local judge argued that his participation in the protests violated his probation for an earlier arrest for driving without a state license. The judge sentenced King to four months in prison in Reidsville State Penitentiary.

Worried about King's safety and sensing an opportunity to court the black vote, Harris Wofford, an aide to John F. Kennedy, convinced the Democratic presidential candidate and his brother, Robert, to make several gestures in support of the jailed civil rights leader. Against the advice of his top political aides, who feared alienating southern white voters, John F. Kennedy called King's wife, Coretta, to express his concern. Shortly thereafter, Robert contacted Judge Oscar Mitchell of Georgia, prodding him to release King from jail. The next day King was released.

While few whites knew about these gestures, the black press reported them widely in the days leading up to the election. Likewise, many black ministers informed their congregations about the Kennedys' good deeds. Even stout Republicans like King's father were touched, and King, Sr., switched his endorsement from Nixon to Kennedy. On election day, John Kennedy defeated Richard Nixon, the Republican candidate, by two-thirds of 1 percent of the popular vote. In 1956 Eisenhower and Adlai Stevenson had nearly split the black vote; this time the Democrats won nearly two-thirds of the black vote. Put another way, SNCC's decision to stage sit-ins, which spurred King to protest, which got him arrested, which prompted the Kennedys to intervene, which increased the black vote for Kennedy in several key states gave Kennedy the edge in one of the closest presidential elections in history.

Of course, the black vote for John F. Kennedy also rested on promises that the Democratic candidate had made during the campaign. "With one stroke of the pen," Kennedy pledged to end discrimination in federally funded housing. (Through this statement JFK conjured up images of FDR, who had prohibited discrimination in the defense industries during World War II simply by signing an executive order.) Kennedy's youth, vigor, and overall platform, calling for a New Frontier, further attracted black support. Yet in the first hundred days of his presidency, Kennedy did not fulfill his specific pledge to end discrimination in public housing, nor did he place racial reforms at the top of his agenda. On the contrary, needing southern support for his foreign and economic policies, he took a very cautious approach to civil rights.

Civil rights forces responded to Kennedy's lethargy by developing new ways to pressure him to live up to his promises. Most prominently, the Congress of Racial Equality (CORE) announced that it would stage a freedom ride. CORE had been founded by a small group of nonviolent activists during World War II. It briefly gained fame through its Journey of Reconciliation in 1947, which sought to desegregate transportation facilities in the upper South. During the 1950s CORE's membership and influence waned, only to be revived by the sit-ins. In the spring of 1961, CORE recruited thirteen individuals, black and white, to take part in the freedom rides. According to CORE's plans, these thirteen men and women would ride two separate buses through the South in a desegregated manner. Blacks would use white restrooms and waiting rooms, while whites would use facilities reserved for blacks. CORE considered these rides a test of the February 1, 1961, *Boynton* decision, in which the Supreme Court had ruled against segregation in interstate transportation. If southern authorities refused to comply with this decision, as CORE expected, the Kennedy administration would be obligated to intervene.

Leaving Washington, D.C., on May 4, the riders experienced little resistance during the first days of their journey. In Rock Hill, South Carolina, white hoodlums attacked John Lewis, a black veteran of the Nashville student movement, when he entered the white waiting room. Otherwise, the rest of the journey through the Carolinas and Georgia took place without incident. Then, on Sunday, May 14, Mother's Day, the riders came face to face with vicious white segregationists. In Anniston, Alabama, a crowd of whites stoned one of the buses and slashed its tires. When the driver pulled over to repair the tires, pursuing whites set the bus ablaze. Not long after this incident, the second bus pulled into Birmingham, Alabama, and was met by a large mob. No police were in sight, although they had been given advance notice of the journey. "As we entered the white waiting room," James Peck, one of the white riders recalled, "we were grabbed bodily and pushed toward the alleyway. . . . As soon as we got . . . out of sight of onlookers in the waiting room, six of them started to swing at me with fists and pipes. Five others attacked Person [one of the black riders] a few feet ahead. Within seconds, I was unconscious on the ground."[11]

Images of these attacks, including a famous photograph of the burning Greyhound bus outside of Anniston, appeared around the world, rousing sympathy and support for the civil rights movement and jolting the Kennedy administration into action. SNCC and Diane Nash, a veteran of the sit-in movement in Nashville, Tennessee, responded by putting out a call for volunteers to rush to Birmingham to continue the rides, explaining that the movement could not allow violence and repression to prosper. Under pressure from the Kennedy administration, Alabama authorities agreed to provide protection for the riders as they traveled from Birmingham to Montgomery. Once again, however, all signs of police or other officials disappeared as the bus pulled into Montgomery's terminal, and the riders were attacked by a mob. Jim Zwerg, a white activist from Madison, Wisconsin, was nearly killed. John Lewis, Kennedy presidential aide John Seigenthaler, who attempted to protect one of the female riders, and others were mauled. Furious that Alabama governor John Patterson had broken his promise to provide protection, President Kennedy sent over five hundred federal marshals into Montgomery to restore order.

That night, much of the civil rights movement assembled at the First Baptist Church in Montgomery. With Martin Luther King, Jr., delivering the keynote address, thousands of whites rioted outside, burning automobiles and clashing with federal authorities. Tear gas poured into the First Baptist Church. Finally, Governor Patterson called in the National Guard to quell the violence. At this point, Robert Kennedy called for a cooling-off period. CORE leader James Farmer retorted that "we'd been cooling off for 350 years and that if we cooled off any more, we'd be in a deep freeze."[12]

To make matters worse, Mississippi, with its long history of lynchings and near-total commitment to segregation, lay ahead. The prospect of more violence prompted the Kennedy administration to broker a deal with Mississippi governor Ross Barnett whereby the governor promised to protect the riders from their moment of entry into the Magnolia State until their arrival in Jackson, the state capital. In exchange, the Kennedy administration agreed to turn a deaf ear while state authorities whisked the riders from the buses into paddy wagons and jail cells on trumped-up charges ranging from trespassing to disturbing the peace. In spite of this Faustian deal, freedom riders kept traveling to Mississippi for the rest of the summer, knowing that they would end up in one of the worst prisons in the nation.

The freedom rides marked an important juncture in the civil rights movement. Like the sit-ins, they showed an increased commitment to nonviolent, direct-action protest and a willingness by many, especially young activists, to confront white segregationists despite or perhaps because of the severity of threats. Calls for cooling off, prison sentences, and terrorist attacks did not deter the freedom riders. At the same time, the rides revealed the Kennedy administration's timidity on civil rights. While CORE prompted the federal government to intervene, it did so in only a limited fashion. Robert F. Kennedy pressured the Interstate Commerce Commission to issue a regulation prohibiting segregated bus facilities, and the Kennedys drummed up liberal foundation support for voter education and registration drives, to be directed by civil rights activists in the South. Yet President Kennedy was still not ready to call for legislation aimed at protecting the rights of blacks in the South, nor was he willing to make civil rights his top priority.

BIRMINGHAM AND THE MARCH ON WASHINGTON

In 1962 and 1963 the civil rights movement reached a new level of intensity, with Martin Luther King, Jr., capturing the public's attention as few other activists in American history had done. Yet it would be inaccurate to suggest that King constituted the movement. On the contrary, he was only a small part of a broad-based struggle for freedom. SNCC, CORE, the NAACP, the Nation of Islam, which counted as one of its members Malcolm X, and many other groups played very active and effective roles during these years as well. In numerous communities freedom movements were led by men and women unaffiliated or only very loosely affiliated with any national organization. While the movement was strongest in the South, it was active in the North as well, fighting for jobs and against residential discrimination from New York City to San Francisco. Somewhat eclipsed by the direct-action protests led by King, CORE, and SNCC, the NAACP continued to push for the desegregation of education, winning a momentous victory in the fall of 1962 when it compelled the University of Mississippi to register James Meredith as its first black student. Medgar Evers, the head of the NAACP in Mississippi, forged a vibrant, multifaceted struggle for equality in Jackson, cut short only by his assassination in 1963. Robert Moses and SNCC set down roots in Mississippi, while other SNCC and CORE members fanned out across the nation, stirring freedom movements from Danville, Virginia, and Cambridge, Maryland, to Pine Bluff, Arkansas, and Albany, Georgia.

King's greatest triumph came in 1963 in Birmingham, Alabama. Ironically, prior to Birmingham, many felt that King had lost his effectiveness as a civil rights leader. In December 1961, black leaders in Albany, Georgia, invited King to their community. Shortly before he arrived, SNCC activists had begun organizing there. SNCC opposed bringing King to Albany, feeling that he would undercut their attempt to build a grassroots movement. But local leaders decided that in the face of mass arrests, they could use King's help and the media attention his presence would generate. King arrived without a suitcase or a toothbrush, expecting only to speak at an evening rally. During the mass meeting at which King spoke, however, Dr. William Anderson, the official leader of the Albany movement, got King to agree to join in a march on city hall the following day. During the march, Albany authorities arrested King, prolonging his involvement in Albany— he remained active there for nine more months, leaving only after being bailed out of jail following another arrest in August 1962. King's willing- ness to be bailed out of jail impressed some militant activists more than his willingness to march, as they viewed his bailing out as selling out. Ironically, it was Albany's police chief, Laurie Pritchett, who bailed King out of jail, although this fact was not known at the time.

Since the protests in Albany produced no concrete gains, many liberals and moderates questioned King's methods. The *New York Times* observed that King had been defeated by Pritchett, who had skillfully responded to King's involvement without a public display of force. An NAACP official commented that for King, "Albany was successful only if his objective was to go to jail."[13] At the same time, SNCC felt that King's departure justified its opposition to his presence in Albany in the first place.

While King and the SCLC felt the sting of these criticisms, they redoubled their efforts to prove that they could mount a successful nonviolent campaign for racial reform. Learning from their experiences in Albany, they carefully chose their next target and mapped out a strategy for rousing the nation. Within a short period of time, they selected Birmingham, Alabama, launching Project C (for confrontation) in the first week of April 1963. King and SCLC chose Birmingham for several reasons, foremost being the city's long history of hostility to race reform, personified by Public Safety Commissioner T. Eugene "Bull" Connor, an unreconstructed white supremacist who routinely used physical force against civil rights activists. Nicknamed "Bombingham" due to its high incidence of bombings, Birmingham had been the site of one of the fiercest mob attacks on the freedom riders. It was also the home of the Reverend Fred Shuttlesworth, who had forged the Alabama Christian Move- ment for Human Rights (ACMHR), the local arm of the SCLC, in the years prior to King's arrival. Building on Shuttlesworth's endeavors, the SCLC organized marches, mass meetings, and boycotts of downtown businesses.

King and his associates assumed that Connor would not be able to contain his anger and that, unlike Laurie Pritchett of Albany, Georgia, who had appeared nonviolent to the outside world, he would explode, garnering national attention for SCLC in the process.

On Good Friday, April 12, 1963, King, along with his closest associate, the Reverend Ralph Abernathy, openly defied a court injunction against marching. They were promptly placed under arrest and thrown in jail. While incarcerated, King wrote "Letter from a Birmingham Jail," one of the most profound statements on the origins and goals of the civil rights movement. King's letter was a direct response to a letter written by a group of white clergymen who had urged him and Birmingham's blacks to stop demonstrating. In addition to calling for restraint, the clergymen condemned the entrance of outsiders into their community, which they felt was on the path to reform— prior to King's arrival, Birmingham had voted against Connor for mayor, favoring, instead, a more moderate ticket backed by the business community. King found the clergymen's position appalling. As a Christian, like the apostles and Jesus, King wrote, he felt "compelled to carry the gospel of freedom beyond my home town." As an American, too, he felt justified combating injustice wherever it existed. In terms of timing, King retorted, "Frankly, I have yet to engage in a direct-action campaign that was 'well timed' in view of those who have not suffered unduly from the disease of segregation." In perhaps the strongest passage of the letter, King declared, "For years now I have heard the word 'wait!' It rings in the ear of every Negro with piercing familiarity. This 'Wait' has almost always meant 'Never.' We must come to see, with one of our distinguished jurists, that 'justice too long delayed is justice denied.' " In language just as strong he added:

We have waited for more than 340 years for our constitutional and God-given rights. The nations of Asia and Africa are moving with jet-like speed toward gaining political independence, but we still creep at a horse-and-buggy pace toward gaining a cup of coffee at a lunch counter. Perhaps it is easy for those who have never felt the stinging darts of segregation to say, "Wait." But when you have seen vicious mobs lynch your mothers and fathers . . . when you see the vast majority of your twenty million Negro brothers smothering in the airtight cage of poverty in the midst of an affluent society . . . when you suddenly find your tongue twisted and your speech stammering as you seek to explain to your six-year old daughter why she can't go to the public amusement park that has just been advertised on television . . . and see ominous clouds of inferiority beginning to distort her personality by developing an unconscious bitterness toward white people . . . then you will understand why we find it difficult to wait.[14]

King's letter, which was not published for another month, did not have an immediate impact on the protest in Birmingham. Nevertheless, it clearly expressed the views of the black masses of the community.

Shortly after his release from jail, the SCLC stepped up its campaign, most notably with daring freedom marches by schoolchildren. With the jails filled beyond capacity, Bull Connor sought to stop these marches. Using police dogs and fire hoses, he brutally turned back protesters. These attacks on nonviolent activists, however, backfired; they emboldened the black community and shocked the nation. For many Americans, the image of Connor's German shepherd dogs biting at the limbs of peaceful protesters became a symbol of the viciousness and ugliness of the southern way of life. Polls showed an outpouring of support for King; letters and telegrams poured into the White House expressing support for the goals of the movement. At the same time, moderate and conservative blacks in Birmingham who heretofore had not joined the protests united with those who had. Put differently, Birmingham represented a masterful moment for King.

In combination with protests that erupted elsewhere during the spring of 1963, Birmingham convinced Kennedy that his strategy of seeking solutions to America's racial problems with minimal federal intervention would no longer work. Everywhere the Kennedy administration looked it saw, in the president's words, the "fires of frustration and discord." The Justice Department reported at least 758 demonstrations in 186 cities across the South in the ten weeks following the Birmingham campaign. President Kennedy's confrontation with Alabama governor George Wallace, who had pledged to maintain "segregation forever" over the admission of blacks to the University of Alabama, reinforced the president's sense that he could no longer remain on the sidelines or respond to crises on an ad hoc basis.

On June 11, 1963, President Kennedy delivered a major television address on civil rights, the most forceful and important speech by a president on race relations since Reconstruction. Noting that the nation was founded on the principle of equality and was committed to a "worldwide struggle to promote and protect the rights of all who wish to be free," Kennedy demanded that America overcome its history of racial inequality. "If an American, because his skin is dark, cannot eat lunch in a restaurant open to the public; if he cannot send his children to the best public school available; if he cannot vote for the public officials who represent him; if, in short, he cannot enjoy the full and free life which all of us want, then who among us," Kennedy rhetorically inquired, "would be content to have the color of his skin changed and stand in his place?" To rectify this situation, Kennedy proposed strong civil rights legislation which, among other things, would make it illegal to discriminate against blacks in public accommodations and would provide increased protection for civil rights workers.

Even before Kennedy delivered this address, A. Philip Randolph, the dean of the civil rights movement, and a coalition of civil rights forces had determined to stage a mass demonstration in Washington, D.C., for "jobs and freedom." Randolph, whose proposed March on Washington Movement in 1941 had prompted President Franklin D. Roosevelt to desegregate the defense industry, saw this new march as a vehicle for advancing the civil rights movement. In a meeting with Randolph and other civil rights leaders, President Kennedy urged that the protest be called off, arguing that it threatened to strip away support for the civil rights bill. Randolph and others unequivocally rebuffed the president, warning that the main issue was not whether the march would take place but who would lead it, those committed to nonviolence or those who were not. (This was a thinly veiled reference to Malcolm X, who was attracting a growing following in the North.)

On August 28, 1963, between 200,000 and 250,000 people, from all across America, black and white, old and young, poured into the nation's capital. Thousands of men and women massed around the reflecting pools of the Lincoln Memorial heard A. Philip Randolph introduce a series of speakers, including Roy Wilkins of the NAACP, Whitney Young of the National Urban League, and Walter Reuther of the United Automobile Workers. Mahalia Jackson; Peter, Paul and Mary; and other performers and dignitaries sang songs and made appearances. The breadth and depth of those assembled served as a fitting tribute to Randolph, who had dreamed of such an event for years.

Behind the scenes, however, trouble brewed. One of the last scheduled speakers was John Lewis, SNCC's chair. Lewis had prepared a very militant speech in which he questioned the value of coalition with liberals, the Kennedy administration, and the civil rights bill itself. As drafted, Lewis's speech concluded with a threat to "march through the Heart of Dixie, the way Sherman did," if the pace of change and the extent of federal intervention did not increase significantly.[15] Lewis's threatened jeremiad was born out of SNCC's experiences in the deep South. For several years its workers and blacks in the communities in which they were active were routinely beaten, jailed, and at times killed. Even though the Kennedy administration professed support for SNCC's goals, channeling foundation funds to voter education projects in the Mississippi Delta, the Federal Bureau of Investigation (FBI) refused to provide protection, insisting that it was only an investigative body. Lewis's views were also based on the fact that Kennedy's bill did little to protect voting rights for blacks. Some lines of Lewis's prepared speech proved so inflammatory that several moderate participants in the march, especially clergymen, threatened to withdraw unless it was rewritten. Only out of respect for Randolph did SNCC agree to alter the speech. Still, it was the most militant address of the day and an omen of things to come.

Very few Americans, however, knew of this behind-the-scenes dispute. For the majority, the most memorable moment of the march was King's moving "I Have a Dream" speech. Unlike his "Letter from a Birmingham Jail," King's oration at the March on Washington exuded optimism and unity. Rather than criticizing moderates, he reached out to them with his vision of a color-blind society. In delivery alone, the speech was spellbinding. Given in cadences familiar to black churchgoers, it provided a fitting climax to a peaceful day of protest, followed only by the singing of the movement's anthem, "We Shall Overcome." Ralph Abernathy called the march the "greatest day of my life." SNCC's newspaper, the *Student Voice*, judged the march a success. Black comedian-activist Dick Gregory remarked, "Never in the history of the world have that many people ever been able to come together with a three hundred year old gripe and [not] fight. That is strength. That is power."[16]

LYNDON B. JOHNSON AND MISSISSIPPI SUMMER

The two years that followed the March on Washington resembled a roller-coaster ride, with civil rights forces experiencing both highs and lows and twists and turns in rapid succession. By the fall of 1965 the movement had gained much, certainly more than many had considered possible when Rosa Parks had refused to give up her seat a decade earlier. Yet the process of attaining change left the movement with many scars and divisions.

On September 15, 1963, less than three weeks after the March on Washington, a bomb exploded in the Sixteenth Street Baptist Church in Birmingham, Alabama (the staging point of the Birmingham movement the previous spring). Four young black girls, all dressed in Sunday white, Denise McNair, Addie Mae Collins, Cynthia Wesley, and Carole Robertson, were killed. Nearly twenty other people were seriously wounded. The bombing tested the mettle of the civil rights movement and the nation. Coming so soon after the March on Washington, it put King and his allies in a somber mood and, just as important, cast doubt on the feasibility of achieving his dream. Birmingham, which had barely averted a major riot in the spring, exploded. Meanwhile, President Kennedy's civil rights bill was stalled in the Senate, leaving many pundits predicting that Congress would pass another watered-down law, at best.

Then, on November 22, 1963, President Kennedy was assassinated in Dallas, Texas. Despite the gap between his rhetoric and his record during the first two years of his presidency, Kennedy enjoyed strong support among African Americans, with the Gallup Poll showing that 83 percent of African Americans who responded approved of the job he was doing. Blacks and their liberal allies not only mourned JFK's death, they feared that Lyndon B. Johnson's ascendancy to the presidency spelled disaster. To their surprise, Johnson, a Texan with a poor record on racial matters, proved a strong ally. Five days after Kennedy's assassination, before a joint session of Congress, Johnson declared, "No eulogy could more eloquently honor President Kennedy's memory [than the] earliest possible passage of the civil rights bill for which he fought so long."[17] Afterwards, Johnson mustered all of his considerable political skills to obtain passage of the Civil Rights Act, sans amendments (except for one that prohibited sexual as well as racial discrimination). Simultaneously, Johnson introduced the War on Poverty. The fact that he won reelection in 1964 in a landslide vote suggests that many Americans approved of these initiatives.

The Civil Rights Act of 1964 was the most significant federal legislation of its kind since Reconstruction. The law increased the federal government's ability to compel local school districts to desegregate and provided more protection for civil rights activists. It made it illegal to discriminate against an individual because of race, color, or sex in public accommodations or employment. The Civil Rights Act, however, did not ensure the right to vote, nor was it clear that it would be obeyed in the deep South.

While the civil rights bill worked its way through Congress, SNCC and its allies in Mississippi put out a call for nearly one thousand volunteers to come to Mississippi to take part in Freedom Summer. According to this plan, black and white volunteers, many of them from prominent northern families and universities, would register blacks to vote and organize Freedom Schools. Whereas Americans had largely ignored the beating and killing of native black Mississippians, SNCC's Robert Moses and others presumed that they would not ignore similar injustices against well-connected activists, many of whom would be white students from elite universities. During the summer of 1964, in spite of the murder of three volunteers, in fact, nearly one thousand men and women established tens of Freedom Schools, where they taught the three R's and citizenship skills, introduced an innovative curriculum on African American history, and organized the

Mississippi Freedom Democratic Party (MFDP), a parallel to the white-controlled regular Democratic Party in the state.

Freedom Summer came to a climax in Atlantic City, New Jersey, at the Democratic Party's national convention, when the MFDP sought recognition as the bona fide delegation from the state of Mississippi. Even though the MFDP's delegates, especially Fannie Lou Hamer, wowed the credentials committee with their testimony, the Democratic Party, facing keen pressure from President Johnson, who feared losing southern white votes in the general election, refused to seat the MFDP slate. Paradoxically, almost all of the delegates from Mississippi's regular Democratic Party walked out of the convention because Johnson had offered the MFDP a "compromise" of two at-large delegates, despite the fact that the MFDP rejected said compromise.

While few outsiders recognized the significance of the MFDP affair at the time, it proved a pivotal event in the history of the civil rights movement. Freedom Summer represented the movement tackling injustice in its most entrenched and repressive form. Thousands of lives were touched by these actions, and in many ways Mississippi and the nation would never again be the same. The mere fact that the MFDP gained an ear at the Democratic convention and came close to unseating the regular Democrats showed how far civil rights forces had traveled in a short time. Just a few years earlier, when Robert Moses first arrived in Mississippi, one of the blacks whom he recruited to register to vote was shot to death in broad daylight. Not only did his assailant go unpunished, the nation paid little notice to this atrocity.

Yet, tensions that had simmered below the surface before the summer came out into the open at summer's end. Many activists in and around SNCC and CORE tired of the nonviolent method and questioned the value of integration. While bringing white volunteers to the state brought valuable national attention and manpower, it also augmented a sense of dependency among blacks. Nonviolence appeared increasingly inadequate in the wake of fierce resistance by local whites. Moreover, the willingness of most liberals to back LBJ as opposed to the MFDP at the convention led many to doubt the dependability of liberals as allies.

SELMA

Before the civil rights movement split into warring factions, however, its more traditional arm, oriented around the goal of achieving integration through nonviolence and coalition with liberals, enjoyed one last shining moment, in Selma, Alabama. There, in the early months of 1965, Martin Luther King, Jr., and the SCLC organized another grand campaign. As in

Birmingham, King and the SCLC carefully selected their target, choosing Selma because of its reputation as a racist town, ruled over by Sheriff Jim Clark, who had used electric cattle prods to intimidate activists. Selma also contained a core of dedicated activists, led by Amelia Platts Boynton, who provided the SCLC with the basis for mounting a broad-based campaign to gain the vote.

King made an initial appearance in Selma on January 2, 1965, delivering an inspirational address at Brown's Chapel African Methodist Episcopal Church in which he spelled out the SCLC's aims. "We will seek to arouse the federal government by marching by the thousands [to] the places of registration." As in Birmingham, King expected that the protests would produce federal legislation, which in turn would protect the rights of blacks to vote. Ultimately, King declared, "When we get the right to vote, we will send to the statehouse not men who will stand in the doorways of universities to keep Negroes out [a reference to Governor George Wallace of Alabama], but men who will uphold the cause of Justice."[18]

Initially responding to the SCLC's protests more like Chief Pritchett of Albany than like Bull Connor of Birmingham, Sheriff Clark nearly upset the SCLC's plans. But following the arrest of Amelia Boynton, which made national headlines, the SCLC gained the upper hand. On January 22 over one hundred black teachers, traditionally one of the more conservative segments of the black community, staged a silent protest at the courthouse. Enraged by their defiance of his authority, Sheriff Clark and his deputies indiscriminately used clubs and cattle prods to clear the streets. Clark personally pinned Annie Lee Cooper to the ground and pummeled her with his fists in front of a cameraman. On February 1, King, Abernathy, and over seven hundred demonstrators, many of them schoolchildren, staged a mass protest. All of them were placed under arrest. More demonstrators were arrested the following day, leaving the jails overflowing.

With King in jail, SNCC, which had been active in Selma for several years, invited Malcolm X to speak at Brown's Chapel. Even though SNCC initially opposed King's decision to target Selma, it used the campaign and Malcolm X's appearance to further its organizing efforts in the region. Malcolm X effectively played up his image as the "violent" black leader to make King's demands appear more reasonable. On the same day that Malcolm X spoke in Selma, President Johnson informed the nation that he supported voting rights legislation.

Less than two weeks later, during a dangerous nighttime march in Marion, Alabama, a rural community outside of Selma, Jimmy Lee Jackson was shot to death by a state trooper while protecting his mother from being wantonly beaten by authorities. Partly with the aim of channeling the anger of Selma's blacks over this incident into something constructive, the SCLC proposed holding a march from Selma to Montgomery, Alabama. Governor George Wallace utterly opposed this idea and proclaimed that he would take whatever measures were necessary to halt it. The SCLC proceeded nonetheless.

On Sunday, March 7, 1965, approximately six hundred blacks led by Hosea Williams and John Lewis headed from Selma to Montgomery. As they crossed the Edmund Pettus Bridge, the main artery out of town, they encountered local and state authorities who ordered them to halt and turn back. Even before the marchers had an opportunity to finish a prayer, Alabama authorities donned their gas masks, mounted their horses, and attacked. As Sheyann Webb, age six at the time, remembered, "I heard all of this screaming and . . . somebody yelled, 'Oh, God, they're killing us!' . . . And I looked and I saw the troopers charging us . . . swinging their arms and throwing canisters of tear gas. . . . Some of them had clubs, others had ropes or whips. . . . It was like a nightmare. . . . I just knew then that I was going to die."[19]

Fortunately for Webb, she survived the rampage. The American public, which viewed scenes of "Bloody Sunday," as the massacre came to be known, was outraged by this vicious attack on nonviolent protesters. SNCC, which had not endorsed the first march, seeing it as a misdirected use of resources, vowed to stage another one. King, who agreed that the movement could not allow itself to be defeated by violence, put out a call for allies of the movement to come to Selma for the second march. On Tuesday, March 9, King led a second group to the Pettus Bridge. But faced with the prospect of breaking a temporary injunction issued by a federal court against marching, and with state troopers, who once again told the protesters to halt, King decided to turn back. SNCC was outraged at King's actions. Others were simply befuddled. King promised that another march would take place. Later that same day, four Unitarian ministers were brutally assaulted in Selma by white ruffians. One of them, James Reeb, died from the attack.

On March 15, the night of Reeb's memorial service, President Johnson delivered a nationally televised address on civil rights. "At times history and fate meet at a single time in a single place to shape a turning point in man's unending search for freedom," Johnson began. "So it was at Lexington and Concord. . . . So it was last week in Selma, Alabama." Observing that the "issue of equal rights for American Negroes" was at the core of the meaning and promise of America, Johnson called on Congress to guarantee blacks the right to vote. Using the language of the movement, Johnson added,

"Their cause must be our cause, too. Because it's not just Negroes, but it's really all of us who must overcome the crippling legacy of bigotry and injustice. And, *we shall overcome.*"

On March 21, after Judge Frank Johnson (no relation to the president) rescinded the federal injunction against marching, thousands of activists set out from Selma to Montgomery. This time Alabama guardsmen, under the president's command, provided protection. Five days later the marchers arrived, approximately twenty-five thousand strong, led by King and a bevy of national civil rights leaders. As Coretta Scott King observed, their arrival represented a homecoming of sorts. In 1955 the civil rights movement had thrust itself into the national consciousness at Montgomery and introduced King to the world. Ten years later, it reappeared in Alabama's state capital much stronger, on the verge of gaining voting rights legislation. From the steps of the state capitol, King delivered a triumphant speech, which he ended by repeating the words of "Battle Hymn of the Republic." "Mine eyes have seen the glory of the coming of the Lord, trampling out the vintage where the grapes of wrath are stored. He has loosed the fateful lightning of his terrible swift sword. His truth is marching on."[20] Later that evening, while driving marchers from Montgomery to Selma, Viola Liuzzo, a white CORE member from Detroit, was shot to death by four KKK members. Her murder served as an ugly reminder of the costs of the struggle for racial equality.

On August 6, 1965, President Johnson signed the Voting Rights Act into law. Liberal politicians and many black leaders hailed the moment, agreeing with President Johnson that the vote represented "the most powerful instrument ever devised for breaking down injustice." In turn, most Americans believed that the era of demonstrations had come to an end, that an age of normalcy would take its place. Even Bayard Rustin, the behind-the-scenes organizer of the March on Washington and confidant of King, called for a shift from "protest to politics." Five days after Johnson signed the Voting Rights Act, however, the ghetto of Watts, Los Angeles, erupted in flames. For over four days blacks rioted, looted, and battled the police and the National Guard. Thirty-four persons were killed; over $40 million in property damages was incurred. The sense of fulfillment felt earlier in the week by Johnson and his supporters, and shared by large segments of the civil rights movement, lay shattered amid the rubble.

BLACK POWER AND WHITE BACKLASH

The Watts riot—which took as its slogan "Burn, Baby, Burn," a phrase coined by the Magnificent Montague, a local disc jockey—and those that followed in Newark, Detroit, Cleveland, and elsewhere in the latter half of the 1960s displayed the rage of millions of black Americans for whom the early civil rights movement had little effect, except, perhaps, to raise their expectations. This rage sprouted from a society pervaded by racial, social, and economic inequality, which itself was the by-product of centuries of racism. The riots also revealed the shortcomings of the mainstream civil rights movement, which until Watts had focused on the problems of southern blacks. With the riots, a new set of figures and organizations emerged, and older or established leaders and groups adjusted their aims and plans. With the riots, the movement became more active in the North, grew more radical, and lost much of its public support.

To a large extent, the civil rights movement of the latter half of the 1960s represented the ascendancy of Malcolm X's black nationalist vision. Ironically, by the time this shift took place, Malcolm X lay dead, assassinated on February 21, 1965, by members of the Nation of Islam. Prior to 1965, Malcolm had caught the ear of some within SNCC and CORE. In the second half of the 1960s, he became their guiding light and earned the admiration of many others. His voice resonated among young blacks in part because of his willingness to upset white allies, to say what he wanted without regard to whether it met liberal standards of approval. In addition, Malcolm X's vision gained adherents because it seemed more attuned to the needs and grievances of northern urban blacks than the visions of King or the NAACP, which had been shaped largely by the needs of southern blacks.

While a new mood swept across the civil rights movement, not until the summer of 1966 did a new slogan that fit this mood take hold. Then Stokely Carmichael, the new chair of SNCC, which had recently jettisoned its commitment to nonviolence and integration, introduced the world to the term "black power." Speaking to an angry crowd of about six hundred in Greenwood, Mississippi, Carmichael declared, "This is the 27th time I have been arrested—I ain't going to jail no more." Then, he repeatedly asked the crowd, "What do you want?," to which they replied upon his cue, "Black Power!"[21] Almost overnight this new slogan replaced the traditional one, "Freedom Now."

In a detailed discussion of the slogan, Carmichael explained that black power meant that blacks wanted political, economic, and social power. In Lowndes County, Alabama, in the heart of the black belt, where SNCC had organized the Lowndes County Freedom Party, for example, it meant that "if a Negro is elected sheriff, he can end police brutality. If a black man is elected tax assessor, he can collect and channel funds for the building of better roads and schools serving black people." As opposed to integration, whereby blacks were expected to assimilate to white ways, blacks would "do things themselves," separately, so as to overcome the notions of black inferiority and white supremacy.[22] Partly because Carmichael and many others used used the term "black power" in a more militant manner, however, as Carmichael admitted in "What We Want," a piece he wrote for the *New York Review of Books*, whites remained convinced that "black power seems to mean that the Mau Mau are coming to the suburbs at night," that black power would lead to vengeance and violence.

White fears about black power were amplified by a wave of riots that followed the riot in Watts and by the emergence of the Black Panther Party (BPP), founded by Huey Newton and Bobby Seale in the fall of 1966 in Oakland, California. The Panthers recruited a number of streetwise and energetic blacks and quickly gained notoriety by organizing armed patrols in the black community. While the Panthers meshed fiery rhetoric with pragmatic programs, such as a free breakfast program for black children, it was the former that won the attention of the national media. For instance, the Panthers made headlines for appearing at the California state capitol building armed with shotguns and sporting black leather jackets and caps to protest against attempts by the state to restrict their use of firearms.

Invariably the rhetoric and actions of black power advocates led to showdowns with the police and repressive counterattacks on them by federal and local authorities. The FBI, which had already embarked on a mission to discredit King, expanded its counterintelligence program, known as COINTELPRO, to "prevent the coalition of militant black nationalist groups." As a Select Committee of the U.S. Senate later reported, "no holds were barred" in this operation against the Panthers and others. The FBI used the same tactics against the BPP that it used against Soviet agents. It intentionally exacerbated tensions between rival black organizations, spreading false rumors and planting *agents provocateurs* among them.[23] By the time COINTELPRO was discontinued, nearly every Panther had been arrested, run out of the country, or killed. Fred Hampton, the Panthers' charismatic leader in Chicago, for example, was shot to death by police, who falsely claimed that they fired on Hampton in self-defense.

From the moment Carmichael uttered the term "black power," Martin Luther King, Jr., objected to the slogan. While he sympathized with the goal of increasing black pride and gaining greater political and economic power, King predicted that use of the term would backfire, scaring away important allies who would not see its positive qualities. Moreover, unlike Carmichael, King remained a fervid advocate of nonviolence and integration, both of which SNCC and CORE rejected. Rather than focus his energy on publicly criticizing his erstwhile allies, however, King turned to mounting another major nonviolent campaign, this time in Chicago. In late January 1966, King moved into a run-down apartment unit at 1555 South Hamlin Avenue. Working with local community action and civil rights groups, with the goal of bringing the condition of the urban slums into the national limelight, he led rent strikes. Yet King and the SCLC quickly learned that it would be much harder to effect change in the North than it had been in the South. Not only was the breadth and depth of the problem much more intense, but King also found that it was more difficult to highlight the problems faced by northern blacks than it had been in the South. In addition, Mayor Richard Daley, Chicago's powerful political boss, proved a much more elusive and highly skilled opponent than the political leaders King had encountered in the deep South. Daley minimized the impact of King's efforts through a combination of intimidation, deflection, and accommodation, sending his advisors to negotiate with King, announcing his own program to end the slums, and pouring millions of dollars of War on Poverty funds, channeled through the hands of loyal black politicians (and ministers), into Chicago's largely black south and west sides.

In the summer of 1966, following riots in the city, which Daley blamed on the civil rights movement, King turned from attempting to forge a broad-based community movement to staging open housing marches in all-white neighborhoods. These protests, King predicted, promised to create confrontations akin to those in the deep South, which King hoped would galvanize national attention and produce new federal legislation. To an extent, King's efforts worked. White mobs at least as vicious as any he had encountered in the deep South attacked the open housing marches, with young whites jeering (to the Oscar Mayer jingle), "I wish I was an Alabama trooper, then I could kill a nigger legally." Yet in other ways, King miscalculated. Mayor Daley's police force, in contrast to those of Connor or Clark in Birmingham and Selma, respectively, protected the activists rather than attacking them. This made it harder to paint northern officials as law breakers and to demand federal intervention. In addition, King's open housing protests placed the civil rights movement at odds with many of the same people who had supported civil rights legislation in the first half of the decade. Daley, for instance, had mobilized his political machine in support of the Civil Rights and Voting Rights Acts; he did not rally behind the goal of open housing, although he skillfully made it look as if he supported the goal of nondiscrimination. To make matters worse, King did not even enjoy the full support of Chicago's black community, part of which remained faithful to Daley's political machine and part of which disdained King's nonviolent methods. As a result, King left Chicago unable to point to a new piece of federal legislation as justification for his vision or method. Not until the spring of 1968 did the federal government enact open housing legislation, and this new legislation was passed only after King was assassinated and another set of riots had erupted, hardly a confirmation of his vision.

At about the same time that black power was becoming the rallying cry of the movement and King was protesting in Chicago, the Vietnam War was heating up. The escalation of the war had a profound effect on the civil rights movement. The war further radicalized many young blacks, contributed to the disintegration of the coalition that had come together during the early 1960s, and augmented white backlash. Malcolm X was among the first prominent Americans to condemn the war. SNCC and CORE declared their formal opposition to the war in early 1966. While King personally opposed the war, he did not align himself with the antiwar movement or publicly clash with the Johnson administration over its foreign policy until early 1967. Then, in a major address at Riverside Church in New York City, King announced his opposition to the war, terming the United States the "greatest purveyor of violence in the world today."[24]

While King's speech reflected the black populace's growing disenchantment with the war, it put him at odds with many of his former allies. The NAACP, the National Urban League, and many white liberals condemned King for breaking with Johnson, who had done more for blacks than any other president in modern history. Black journalist Carl Rowan wrote, "Many who had listened to him with respect will never accord him the same confidence. He has diminished his usefulness to his cause, to his country and to his people."[25] J. Edgar Hoover, the director of the FBI, used King's stance on Vietnam to justify further attempts to neutralize him as a leader. Other black activists similarly found themselves attacked because of their antiwar views. Because of his opposition to the war, Julian Bond, a veteran of SNCC, was denied the seat in the Georgia state assembly to which he was elected twice. Muhammad Ali was stripped of his boxing title for refusing to submit to the draft.

The nation's response to the *Report of the National Advisory Commission on Civil Disorders* (1968) provided evidence of the public's declining support for the civil rights movement. In the aftermath of the largest race riots in American history, President Johnson appointed a special committee to investigate the causes of the riots and to suggest reforms to prevent future unrest. Headed by Otto Kerner, the former governor Illinois, the commission reported that the nation was becoming more racially polarized and that the riots grew out of the social conditions of the ghetto, which "white institutions created . . . maintain . . . and condone." In terms of prevention, the commission recommended that the nation commit itself to "a massive and sustained effort" to build a better society.[26]

Conservatives immediately and universally condemned the Kerner Commission's findings, arguing that it let the perpetrators of violence off the hook, coddled criminals, and prescribed rewards for those who broke the law. President Johnson, who was shell-shocked by the Vietnam War and the disintegration of the liberal coalition, offered few words of encouragement. Hubert Humphrey, Johnson's liberal vice president and the Democrats' presidential nominee in 1968, stated that the report's conclusions were "open to some challenge."[27]

This does not mean that all Americans disagreed with the commission's findings or with its recommendations. Robert F. Kennedy and Martin Luther King, Jr., sought to use the report to mobilize support for a broad-based attack on poverty. King and the SCLC organized a "Poor People's Campaign." Robert Kennedy re-energized the left-liberal coalition that had rallied around the Voting Rights Act of 1965. Yet by the end of the spring of 1968 both of these leaders lay dead by assassins' bullets. Whatever possibilities existed for reviving the civil rights coalition seemed to die with them.

LEGACY

Ironically, almost no one at the time realized that the civil rights movement, defined as a specific moment in the ongoing struggle for racial equality, was nearing its end. On the contrary, in the crazy days of the late 1960s, many were predicting that America was on the verge of a revolution. Such fantasies about the potential for change, however, tended to give rise to impractical and unwise proclamations by black radicals, which in turn fueled white backlash and justified repressive measures by federal, state, and local authorities. At the same time, the steady growth of the economy that underlay many of the liberal achievements of the 1960s was coming to an end. Twenty-five years of economic stagnation followed, further weakening the liberal coalition and many of its reforms.

The reaction of the nation to busing and affirmative action reflected the changing political mood. Whereas liberals benefitted in the mid-1960s by supporting racial equality, advocating busing to achieve school integration and other federal programs now became a political liability. In the early 1970s, when the federal courts first began to order busing as a means to overcome segregation, they did not foresee the political firestorm that would follow. Busing was not even one of the demands of black radicals, who instead were busy promoting "community control" and black study programs as the best means of educational advancement. Nonetheless, conservatives seized on busing as an issue that they could use to divide the liberal coalition and to gain the support of some of the Democratic Party's core constituents.

In the long run, affirmative action proved even more politically explosive than busing. Ironically, affirmative action had initally been conceived as a moderate means to rectify racial inequality, with both SNCC and the SCLC favoring much more radical, redistributionary measures. SNCC's executive secretary, James Forman, for example, called for white churches to pay massive reparations to blacks, much as the Germans had been compelled to pay Great Britain and France after World War I. Nonetheless, by the 1980s, conservatives were effectively arguing that affirmative action was not only a bad policy but that it violated the very principles King had espoused. In one of the greater ironies of the civil rights movement, a growing number of middle- and upper-class black conservatives, themselves often the beneficiaries of affirmative action programs, joined white conservatives in criticizing affirmative action, arguing that it stigmatized blacks as inferior. Clarence Thomas, for one, who replaced Thurgood Marshall as the only black man on the Supreme Court, rather than following in Marshall's footsteps as an advocate of further government action to overcome centuries of racial discrimination, decried affirmative action as a violation of the Constitution. Perhaps if the economy had been expanding as fast as it had during the 1950s and 1960s, there would have been less opposition to affirmative action. But in the economic climate of the 1980s and 1990s, it was difficult to counter the claim that the gain of one group did not come at the expense of another.

So where does this bring us? While it is easy to emphasize the movement's shortcomings and to focus on the persistence of racial inequality, the rise of conservatism in the 1970s, 1980s, and 1990s (to a large part as a reaction to the civil rights movement), and the seeming increase in racial tensions and pessimism, this interpretation fails to judge the movement accurately in the context of its times. At the dawn of the civil rights years, the odds against toppling the legal system of Jim Crow in about ten years' time appeared ridiculously long. Virtually no one predicted that all the branches of government would support racial reforms. Yet by 1964, Jim Crow or de jure segregation lay dead, a testimony to the strength and achievements of the civil rights movement. Moreover, unlike the racial reforms enacted during Reconstruction, those of the civil rights years have not been reversed or undermined through a new set of black codes or legal evasions. Nearly thirty years after King's assassination, all of the major civil rights legislation and court decisions of the 1950s and 1960s remain intact, and in many cases are stronger and more far-reaching than they were initially crafted to be. And King, the symbolic embodiment of the modern civil rights movement, has become enshrined as a national hero, with a national holiday in his honor devoted to reflection on the meaning of civil rights.

The civil rights movement also inspired many other social movements, most notably the women's movement, to battle against discriminatory barriers. These movements often ally with civil rights forces to defend the achievements of the past and to fight for more guarantees of equality. Moreover, the civil rights movement changed the agenda and the language public figures use in their debates about public policy. White supremacy and racial segregation, openly and proudly defended by many through much of American history, have virtually disappeared from public discourse. Today, even southern conservatives staunchly defend the notion of a color-blind society.

Finally, the civil rights movement made the nation more aware of the persistence of poverty among large segments of the African American population, rooted, according to many, in the history of racism and race relations in the United States. While it did not solve the problem, the civil rights movement deserves credit, not criticism, for bringing this aspect of the American experience to the fore. No longer are the black poor invisible, as they were through much of American history. Furthermore, while policy makers disagree over the solution to poverty, few if any contend that blacks are "naturally" inferior, making any and all attempts to eradicate poverty futile.

This does not mean that we should underestimate the persistence of racism and racial inequality in American society. Events ranging from an attack on blacks by whites in the predominantly white neighborhood of Howard Beach, New York, in 1986, to the beating of Rodney King, a black man, by white police in Los Angeles in 1991, testify to the persistence of the color line. Yet these incidents should not compel us to claim that the civil rights movement achieved little. Such a view not only fails to appreciate the magnitude of the strides toward freedom that the civil rights movement made, it also dishonors those who risked their lives in the struggle for racial equality.

NOTES

1. Chris Mead, *Champion: Joe Louis, Black Hero in White America* (New York: Penguin, 1985), 296–97.

2. Martin Duberman, *Paul Robeson* (New York: Alfred A. Knopf, 1988), 342, 373.

3. Thurgood Marshall and Roy Wilkins, "Interpretation of Supreme Court Decision and the NAACP Program," *Crisis* (June 1955), 329–34; Juan Williams, *Eyes on the Prize: America's Civil Rights Years, 1954–1965* (New York: Viking, 1988), 34–35.

4. Association of Citizens' Councils, "Why Does Your Community Need a Citizens' Council?," in Peter B. Levy, ed., *Let Freedom Ring: A Documentary History of the Modern Civil Rights Movement* (Westport, Conn.: Praeger, 1992), 214–15.

5. Quoted in Howell Raines, *My Soul Is Rested* (New York: Penguin, 1983), 40–42.

6. Martin Luther King, Jr., *Stride toward Freedom* (New York: Harper & Row, 1958), 61–63.

7. Quoted in Williams, *Eyes on the Prize*, 94.

8. See Levy, *Let Freedom Ring*, 43–44.

9. Quoted in Williams, *Eyes on the Prize*, 103.

10. Franklin McCain, "Interview," in Raines, *My Soul Is Rested*, 75–82.

11. James Peck, *Freedom Ride* (New York: Simon & Schuster, 1962), 124.

12. Quoted in Williams, *Eyes on the Prize*.

13. Quoted in Taylor Branch, *Parting the Waters: America in the King Years, 1954–1963* (New York: Simon & Schuster, 1988), 631.

14. Martin Luther King, Jr., "Letter from a Birmingham Jail," in Levy, *Let Freedom Ring*, 110–14.

15. John Lewis, "Address at the March on Washington," in Levy, *Let Freedom Ring*, 120–21.

16. Henry Hampton and Steve Fayer, eds., *Voices of Freedom: An Oral History of the Civil Rights Movement from the 1950s through the 1980s* (New York: Bantam Books, 1990), 170; Peter B. Levy, *The New Left and Labor* (Urbana: University of Illinois Press, 1994), 9.

17. Quoted in Hugh Davis Graham, *Civil Rights and the Presidency* (New York: Oxford University Press, 1992), 74.

18. Quoted in Williams, *Eyes on the Prize*, 258.

19. Sheyann Webb, *Selma, Lord, Selma* (Tuscaloosa: University of Alabama Press, 1980), 92–99.

20. Martin Luther King, Jr., "Our God Is Marching On!," in Levy, *Let Freedom Ring,* 162–64.

21. Carmichael quoted in Harvard Sitkoff, *The Struggle for Black Equality*, rev. ed. (New York: Hill & Wang, 1993), 199.

22. Stokely Carmichael, "What We Want," *New York Review of Books*, September 26, 1966.

23. U.S. Senate, "Final Report of the Select Committee to Study Government Operations with Respect to Intelligence Activities," in Levy, *Let Freedom Ring*, 220–22.

24. Martin Luther King, Jr., "Beyond Vietnam," in Levy, *Let Freedom Ring*, 207–10.

25. Quoted in David Garrow, *Bearing the Cross: Martin Luther King, Jr. and the Southern Christian Leadership Conference* (New York: William Morrow, 1986), 429–30.

26. National Advisory Commission on Civil Disorders, "Report" (Washington, D.C.: GPO, 1968).

27. Quoted in Irwin Unger, *Turning Point: 1968* (New York: Charles Scribner's Sons, 1988), 185.

2

Freedom's Coming and It Won't Be Long: The Origins of the Civil Rights Movement

On March 25, 1965, Martin Luther King, Jr., and upwards of twenty-five thousand marchers converged on the state capitol building in Montgomery, Alabama, the cradle of the old Confederacy. Their demonstration brought to a climax one of King's and the civil rights movement's greatest moments, the march from Selma to Montgomery, itself the culmination of weeks of bloody protests in and around Selma. Addressing the crowd from the capitol steps, King reviewed the progress that the movement had made over the past decade. It was fitting that King found himself in Montgomery. Just ten years earlier he and the modern civil rights movement had burst into public view with the Montgomery bus boycott, which began when Rosa Parks, who was one of the honorees at this demonstration, refused to give up her seat to a white man. So much had happened since then: Little Rock, the sit-ins, freedom rides, Birmingham, Freedom Summer. Now thousands of protesters, black and white, stood together in defiance of Alabama's segregationist governor, George Wallace, and all of the other forces of resistance that had fought to maintain Jim Crow. "We are on the move now," King asserted. "Yes we are on the move and no wave of racism can stop us. . . . The burning of our churches will not deter us. . . . Like an idea whose time has come, not even the marching of armies can halt us." While the movement still needed to fight for the end of segregated housing and for social and economic equality, King continued, the end of the struggle was in sight. How long would it take to get there? "Not long," King responded, "because the truth pressed to earth will rise again. How long? Not long, because no lie can live forever. . . . How long? Not long, because the arm of the moral universe is long but it bends toward justice. How long? Not long, 'cause mine eyes have seen the glory of the coming of the Lord, trampling out the vintage where the grapes of wrath are stored. He has loosed the fateful lightning of his terrible swift sword. His truth is marching on."[1]

King's poetic speech fit the occasion, but how accurately did it reflect the course of the civil rights movement? More precisely, how accurate was King's view of the origins of the civil rights movement? Like many others, he perceived the movement as rooted in the "American dilemma," the term Swedish sociologist Gunnar Myrdal coined to describe the contradiction between America's promise of equality for all and the reality of persistent discrimination and inequality.[2] The movement had come into being and would continue to triumph because, as King asserted, "no lie can live forever." Its achievements demonstrated that good triumphs over evil, that America's history is one of progress toward a realization of its ideals, and even more broadly that God intervenes in the affairs of man in favor of the righteous.

King was not the only one to put forth this view of the origins of the movement. "Now the time has come for this nation to fulfill its promise," John F. Kennedy declared in his first major address on civil rights, in the spring of 1963. "At times history and fate meet at a single time in a single place to shape a turning point in man's unending search for freedom. So it was at Lexington and Concord. . . . So it was last week in Selma, Alabama," proclaimed Lyndon Johnson in his 1965 speech on voting rights. Sounding much like King and Kennedy, he added, "This was the first nation in the history of the world to be founded with a purpose. The great phrases of that purpose still sound in every American heart, North and South: 'All men are created equal'—'government by consent of the governed'—'give me liberty or give me death.' . . . The time of justice has now come. I tell you that I believe sincerely that no force can hold it back. It is right in the eyes of man and God that it should come."[3]

Certainly it is comforting to believe that history progresses in such a manner. Yet, even if one could develop a cogent argument that the civil rights movement was inevitable, how does one account for its timing and shape? Why did it take place when it did? Why didn't these ideas prove compelling at an earlier or later time? Why did "man's unending search for freedom" reach such heights in the early and mid-1960s? Why did certain actors emerge as leaders and not others? Why were certain goals or demands given priority? And to a lesser extent, why did the movement achieve some objectives but not others?

The modern civil rights movement had both external and internal origins and causes. It came into being when and in the way it did because of both structural and human factors. Forces that were only indirectly related to the movement helped give rise to it and sustained it, as did complex developments within the African American community. Demographic shifts, particularly the great migration, the emergence of the United States as a world power, and the overall process of modernization played key roles. So too did several internal factors, most importantly the accumulation of resources by the African American community. These developments were intertwined and reinforced one another. In addition, the success of the civil rights movement depended on human agency. If individual men and women had not primed themselves to take advantage of new opportunities and then in fact acted, in spite of considerable barriers and personal costs or risks, then the modern civil rights movement would never have taken place.

THE GREAT MIGRATION

In his essay on the origins of the civil rights movement, David Levering Lewis, the Pulitzer Prize–winning biographer of W.E.B. Du Bois, asserts, "Political demographics may truly be said to be racial destiny." While Lewis overstates his case, an understanding of the origins of the civil rights movement must take into account the impact that the great migration had on race relations in the United States of America.[4] As the twentieth century dawned, 90 percent of all African Americans still lived in the South, mostly in rural areas. They continued to work largely as laborers or sharecroppers, growing cotton, rice, sugar, and tobacco, as had their ancestors. Beginning with World War I, African Americans began to migrate northward, particularly to the industrial heartland, to cities such as Chicago. While the flow of African American migrants slowed during the Great Depression of the 1930s, it resumed and sped up during and after World War II. Drawn by the promise of better-paying jobs and pushed out of the rural South by the mechanization of agriculture and a repressive social and economic system, over a million blacks migrated north each decade between 1940 and 1970. By 1970 about one-half of all African Americans lived in the North or the West (see Figure 2.1). Moreover, many of those who remained below the Mason-Dixon Line left the agricultural fields for the South's burgeoning urban areas.

The great migration had a clear and dramatic impact on the lives of the migrants and on the American experience in general. By moving out of the South, blacks gained political rights—most importantly the vote. (To a lesser extent the same can be said for blacks who migrated out of rural areas to urban ones within the South.) Throughout the middle decades of the

Figure 2.1
Distribution of Black Population, 1930–1990

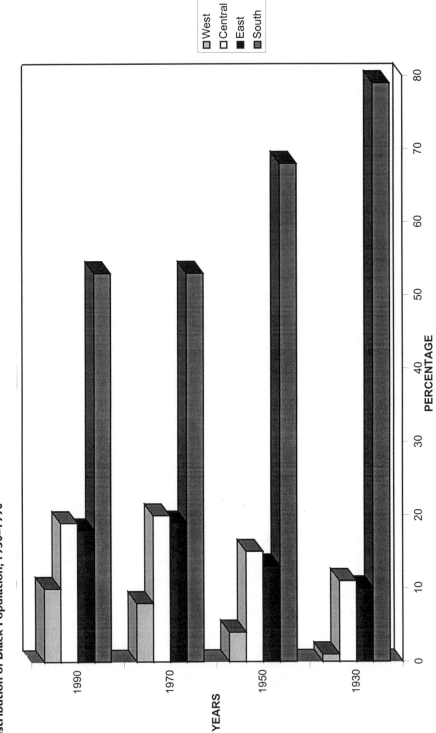

twentieth century, African Americans often constituted the swing vote in hotly contested elections. Neither the Democrats nor the Republicans could assume their allegiance, and both parties vied for their support. In the face of a growing black electorate, northern states enacted their own civil rights legislation, and the national parties pledged themselves to the same. Furthermore, with the great migration, African Americans began to win elections for local and national offices for the first time since Reconstruction. New York City, Detroit, Chicago, and other northern cities with large black communities sent African Americans to Congress, where some of them advocated the enactment of civil rights measures.

In New York City, for example, Adam Clayton Powell, Jr., built a powerful political organization based in Harlem, which he used as a springboard to a seat in the House of Representatives. For over twenty years Powell championed the cause of civil rights, frequently attaching a pro–civil rights amendment, known as "Powell Amendment," to various bills. Powell, along with a handful of other black and white liberal members of congress, became a thorn in the side of the Democratic Party, which felt that the Powell Amendment endangered other party priorities. Powell nonetheless persevered, establishing the base around which other black representatives and white liberals coalesced.

To a lesser extent, in some communities in the rural South—most notably Tuskegee, the onetime home base of Booker T. Washington—African Americans gained a degree of political power, ironically by accommodating themselves to segregation. Washington had argued that political rights would follow from the accumulation of economic power. And as historian Robert Norrell has masterfully shown, African Americans in Tuskegee used their economic power to gain a modicum of political power well before the *Brown* decision and the rise of the modern civil rights movement. Subsequent efforts by whites in Alabama to strip Tuskegee blacks of political power, in turn, virtually transformed this longtime bastion of Booker T. Washington's political philosophy into a hotbed of political activism aimed at attaining black power. In 1966, for instance, Lucius Amerson was elected sheriff of Macon County, Alabama, largely by building on the votes of Tuskegee's blacks.

With the great migration, African Americans also advanced economically. Even though they continued to work for less pay and under worse conditions than whites, blacks in the industrial North began to enjoy a standard of living heretofore unknown to them or their counterparts in the rural South. Between 1940 and 1970, the mean income for black men, adjusted for inflation, more than tripled. During the same years, home ownership by blacks virtually doubled and the number of school years completed by African Americans rose rapidly (see Figure 2.2). Increased income, economic security, and education all benefitted the cause of civil rights. Such advances afforded African Americans the opportunity to contribute financially to civil rights organizations, such as the NAACP, and to build black-owned institutions, such as the black press, which provided support for the cause of racial reform. Blacks also increased their power as consumers, a power that they used to influence white businesses.

The great migration grew out of and reinforced changes in the South that in turn fostered the civil rights movement. Mechanization in the cotton

Figure 2.2
Economic and Educational Progress

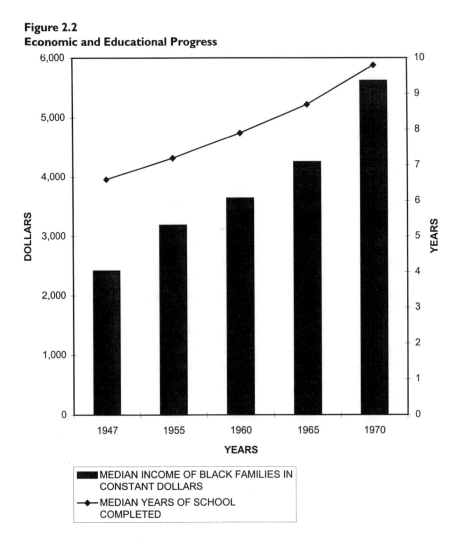

fields, which spurred the out-migration of blacks, decreased the commitment of planters, the traditional power brokers in the region, to maintaining segregation and other repressive measures that had been established to a large degree to ensure a ready supply of cheap and compliant labor in the first place. The concurrent rise in the South of the urban middle class, which was interested in attracting industries and capital to their communities and to tapping into the pocketbooks of black consumers, diluted white commitment to many repressive traditions. Lynchings, for example, declined in the late 1940s and early 1950s and became a very rare occurrence by the 1960s. (Of course, these were long-range trends that were often resisted due to political and cultural factors and sometimes irrational economic behavior.)

More broadly, the great migration destabilized the South, and instability, according to many scholars, is one of the preconditions necessary for the emergence of a social movement. New conditions created an opportunity for blacks, heightening their expectations, and then, when racial reforms proved slow in coming, increasing their frustration and anger, which in turn fueled even more militant demands for change. At the same time, the destabilization of the deep South opened or reopened schisms among whites, which created even more instability and thus opportunities for change.

Lastly, the great migration made race a national problem, or more precisely made northerners more aware of race as *their* problem. Initially, northerners focused on the southern dimension of racism, but by the latter half of the 1960s they could no longer ignore the existence of racism and racial inequality in their own communities. Indeed, some have suggested that by seeing race as a southern problem, northerners and the nation at large ensured that the problem would fester and, like a raisin in the sun, ultimately explode.

THE INTERNATIONAL SETTING

The great migration coincided with the emergence of the United States as a world power, symbolized by its dominant role in World War II. World War II dramatically affected American life, especially the lives of African Americans. It spurred the great migration again, increased the power of the federal government, and ended America's sense of isolation from world affairs. Cognizant of the power that the federal government exercised during wartime, black leaders did their best to prosper by the war. A. Philip Randolph, the president of the Brotherhood of Sleeping Car Porters, called for a Double V strategy, victory abroad and against racial inequality at home. He understood that with total mobilization, the nation needed black labor and support, and he seized the moment to press for civil rights. In 1941 Randolph announced that he would organize a mass march on Washington if President Roosevelt did not address the subject of racial discrimination. Roosevelt told Randolph to wait until the war was over, but Randolph demanded immediate action. Not wanting to present a divided front to the Axis powers, Roosevelt ordered defense contractors to eliminate the color ban rather than risk the march. This said, the war could cut both ways. Particularly after American involvement overseas deepened, it became more difficult to protest over domestic problems lest one be accused of endangering the lives of American troops in Europe and the Pacific.

With the war, a half a million African Americans served in the military, some as officers. Even though blacks were confined to segregated units and often relegated to fatigue duty, service in general and the existence of black officers increased blacks' collective self-esteem and added to the drive to gain equality after the war's end. Medgar Evers, for one, a black native of Mississippi who fought in both France and Germany, returned to his home state determined to exercise his rights as an American citizen. Evers and many other black veterans were rebuffed in the years that followed the war, but they never wavered in their commitment to winning equality.

The impact of World War II on the nation's ideology cannot be understated. The war put white supremacy on the defensive through propaganda put forth by the United States in opposition to the Nazi regime and by means of official proclamations, such as the Atlantic Charter and the founding documents of the United Nations, which reaffirmed America's belief in the principles expressed in the Declaration of Independence. Despite segregation in the armed forces and racial violence at home, the overall message of the war effort was that proponents of racial supremacy were wrong and that America would prosper because of its faith in equality and freedom for all. The Holocaust, which revealed to the world the atrocities that could be committed by a people driven by the ideology of racial supremacy, strengthened the American public's belief in the ideal of equality for all and marginalized open advocates of white supremacy. The nation did not immediately act upon its ideals, but as Vincent Harding, a participant in the civil rights movement and a scholar of African American history, put it, "By the time the war ended in 1945, it was clear to sensitive observers that nothing at home or overseas would ever be quite the same again where the black struggle for freedom and justice was concerned."[5]

Like World War II, the Cold War gave a boost to the civil rights movement. As the rivalry between the Soviet Union and the United States heated up, the Soviets pointed to the "U.S. policy" of discriminating against minorities and used virtually every incident of violence toward or mistreatment of African Americans as a propaganda weapon to embarrass the United

States and to win favor with the numerous developing, newly independent nations, many of which were nonwhite. So fearful did the United States government grow of unfavorable foreign opinions that it stripped some prominent African Americans who were critical of U.S. foreign policy of the right to travel abroad, lest they confirm the Soviets' propaganda. Henry Cabot Lodge, the ambassador to the United Nations, alarmingly referred to racial discrimination at home as the nation's Achilles' heel in its struggle against international communism. President Truman's Committee on Civil Rights concurred: "The United States is not so strong, the final triumph of the democratic ideal is not so inevitable that we can ignore what the world thinks of our [racial] record." The contradictions between the rhetoric of democracy and the reality of race relations in the United States compelled Presidents Truman, Eisenhower, and Kennedy to support civil rights measures that otherwise they might not have. The Supreme Court considered the foreign policy implications of racial inequality in arriving at its decisions in key civil rights cases, including *Brown* v. *Board of Education*.[6]

Paradoxically, the Cold War also acted as a double-edged sword, cutting into the momentum that civil rights forces made during World War II as well as giving it a boost. America's phobia about communists at home, often referred to as McCarthyism, erected one more hurdle for civil rights activists to overcome. The red scare of the late 1940s and the early 1950s created a climate inhospitable to social change in general, and handed white supremacists a potent weapon that they repeatedly wielded to smear the black freedom struggle red. A number of leading African American figures, organizations, and their allies, from W.E.B. Du Bois and the Civil Rights Congress to the Southern Conference for Human Welfare (SCHW) and former Vice President Henry Wallace, were so tarnished by the communist label that they disappeared as factors in American life. Other organizations such as the NAACP and the CIO survived the red scare, but were put on the defensive by McCarthyism. Not until McCarthyism subsided did the civil rights movement regain momentum.

MODERNIZATION

To an extent, the great migration and the emergence of the United States as a world power were part of a much broader process of modernization that affected nearly all facets of American life. America in the 1960s was a much different place politically, socially, culturally, and economically than it had been at the dawn of the century. Politically, the most significant change was the growth in the size and prominence of the federal government, which, by the 1960s, directly touched upon numerous aspects of life. It set minimum wages, oversaw labor relations and financial markets, regulated interstate trade, levied and collected taxes, constructed highways, subsidized farming, and controlled a vast military-industrial complex. Americans looked to the federal government to solve their problems and now tended to have greater faith in Washington than in previous eras.

Sensing that the federal government would play an important role in the arena of race relations, both advocates and opponents of civil rights developed strategies aimed at winning its favor. In the mid-1930s, southern politicians, all solidly members of the Democratic Party, joined hands with northern Republicans to create a conservative coalition. Ostensibly, the coalition aimed at blocking New Deal initiatives, with southern Democrats justifying their alliance with their erstwhile rivals by highlighting the coalition's defense of states' rights, a traditional Democratic position. Yet the voting record of southern Democrats suggested a deeper intent, the blocking of racial reforms. Southern Democrats continued to support federal programs that benefitted the region economically, from the Tennessee Valley Authority to veterans' benefits and agricultural subsidies, but they stood fast against antilynching proposals and fair employment measures.

In the same years, the NAACP used the federal courts to launch a sustained attack on Jim Crow. They adopted a strategy of filing "equalization" suits, which demonstrated that southern states had failed to provide equal facilities as mandated by *Plessy* v. *Ferguson* (1896). Building on favorable court rulings in these suits, they turned their attention to overturning *Plessy* itself. In many cases, NAACP lawyers based their arguments for desegregating schools and ending discriminatory voting practices on court cases and legal theories developed outside the realm of civil rights law that had expanded the reach of the federal government in the first place.

As an example of how an empowered federal government could aid the cause of civil rights, during the 1960s Lyndon Johnson effectively leveraged Washington's control of non–civil rights expenditures, from highway construction to the space program, both of which southerners wanted, to win support for his civil rights proposals. Without the growth of federal programs and expenditures, Johnson would have found it more difficult to win the votes of key representatives.

At the same time, policies enacted by the federal government often reinforced segregation and racial inequality. The Federal Housing Authority (FHA) adopted explicit rules that mandated segregation to ensure community stability in urban areas. Federal agricultural policies encouraged mechanization, which threw large numbers of African Americans off the land while benefitting large white landowners. Similarly, urban renewal projects in the

1950s and 1960s tended to help large developers and middle-class whites while destabilizing poorer African American communities.

In the middle years of the twentieth century, America also experienced a social and cultural transformation. As late as 1920, as many Americans lived in rural areas as in urban ones. By the 1960s America was an urban/suburban nation, with only a small fraction of the population still living in remote rural regions. Urbanization broke down provincial mores and nourished cosmopolitan ones. Breakthroughs in mass communication, from the radio to the television, further reduced provincialism, including ethnic, religious, and racial prejudices. Civil rights forces learned to use the mass media effectively and to play upon emerging cosmopolitan attitudes in their attacks on Jim Crow. In contrast, opponents of the civil rights movement, with few exceptions, found it much more difficult to play to a national audience, perhaps because they were so accustomed to concerning themselves only with local or provincial ones.

Economic developments paralleled (some would argue underlay) political, social, and cultural ones. By the dawn of the twentieth century, large corporations had created the infrastructure necessary for the emergence of a national mass consumer-driven economy. Signs of this economy emerged during the 1920s. In the 1950s it arrived full-blown. National retail and grocery stores grew ever more prominent; hotel and restaurant chains were not far behind. Perhaps the entertainment industry represented the most obvious manifestation of the national mass consumer economy, as national sports figures and motion picture and music stars attracted attention and admiration east, west, north, and south. The national mass consumer economy further undercut provincialism. Knowing that national chain stores, such as Woolworth's, were susceptible to national boycotts and protests, civil rights protesters targeted them for the discriminatory practices of their southern franchises alone. Southern businessmen who sought capital and industries from the North found that Jim Crow practices, and the protests over them, ran counter to their economic interests. Entertainment moguls who had vacillated for years, unwilling to offend white southern consumers who demanded Jim Crow entertainment, ultimately yielded to the demands of the larger market. For instance, the sports world broke the color line, first in boxing and then in baseball. Watching Joe Louis, Jackie Robinson, and other black sports figures and entertainers perform eroded traditional negative stereotypes of blacks and inspired other blacks to try to crack other color lines. In turn, prominent African American entertainers and sports figures, from Lena Horne to Muhammad Ali, could and did use their national stardom to drum up even more support for civil rights.

With modernization came interdependence. America, along with the rest of the world, became less provincial. The opinions of foreigners and co-nationals from different regions, which previously had little impact on daily life, took on new significance. The plight of local shopkeepers became intertwined with the interests of the national business community. African Americans found themselves able to take advantage of niches that opened to them in sports, the art world, and entertainment to win admiration and to break down provincial mores. While the president and the federal government became more powerful, at the same time they came to recognize their vulnerability to the opinions of the world community. Without a strong federal government, African Americans would have had to fight for equal rights on a state-by-state basis. Civil rights protests would not have proven as effective had a national mass media not existed. Perhaps a civil rights movement would have taken place without these developments. This movement might have built on earlier campaigns, such as the antilynching crusades organized by Ida Wells Barnett and Mary Church Terrell, the black nationalist drives led by Marcus Garvey in the 1920s, and the unemployment councils promoted by the Communist Party in the 1930s. Perhaps racial equality was an idea whose time had come. But it seems obvious that it would have been a much different movement if not for the great migration, the rise of the United States as a world power, the growing reach of the federal government, and the development of a mass consumer economy.

MOBILIZING RESOURCES

Conditions alone do not create change. Ideas do not come to fruition on their own. Individuals and communities must be in a position to take advantage of changed conditions and then act when the opportunity arises. Even before the Civil War, African Americans fought for equality. They pressured Lincoln and the Republican Party to end slavery and later to grant equal citizenship rights during Reconstruction. After Reconstruction, when the nation stripped them of their newfound rights, African Americans did not accept the myth of white supremacy. Even during the bleakest days of Jim Crow, when lynchings were routine, blacks sustained their faith in their own equality and struggled to carve out as much freedom as possible. In the process they accumulated the resources and skills necessary to launch and sustain the modern civil rights movement.

One of the most important institutions they established was the church, which served as an invaluable resource during the civil rights movement. Over the course of their history in America, blacks established churches of their own that served their needs. African American churches were a seedbed for leadership, fostering oratorical and organizational skills. African American ministers enjoyed a greater degree of autonomy than did most other black workers, leaving them relatively free from white pressure. Inside their churches, unlike in the outside white world, individual black men and women found a place where they were considered equal. As evidenced by the Montgomery bus boycott, when it became necessary to mobilize the black masses, African Americans already had the tools at their disposal. They had a gathering spot. Their leadership, in the persons of charismatic ministers, was in place. By changing the lyrics to some old gospel tunes, they even had ready-made freedom songs.

Of course, not all African American churches and ministers were in favor of the fight for civil rights. As several case studies of the movement have suggested, many ministers and their churches remained at the rear of the struggle rather than in the vanguard. Some ministers had a vested interest in maintaining the status quo. Others disapproved of stressing social and material concerns over spiritual ones. Still others feared that their churches would be burned to the ground by nightriders if they opened their doors to young black militants. Nonetheless, even in cases where church leaders did not rally around the cause of civil rights, faith in God and the Christian belief in the equality of man played an indispensable role in sustaining the movement. For example, during the Montgomery bus boycott, white supremacists planted a bomb in Martin Luther King, Jr.'s home that nearly killed his family and destroyed his house. Instead of withdrawing from the boycott, King remained at the forefront, explaining that God directly helped him overcome his uncertainty and fears. "It seemed as though I could hear the quiet assurance of an inner voice saying: 'Stand up for righteousness, stand up for truth; and God will be at your side forever.' "[7]

Similarly, the Reverend L. Griffin, a minister in Prince Edward County, Virginia, drew on the New Testament to justify and fortify his congregation's support of a challenge to segregated education. In the end, Griffin declared, as the Bible said, " 'Every valley shall be exalted and every mountain and hill shall be made low; and the crooked shall be made straight and the rough places made plain; and the Glory of the Lord shall be revealed, and all flesh shall see it together, for the Mouth of the Lord hath spoke it.'—Isaiah 40:4–5."[8] Perhaps if African American churches had frowned on personal religious experiences or emphasized hierarchy and the salvation of the elite alone, they would have proved an impediment to change, but this was not the case.

By the mid-1950s African Americans also had established both national and local institutions and organizations explicitly committed to the cause of civil rights. These groups paved the way for the blossoming of the civil rights movement in the latter part of the 1950s and the early 1960s. Most important among these was the NAACP, founded in 1909. By the end of World War II, the NAACP had about a half million dues-paying members with chapters all across the nation, a growing treasury, a small army of lawyers trained in the intricacies of civil rights law, and a circle of allies prepared to join the crusade against Jim Crow. Even though the NAACP played a somewhat diminished role during the direct-action protest days of the 1960s, it did much of the spade work and provided legal counsel to many imprisoned and abused civil rights workers. As Charles M. Payne's detailed examination of the freedom struggle in Mississippi shows, SNCC, which forged a mass movement in the Delta during the 1960s, built on efforts by numerous local people, from Amzie Moore and Medgar Evers to Aaron Henry and C. C. Bryant, all NAACP members. And even though the NAACP feuded with several rival civil rights organizations during the early 1960s, this feud produced what Nancy Weiss has termed "creative tensions," with the NAACP's expertise and its emphasis on federal legislation complementing SNCC's, CORE's, and the SCLC's focus on direct action. In some places, such as Philadelphia, Pennsylvania, strong leadership in the local NAACP chapter actually prodded other civil rights groups to action by pointing out targets for protest and organizing demonstrations.[9]

Two other valuable resources available to the civil rights movement were the black press and black schools and colleges. *Jet* magazine, for example, helped transform the lynching of fourteen-year-old Emmett Till in Mississippi in 1955 into a cause célèbre nationwide, especially among the black middle class. Black newspapers, such as the *New Amsterdam News*, provided some of the first detailed coverage of the movement. All-black colleges, such as North Carolina Agricultural and Technical College, Fisk University, and Tougaloo College, operated as launching pads for the sit-ins in Greensboro, Nashville, and Jackson, respectively. Other black colleges, most notably Howard University, Atlanta University, Morgan State College, and Albany State College, served as a constant source of attacks on the status quo. Stretching back to the 1930s, Charles Houston, dean of Howard's Law School, used the university's law students and professors to fine-tune the legal attack on Jim Crow. Later, Howard University gave rise to the National Action Group, or NAG, one of the prime agents for militancy within SNCC and the civil rights movement in general.

Even in the many cases where black schools did not act as agents of change, in part because middle-class teachers and administrators had a vested interest in the status quo and feared reprisals from white authorities, such as loss of their jobs, they employed individual teachers who inspired their students to protest. William Chafe's case study of Greensboro, North Carolina, for instance, describes the impact that two teachers, Nell Coley and Vance Chavis, had on black students at Dudley High School. "By their own examples," Chafe writes, "each held forth a standard of pride and assertiveness that students found hard to forget. Chavis taught physics, but as one student recalled, he also taught the importance of 'not selling one's soul.' . . . Coley drove home the theme that nothing was beyond the reach of those who dared."[10] If these schools, magazines, newspapers, and individual mentors had not existed, the civil rights movement might have been stillborn.

In addition to these black-led or -controlled institutions, an assortment of interracial organizations and "halfway houses," a termed used by Aldon Morris in his book *The Origins of the Civil Rights Movement*, provided important resources for the burgeoning crusade for racial equality.[11] The Southern Conference for Human Welfare exemplified the role that several interracial organizations played on the eve of the modern civil rights movement. Formed in 1938 by prominent southern liberals, SCHW fostered interracial communication and promoted economic, educational, and social reform in the South. Even though it was red-baited out of existence, many of its ideals lived on in the Southern Christian Education Fund, which lent support to civil rights activists throughout the early 1960s. The Highlander Folk School of Tennessee, founded by Myles Horton in the 1930s to help workers and organized labor in the South, was another key halfway house. It sponsored retreats, training sessions, and symposia, which, among other things, gave a wide variety of activists, black and white, the space (both physical and emotional) to interact. At Highlander, veteran activists introduced a generation of younger men and women to organizing skills and tools which they then taught to others. Martin Luther King, Jr., learned the tune "We Shall Overcome" at Highlander. Rosa Parks attended a retreat at Highlander shortly before refusing to give up her seat. In the wake of the first wave of sit-ins, young protest leaders gathered at Highlander Center, where they developed contacts and strategies for the next phase of the movement.

To a lesser extent, organized labor bolstered the civil rights movement. For years, the American Federation of Labor (AFL) had done little to advance racial equality. Many of its unions (or locals) were racist to the core, and its overall philosophy of craft unionism reinforced the racial segmentation of the labor market. In contrast, the Congress of Industrial Organizations (CIO), which merged with the AFL in 1955, was born in the 1930s with the express goal of establishing interracial unions and at least the implicit promise of fighting for racial equality in society at large. By the time of its merger with the AFL, the CIO's commitment to the latter goal had diminished. Operation Dixie, whereby the CIO sought to organize black and white workers in the South, lay on its deathbed, and as studies by Bruce Nelson, Herbert Hill, and Robert Norrell have noted, the largest CIO unions—the United Automobile Workers, the United Steelworkers of America, and the electrical and garment workers' unions—displayed disturbing signs of racism within their ranks and leadership. Nonetheless, the number of blacks who belonged to labor unions grew steadily, and perhaps because of their presence the labor movement provided funds and political support for the civil rights movement. Labor leaders lobbied hard for civil rights legislation and gave financial aid to nearly all of the different civil rights organizations. In addition, a select number of unions, most particularly the Brotherhood of Sleeping Car Porters and the United Packinghouse Workers, became directly intertwined with the civil rights movement. E. D. Nixon, an officer with the Sleeping Car Porters, helped launch the Montgomery bus boycott. Other members of this all-black union helped jump-start the civil rights movement in their communities. The packinghouse workers' union provided funds for SNCC from its birth and conducted antiracist education campaigns within its ranks. In addition, these unions constantly pressured the federal government to intervene in the South and to enact civil rights legislation.

TRAILBLAZERS AND TORCHBEARERS

The modern civil rights movement also owed much of its success to numerous trailblazers and torchbearers, individual men and women who fought against Jim Crow, built the institutions upon which men like Martin Luther King, Jr., depended, and provided the foothold that new organizations such as SNCC needed to propel the movement forward.[12] Some of these men and women, among them W.E.B. Du Bois (co-founder of the NAACP), the poet Langston Hughes, and the educator Mary McLeod Bethune, have received their deserved spot in the history books. Others, such as Ida Wells Barnett and Mary Church Terrell, prominent early crusaders against lynching, have only just begun to receive attention. Still others, like Septima Clark, director of the Citizenship Schools, and Ella Baker, an organizer with the NAACP during the 1940s and a mentor to SNCC during the 1960s, probably will never be known outside a small circle of civil rights activists and scholars. Nonetheless, their contributions were large.

Indeed, the more closely scholars examine the civil rights movement, the more clearly they see the interconnections between these trailblazers and torchbearers and the movement itself. Rather than contending that racial equality was an idea whose time had come or seeing the burst of activism of the 1950s and 1960s as the result of amorphous, generally idealistic forces, scholars now see the movement as an outgrowth of years of struggle by numerous men and women. Charles Payne's *I've Got the Light of Freedom* uncovers a world of unknown activists in Mississippi who struggled against one of the most oppressive regimes in history over the course of decades. A number of them, such as the Reverend T. A. Allen, who sought to organize sharecroppers during the 1930s, the Reverend George Lee and Gus Courts, who founded the Belzoni, Mississippi, branch of the NAACP in the early 1950s, and Medgar Evers, Mississippi's most prominent activist during the 1950s and early 1960s, were either run out of the state or killed before the federal government ever passed civil rights legislation that affected the daily lives of African Americans in Mississippi. Others, such as Aaron Henry and Amzie Moore, leaders in the NAACP and/or the Mississippi Freedom Democratic Party, played an active role in the struggle for racial equality in Mississippi long before the nation paid any attention to the Magnolia State and after the public had cast its gaze elsewhere.[13]

Richard Kluger's *Simple Justice*, a masterful examination of the struggle to desegregate public education in the South, similarly shows that the *Brown* case was built on the sacrifices of many virtually anonymous plaintiffs. Harry Briggs of Clarendon County, South Carolina, who filed one of the four suits that was joined to the *Brown* suit against the Board of Education of Topeka, Kansas, was as responsible for toppling Jim Crow as Chief Justice Earl Warren of the Supreme Court. For filing this suit, Briggs, his wife, and other petitioners endured years of harassment, ranging from loss of credit and jobs to arrest to threats on their lives. Ultimately, the Briggses were forced to move to Florida, returning only long after their children had grown up, unable to take advantage of improvements in education that grew out of their early efforts.[14]

Several studies have suggested that a disproportionate number of the torchbearers and trailblazers were women, who drew on a tradition of activism within the African American community, stretching back to Harriet Tubman and Sojourner Truth. While these women rarely made the headlines or played official leadership roles during the 1960s, they did the organizing. Other scholars have suggested that World War II veterans played a seminal role, sowing the fields that younger activists reaped. Together these scholarly arguments reinforce the point that the modern civil rights movement depended on the actions of largely anonymous individual men and women.

In sum, many see the civil rights movement as an inevitable development, part of the nation's natural evolution. The standard dating of the movement in textbooks and popular accounts of the topic, beginning with the *Brown* decision and culminating with the Voting Rights Act of 1965 signed by President Johnson, reinforces this view. All that was necessary, according to this interpretation, was for the nation's leaders to hand down these edicts. Yet, this view of the past misses the underlying causes of the civil rights movement, from the deep structural changes that created the climate for change, to the development of resources by the African American community so that it could take advantage of the improved climate, to the courage and bravery of individual men and women who acted to alter the course of history. It also risks misrepresenting one of the main lessons of the civil rights years. The civil rights movement did not take place because a handful of leaders determined that the time was right for enacting certain reforms. Rather, thousands of ordinary men and women, taking advantage of existing conditions, forged a movement that compelled the nation to begin to live up to its ideals.

NOTES

1. Martin Luther King, Jr., "Our God Is Marching On!," in Levy, *Let Freedom Ring*, 162–64.

2. Gunnar Myrdal, *An American Dilemma* (New York: Harper & Row, 1944).

3. John F. Kennedy, "Address," June 11, 1963, in Levy, *Let Freedom Ring*, 117–19; Lyndon B. Johnson, "Address before a Joint Session of Congress, March 15, 1965," ibid., 159–62.

4. David Levering Lewis, "The Origins and Causes of the Civil Rights Movement," in *The Civil Rights Movement in America*, ed. Charles Eagles (Jackson: University Press of Mississippi, 1986), 3.

5. Vincent Harding, "We the People: The Long Journey toward a More Perfect Union," in Juan Williams, *Eyes on the Prize: America's Civil Rights Years, 1954–1965* (New York: Viking, 1988), 21.

6. Mary L. Dudziak, "Desegregation as a Cold War Imperative," *Stanford Law Review* 41, no. 1 (November 1988): 66–120.

7. King reflected on the bombing in *Stride toward Freedom*, excerpted in Levy, *Let Freedom Ring*, 60.

8. Griffin quoted in Levy, *Let Freedom Ring*, 32.

9. Nancy Weiss, "Creative Tensions in the Leadership of the Civil Rights Movement," in Eagles, *The Civil Rights Movement in America*, 39–64.

10. William Chafe, *Civilities and Civil Rights: Greensboro, North Carolina, and the Black Struggle for Freedom* (New York: Oxford University Press, 1980), 23.

11. Aldon D. Morris, *The Origins of the Civil Rights Movement: Black Communities Organizing for Change* (New York: Free Press, 1984).

12. The phrase, "trailblazers and torchbearers" is borrowed from Vicki L. Crawford, Jacqueline Anne Rouse, and Barbara Woods, eds., *Women in the Civil Rights Movement: Trailblazers and Torchbearers, 1941–1965* (Bloomington: Indiana University Press, 1993).

13. Charles M. Payne, *I've Got the Light of Freedom: The Organizing Tradition and the Mississippi Freedom Struggle* (Berkeley: University of California Press, 1995).

14. Richard Kluger, *Simple Justice: The History of Brown v. Board of Education and Black America's Struggle for Equality* (New York: Random House, 1975).

Mississippi and Its Environs

3

Mississippi: "Is This America?"
A Case Study of the Movement

THE CLOSED SOCIETY

On July 2, 1946, Medgar Evers, a black native of Mississippi and a World War II combat veteran, along with several other black GIs, headed down to the courthouse in Evers's hometown of Decatur, Mississippi. Evers hoped to celebrate his return from service and his twenty-first birthday by voting in the Democratic primary. When the group arrived at the courthouse, however, they encountered a mob of fifteen to twenty armed white men intent on stopping them or any other blacks from exercising their franchise. "We had all seen a lot of dead people on Omaha beach," Evers recalled. "All we wanted to be was ordinary citizens. We fought during the war for America, Mississippi included. Now after the Germans and Japanese hadn't killed us, it looked as though white Mississippians would." Rather than risk sure death, Evers and the other black veterans retreated. Even in retreat Evers could see a white man with a gun "keeping a bead on us all the time," a reminder of the precariousness of the life of a black person in Mississippi.[1]

Nearly a decade later, in August 1955, Emmett Till, a fourteen-year-old black youth from Chicago, traveled to Money, Mississippi, to visit with his mother's family. Shortly after he arrived, Till, his cousins, and their friends ventured to the town drugstore to buy some candy. On his way out of the store, Till allegedly whistled at and said "bye baby" to the female shopkeeper. Later that night, the shopkeeper's husband, Roy Bryant, and his half-brother, J. W. Milam, knocked at the door of the home of Mose Wright, Till's great-uncle, where Till was staying. Shining a flashlight into Wright's eyes and brandishing a revolver, Bryant asked for the boy who had been "talking fresh." Bryant and Milam dragged Till out of the house, beat and shot him, and then threw his dead body, attached to a cotton gin fan, into the Tallahatchie River.

Till's murder outraged African Americans nationwide. Till's mother insisted upon an open-casket funeral so that "the whole world could see what they've done." *Jet* magazine featured a photograph of Till's bloated and mutilated body. The NAACP kept the Till incident in the limelight in order to generate support for the fight against segregation. Bryant and Milam were arrested and brought to trial for murder. At the end of the trial, their defense attorney turned to the jury and declared. "I am sure that every last Anglo-Saxon one of you will have the courage to free these men." After adjourning for lunch, the jury acquitted the accused of all charges. Afterwards, in a paid interview with William Bradford Huie for *Look* magazine, Bryant and Milam admitted that they had killed Till in cold blood. As Milam recalled: "I just decided it was time a few people got put on notice. As long as I live and can do anything about it, niggers are gonna stay in their place."[2]

To a large extent, Till's murder achieved Bryant and Milam's purpose. In the face of constant threats and actual acts of violence, fear and passivity predominated in Mississippi's African American community. When Anne Moody, who grew up near Money, Mississippi, and was Till's age, tried to broach the subject of his murder, her mother nervously responded, "Where did you hear that?" When Moody said that she had learned about the murder from her friends, her mother retorted that more talk about the incident would just lead to further trouble. As Moody prepared for work at a local white woman's home, her mother advised her to "just do your work like you don't know nothing." While at work, Moody was so nervous that she found it hard to clear or wash the dishes without dropping them. Her employer's remark, that Till had been killed because he didn't know his place, left Moody even more scared. As she recalled:

Before Emmett Till's murder, I had known the fear of hunger, hell, and the Devil. But now there was a new fear known to me—the fear of being killed just because I was black. This was the worst of my fears. I knew once I got food, the fear of starving to death would leave. I also was told that if I was a good girl, I wouldn't have to fear the Devil or hell. But I didn't know what one had to do or not do as a Negro not to be killed. Probably just being a Negro period was enough.[3]

Although not representative of everyday life in Mississippi, these two incidents provide keen insight into race relations there at mid-century. Evers responded to being driven away from the polls by committing his life to the fight for racial equality, and Moody determined to ignore her mother's advice and later joined the movement, but they were, for awhile, the exception to the rule. As of 1955 only about twelve thousand, or 2 percent, of all African Americans who were eligible to vote in the Magnolia State were registered. In many counties, especially those with a high percentage of black residents, the percentage of those registered was even lower. The NAACP, which had shown signs of life in the mid-1940s, lay in disarray. The black press and black educators maintained an accommodationist posture rather than risk further trouble. The black middle class stayed to itself. While the SCLC, Martin Luther King, Jr.'s organization, spread through most of the South, it formed no chapters in Mississippi during the 1950s or early 1960s.

To make matters worse, the cotton economy of the Mississippi Delta, the mainstay of African American life for over a century, was in the midst of a revolution, one that began with the introduction of mechanical pickers during the 1940s and continued with the development of chemical fertilizers and defoliants in the 1950s and 1960s. These technological breakthroughs underlay the great migration of African Americans out of the state, with over three hundred thousand blacks leaving Mississippi between 1930 and 1970. Whereas the mechanization of cotton plantations tended to give rise to a progressive business class elsewhere, Mississippi remained committed to the old ways of life. The small business community united behind the White Citizens' Council, which devoted itself to maintaining segregation regardless of the economic costs of doing so, and the Klan enjoyed a revival. Even the voices of moderation, such as that of Mississippi sage William Faulkner, advised blacks to go slow. "The South is armed for revolt," Faulkner observed. "These white people will accept another Civil War knowing they're going to lose."[4]

Politics reflected the white majority's commitment to maintaining Jim Crow and the utter lack of dissent. Mississippi remained a one-party state: all members of the state legislature, its governor, and U.S. Senators and Congressmen were Democrats. The only time Mississippi did not stand in the Democratic column was during presidential elections. In 1948 Mississippians supported Strom Thurmond and the Dixiecrat or States' Rights Party. In 1960 Mississippi was the only state to cast its entire electoral college vote for Senator Harry Byrd, an independent and segregationist, rather than support either John F. Kennedy or Richard Nixon. In the same years, Mississippi's representatives in Washington, through filibusters and committee work, blocked or watered down civil rights legislation and red-baited civil rights organizations and leaders, from the NAACP to Martin Luther King. James Silver, a University of Mississippi professor at the time and author of the classic *Mississippi: The Closed Society*, captured the essence of politics in the state: "There can be no real debate on issues for there is no issue beyond the supremacy of the white man."[5]

Due to the intensity of repression, Mississippi presented the greatest challenge to the civil rights movement. Activists had to overcome both extraordinary white resistance and a deep sense of fatalism and fear among Mississippi's blacks. Failure to take on Mississippi, the citadel of segregation and white supremacy, would have signified a tremendous flaw in the movement. Evading the state to concentrate limited resources on more fertile ground would have left victories won elsewhere with a hollow ring. By taking on the closed society, the civil rights movement displayed its commitment to attaining equality for all of America's citizens. The risks were the greatest and the odds the longest, but ultimately the prize was the grandest.

For the historian, the rewards of examining the civil rights movement on a local or regional level, as this chapter will do, are also great. By focusing on Mississippi, we will gain a richer sense of the movement than can be garnered from a study of it from a national perspective. We will see the crucial role that local people played in the struggle for equality and come to understand how the movement developed in the face of mass resistance and fear. Moreover, by concentrating on a single region, we will have the opportunity to assess the significance of the movement, to determine what did and did not change in the lives of ordinary people.

IN THE MIDDLE OF THE ICEBERG

As the 1960s dawned, few if any national observers predicted that Mississippi would become the focal point of the most vibrant civil rights movement in the nation. On the contrary, Mississippi seemed the least likely candidate for such a movement. The Magnolia State's tradition of violence and repression (physical and psychological) deterred the NAACP and the SCLC from devoting resources to a campaign there. In addition, the indigenous civil rights movement appeared dead, crushed by the White Citizens' Councils and the Ku Klux Klan.

More so than any other organization, the Student Nonviolent Coordinating Committee (SNCC), which ignored these odds, helped galvanize a broad-based movement. Led by Robert Parris Moses, a black New York City native, it took on the challenge of transforming the Magnolia State. A graduate of Hamilton College (B.A.) and Harvard University (M.A.), Moses was teaching mathematics at Horace Mann High School in the Bronx when the sit-ins erupted in February 1960. Inspired by them, he traveled to Atlanta to join the freedom movement as soon as he could. Upon arrival at the SCLC's headquarters in Atlanta, he spent some time helping the SCLC prepare a fund-raising drive, picketed supermarkets as part of the Atlanta student movement's campaign for desegregation and jobs, and discussed Camus, Gandhi, and other philosophers with Jane Stembridge, a white volunteer who worked as SNCC's secretary.

As a New Yorker, Moses did not totally fit into Atlanta's movement; indeed, some local activists suspected him of being a communist. At the same time, Moses found that the situation in Atlanta did not meet his expectations or suit his nature. Thus, partly on the suggestion of Ella Baker, he jumped at the opportunity to journey to Mississippi to recruit people for an upcoming SNCC conference. With introductions provided by Baker, he met several enthusiastic and committed activists, the most important of whom was Amzie Moore, a leader of the local NAACP in Cleveland, Mississippi. Moore helped convince Moses to return the following summer after completing the final year of his teaching contract.

In the interim, CORE staged the freedom rides, which ultimately landed over three hundred activists in Mississippi's Parchman Penitentiary. Many of these riders belonged to SNCC and were perfectly situated to join Moses upon their release. The freedom rides had prodded the Kennedy administration to garner foundation support for voter registration efforts in the South, which the administration considered less confrontational than direct-action protests like sit-ins or the freedom rides themselves. While many within SNCC did not want to bow to the Kennedy administration's calls for it to steer clear of direct-action protest, the promise of federal support and funds for voter registration dovetailed with Moses's vague plans.

In mid-July 1961, Moses arrived in Mississippi. Armed with the promise of some foundation support and the likelihood that numerous SNCC members would join him, he embarked upon an ambitious and idealistic voter registration drive. He quickly came into contact with what sociologists have termed an assortment of preexisting networks of activism. These networks gave Moses and others an entrée into the local African American community, which in turn provided the resources vital to building and sustaining a movement. They gave SNCC members places to live (often their homes), sites to hold meetings, and encouragement to continue in the face of Mississippi justice.

In McComb, Mississippi, where Moses first set down roots, he enjoyed the support of C. C. Bryant, the head of the local NAACP, which had been driven underground in the mid-1950s. In the Mississippi Delta towns of Clarkesdale and Cleveland, Moses gained backing from Aaron Henry and

Amzie Moore, two other NAACP veterans. Bryant, who had read about Moses's plans to register voters in Mississippi in *Jet* magazine, welcomed the twenty-six-year-old New Yorker into his home when he arrived in July 1961. In the next several weeks, Webb Owens, Bryant's co-worker on the Illinois Central Railroad and co-leader of the local NAACP, introduced Moses to numerous townspeople. Partly because they respected Owens and Bryant, blacks in McComb listened to Moses and granted him access to their mimeograph machine and to the Masons' meeting hall. Sensing an opportunity, SNCC sent two other organizers, Reginald Robinson and John Hardy, to McComb. Along with Moses, they canvassed the black community door to door, encouraging local people to register to vote. Subsequently, Hardy and several other SNCC members, fresh from the freedom rides, along with several black Mississippi college students, journeyed into Amite County where, with the help of E. W. Steptoe, another NAACP member, they set up a second voter registration campaign.

Quite often black youths proved the first recruits, even though they were not themselves always old enough to vote. Hollis Watkins, a farm boy from the Mississippi Delta, heard one day that Martin Luther King was in McComb. Having been excited by the freedom rides, he and his friend, Curtis Hayes, traveled to town, where they found Moses rather than King. After listening to Moses describe his project, Watkins and Hayes agreed to start work the following day. Not long after, they met Marion Barry (the future mayor of Washington, D.C.), a native of Itta Bena, Mississippi, and SNCC's first national chair, who explained another aspect of SNCC's venture in the state, direct-action protests against segregation. Inspired by Barry's vision, Watkins and Hayes, joined by several other local youths, staged McComb's first sit-in.

The parents of youths who became active frequently followed their sons and daughters into the movement. In Greenwood, for example, June Johnson's mother, Belle, like many other adults, initially tried to ward her children away from SNCC, fearing, somewhat correctly, that it would only lead to trouble. Following the beating of her daughter, however, she decided to commit herself to overcoming racial injustice rather than withdrawing from public action.

While churches played a less important role in Mississippi than they did in several other southern states, most likely because years of repression had prompted black ministers and church elders to adopt an accommodationist stance, religion occupied a key place in the movement's activities. Moses and other SNCC activists were steeped in the traditions of the African American church, and they played to the black community's underlying

Christian faith to recruit people to the movement. SNCC often began its meetings with a prayer. Freedom songs, based on old or updated gospel tunes, constituted a central part of these gatherings. Some activists even put on the airs of a minister to win support for the movement.

Although men usually provided SNCC with its first entrée into Mississippi's black communities, women quickly took on leading roles. In Canton there was Annie Devine; in Mayersville and Hattiesburg, Unita Blackwell and Victoria Gray, respectively. Lou Emma Allen led the singing at mass meetings in Greenwood; Winnie Hudson stood at the center of the movement in Harmony. More famous yet was Fannie Lou Hamer, a sharecropper from Ruleville.

By tapping these preexisting networks, Moses and SNCC built a movement in McComb and its environs more quickly than many thought possible. Whites, nonetheless, quickly mobilized a counterattack. On August 15, 1961, Billy Jack Caston, the cousin of the local sheriff, assaulted Bob Moses with a knife. After receiving eight stitches for his head wound, Moses defied Mississippi tradition by pressing charges against his white assailant. At the trial, after a half-dozen whites lied from the witness stand, claiming that the defendant had acted in self-defense, Caston was acquitted of all charges. Not long after this, a white voter registrar pistol-whipped John Hardy into near-unconsciousness, and Hardy, not the registrar, was placed under arrest for disturbing the peace. On September 25, Herbert Lee, a black farmer and NAACP member, and one of Moses's first recruits to the voter drive, was shot to death in broad daylight in Liberty, Mississippi, by state assemblyman E. H. Hurst. Hurst was never charged with committing a crime, and the only black eyewitness was killed before the FBI could take his deposition.

In response to this counterattack, local black students, over one hundred strong, staged a freedom march. After proceeding through the black community and the business district, they assembled at McComb's City Hall. Not surprisingly, authorities promptly placed them under arrest. Before they were taken into custody, however, a white mob surged forward and attacked Robert Zellner, SNCC's most prominent white organizer. Moses and Charles McDew, another SNCC member, tried to pull Zellner into City Hall while white ruffians pulled him in the opposite direction, gouging his eyes and beating him unconscious in the process. Despite the fact that all of the civil rights activists had acted nonviolently, none of the whites in the mob were arrested. Instead, Moses, Zellner, and the other activists were arrested and tried for disturbing the peace and sentenced to prison terms of four to six months. (Brenda Travis, age fifteen, who was tried as a juvenile, received an indeterminate sentence at the facility for "Negro delinquents.") From his jail cell, Moses penned "Letter from a Mississippi Jail Cell," one of the most profound documents of the decade. "This is Mississippi, the middle of the iceberg," Moses wrote. "This is a tremor in the middle of the iceberg—from the stone that the builders rejected."

In December 1961, Moses and the others were released from jail. (Travis remained in detention until May 1962.) By this time, the movement in McComb lay dead. Nevertheless, over the course of the summer and fall, SNCC had learned some important lessons. It discovered that black youths would respond to its initiatives, that a core of older blacks yearned for change and would provide support, though perhaps not for direct-action protests, and that whites would fight back with all the weapons at their disposal to maintain white supremacy. SNCC, which had undertaken the voter registration drive in Mississippi partly due to the encouragement it had received from the Kennedy administration, also learned that the federal government could not be depended on to protect them or local blacks who sought to register to vote. (FBI agents took notes while Zellner was mauled, refusing to intervene because, according to J. Edgar Hoover, its director, it was only an investigative body.) Whether SNCC could mobilize enough local blacks to overcome white repression without effective support from the federal government remained unclear, but the violence SNCC activists encountered and the prison sentences they received did not deter them from trying. On the contrary, they hardened their resolve to push on.

JAMES MEREDITH AND MEDGAR EVERS

SNCC was not the only civil rights organization to tackle racial inequality in the state. CORE, led by Dave Dennis, established a voter registration drive in the Fourth Congressional District, which included Madison County, whose population was 70 percent black. The NAACP, led by Medgar Evers, enjoyed a revival despite the systematic repression of its members. Evers, who had been chased away from the voting booth in 1946, spent much of the 1950s traveling around the state trying to build and sustain local NAACP chapters. Massive white resistance following the *Brown* decision stalled Evers's organizing efforts. Still, he managed to keep the organization alive, putting it in a position to move when the opportunity presented itself, as it did in January 1961. About the same time that John Kennedy was being sworn in as president, James Meredith informed Evers that he wanted to enroll at the all-white University of Mississippi. Upon Evers's advice, Meredith wrote to Thurgood Marshall, the director of the NAACP Legal Defense Fund, asking for the organization's support. That Meredith had spent nine years in the air force, rising to the rank of staff sergeant, had already completed twelve credits at all-black Jackson State College, and appeared an exemplary citizen convinced the NAACP to pursue Meredith's case.

In a sense, Meredith was to education in Mississippi what Jackie Robinson was to major league baseball. He was the person on whose shoulders the breaking of the color line rested. Evers, like Branch Rickey of the Brooklyn Dodgers, stood behind the scenes, offering his full support. Unlike major league baseball, however, the state of Mississippi committed itself to maintaining segregation, especially at Ole Miss, a symbol of the southern way of life.

When the NAACP got a federal district court to order the University of Mississippi to admit Meredith, Governor Ross Barnett, the White Citizens' Council candidate in 1960, rallied the state (indeed the region) behind segregation. In a televised address, Barnett compared the crisis at Ole Miss to the War Between the States (the southern term for the Civil War). "There is no case in history where the Caucasian race has survived social integration," Barnett exclaimed. In response to the orders that the state accept integration, Barnett retorted, "Never." As a showdown with the federal government over Meredith's admission to the university grew closer, Barnett whipped up even more support for southern resistance. Speaking at halftime to tens of thousands of diehard University of Mississippi football fans, Barnett declared: "I love Mississippi. I love her people, her customs! And I love and respect her heritage." Waving Confederate flags, the crowd interrupted Barnett's speech with chants of "Never, Never, Never, Never, N-o-o-o Never. . . . Ross's standing like Gibraltar. He shall never falter. Ask us what we say, it's to hell with Bobby K. Never shall our emblem go, from Colonel Reb to Old Black Joe."[6]

On Sunday, September 30, 1962, the day after the game, as students returned from the football stadium in Jackson to the university's campus in Oxford, U.S. marshals secretly escorted Meredith onto campus, with the plan of registering him for classes the following morning. Toward nightfall, rumors of Meredith's presence spread. Enraged students and nonstudents, including many from outside the state, lit bonfires and joined in cheers of "Two, four, six, eight, we don't want to integrate." In time, a full-scale riot erupted. While federal marshals battled the rioters, President Kennedy delivered a televised address on the confrontation at Ole Miss. "Americans are free . . . to disagree with the law," Kennedy declared, "but not to disobey it. For any government of laws and not of men, no man, however prominent and powerful, and no matter however unruly and boisterous, is entitled to defy a court of law." The mob either did not hear or chose not to heed

Kennedy's words, as the situation on campus worsened. By daybreak, over 150 marshals had been injured; over 25 had been shot. Two men, including a French reporter, were killed.[7]

Just before 8 A.M., with federal troops having finally restored order on campus, Meredith registered as a full-time student. An hour later he attended his first class, in American colonial history. None of the white students who participated in the riots were expelled from the university. Meredith, who had to endure constant harassment, graduated in 1963, after which he traveled to Africa and earned his law degree from Columbia University in New York City.

Even though the university was desegregated only in a token manner, the Meredith incident emboldened blacks in the state. For Medgar Evers, in particular, who had been denied admission to Ole Miss, Meredith's enrollment represented a personal victory. As the spring of 1963 approached, he organized a massive freedom campaign in Jackson. Responding to the claim of Jackson's mayor, Allen Thompson, that blacks in Mississippi were content and that racial turmoil was the product of outside agitators, Evers declared, "I speak as a native Mississippian. . . . I was educated in Mississippi schools and served overseas in our nation's armed forces in the war against Hitlerism and fascism." "Never in its history," he continued, "has the South as a region, without outside pressure, granted the Negro his citizenship rights." To make matters worse, the pace of change was abominable, slower than that in Africa, where blacks had more opportunities than they did in the deep South. When the Negro looks about his home community, what does he see?, Evers inquired. "He sees a city where Negro citizens are refused admittance to the city auditorium and the coliseum; his children refused a ticket to a good movie in a downtown theater; his wife and children refused service at a lunch counter in a downtown store where they trade. . . . He sees a city of over 50,000, of which forty percent is Negro, in which there is not a single Negro policeman or policewoman . . . fireman, clerk, stenographer. . . . He sees local hospitals which segregate Negro patients."[8]

Evers's address helped launch a mass movement in Jackson that rivaled Martin Luther King, Jr.'s crusade in Birmingham, Alabama. Despite the national NAACP's aversion to direct action, the campaign included sit-ins, boycotts, and mass demonstrations. Many of the participants, such as Anne Moody, came from all-black Tougaloo College or Jackson State. Sensing the power of the movement, Mayor Thompson sought to negotiate a settlement providing for some desegregation. But Thompson's efforts were derailed by the White Citizens' Council, which threatened to punish all who complied with the deal. Given the council's power, neither the mayor nor

Jackson's merchants could afford to take this threat lightly. As the number of arrests increased, the national office of the NAACP warned that it could no longer afford the legal costs of a mass campaign. Rather than calling the protests off, however, Evers turned to black entertainer Lena Horne for help. On June 7, she performed a benefit concert that raised funds for bail and kept the movement going. At the concert, Evers told the audience, "I love my children and I love my wife with all my heart. And I would die, and die gladly, if that would make a better life for them."[9] Five days later, shortly after President Kennedy delivered a televised address on civil rights, Evers was assassinated on his front doorstep.

In the wake of Evers's funeral, only the personal intervention of Justice Department official John Doar averted a riot between angry blacks and police. Evers was buried at Arlington National Cemetery. Byron de la Beckwith, an arch–white supremacist whose fingerprints were found on the rifle used to kill Evers, was arrested. Two murder trials, however, ended in hung juries, and Beckwith was released from jail, heralded by many whites as a hero.

FREEDOM SUMMER

In the late fall of 1963, Robert Moses proposed that SNCC alter its tactics in the Delta, calling on the Council of Federated Organizations (COFO), the umbrella organization that coordinated the activities of SNCC, the NAACP, and CORE in Mississippi, to mount a major campaign, known as Freedom or Mississippi Summer. According to his plans, COFO would recruit about one thousand students, many of them white, from elite colleges and universities to join the movement in Mississippi in the summer of 1964. These volunteers would head up Freedom Schools and help organize a Freedom Democratic Party.

The decision to organize Freedom Summer grew out of Moses's sense that the movement in Mississippi had reached its limits and that it needed more resources and national attention, which, presumably, would follow the well-connected volunteers. The plan also flowed from a smaller-scale project that Allard Lowenstein, a liberal New Yorker, had organized in Mississippi in the fall of 1963, in which one hundred Yale and Stanford students had encouraged black Mississippians to participate in a mock election, a "freedom vote."

While many within the state shared Moses's view that something new needed to be done, some veteran activists worried that Freedom Summer would undermine SNCC's goal of developing local or indigenous leader-ship and empowering ordinary people. Whites, they observed, would take the lead; the uneducated would give way to the highly educated. This in turn would reinforce the old patterns of dependency and deference SNCC had struggled to overcome. To a degree these fears grew out of Lowenstein's earlier efforts. Unlike Moses, Lowenstein operated in a paternalistic, somewhat patronizing manner, showing little concern about the impact he was having on ordinary people. Nonetheless, SNCC's national leaders, especially John Lewis and James Forman, threw their support behind the Freedom Summer idea. Moses also won support from several key Mississippi-born activists, most notably Fannie Lou Hamer and Aaron Henry, with Hamer observing that the freedom movement could not segregate itself as long as it sought to topple Jim Crow. As a result, in December 1963, SNCC committed itself to Freedom Summer. The following month COFO officially endorsed the plan.

As noted above, Freedom Summer had two main foci, Freedom Schools and the Mississippi Freedom Democratic Party (MFDP). The schools were directed by Staughton Lynd, a young white history professor at Spelman College, and staffed by experienced teachers as well as novices. At nearly fifty schools, housed in a variety of structures ranging from churches to abandoned school buildings, summer volunteers and Mississippi natives taught an innovative curriculum to about twenty-five hundred students. Howard Zinn, a colleague of Lynd's at Spelman and one of the first historians of the movement, described the program thus: "Nine-year-old Negro children sounded out French words whose English equivalents they had not yet discovered. . . . They learned about Frederick Douglass, wrote letters to the local editor about segregation, and discussed the meaning of civil disobedience. Some wrote short stories about their lives, and others wrote poems."[10]

At the least, COFO felt that the MFDP would educate blacks in the state about the intricacies of politics. More optimistically, COFO entertained hopes that the MFDP would be seated at the national convention by the Democratic Party. These hopes grew over the course of the summer due to support that the MFDP received from many influential liberals, especially Joe Rauh, who was both the legal counsel for the United Automobile Workers, one of the largest and most influential labor unions in the nation, and the leader of the Americans for Democratic Action, a key liberal organization.

Since the regular Democratic Party of the state prohibited all but token participation by blacks in the electoral process, the MFDP sought to gain recognition at the 1964 Democratic convention in Atlantic City as the legitimate representative of the citizens of Mississippi. To this end, the MFDP followed all of the rules that the regular party followed, ranging from gathering the right number of signatures on petitions required for placing candidates on the ballot, to holding elections for a slate of delegates to attend a state convention on the date prescribed by state law for said convention. At the end of this process, the MFDP held a convention that elected a slate of delegates to represent the state at the Democratic convention, whom it then sent to Atlantic City. Unlike that of the regular Democrats, the MFDP's slate consisted of both black and white delegates.

The summer was a terribly violent one. Even before the bulk of volunteers arrived, three activists, Michael Schwerner, James Chaney, and Andrew Goodman, disappeared after investigating the burning of a remote church in Philadelphia, Mississippi. Following a massive manhunt ordered by President Johnson, they were found murdered, shot, according to the autopsy, on or around the date of their disappearance. Meanwhile, white nightriders bombed or burned numerous local civil rights sites, including thirty-five churches, and over one thousand activists were arrested by Mississippi authorities.

Mississippi Summer came to a climax in late August 1964 in Atlantic City, when Joe Rauh and several other lawyers, including Eleanor Holmes Norton, a future political leader in Washington, D.C., presented the MFDP's case for representation at the convention. The most dramatic moment of this challenge came with Fannie Lou Hamer's testimony; she awed the committee with her description of the repression she had encountered for trying to participate in the political process. For registering to vote, she explained, she had been evicted from her home of eighteen years on less than twenty-four hours' notice. The homes of the friends with whom she sought refuge had been fired on by nightriders. After attending a citizenship class, she had been beaten and abused by police and state patrolmen. "All of this on account we want to register, to become first-class citizens." In conclusion, Hamer rhetorically inquired in her testimony before the Credentials Committee: "And if the freedom Democratic Party is not seated now, I question America, is this America, the land of the free and the home of the brave where we have to sleep with our telephones off the hooks because our lives be threatened daily because we want to live as decent human beings, in America?"

Even before Hamer reached this point in her testimony, President Johnson, fearing its impact, requested television time to hold an immediate press conference. In an era where the press still jumped to the president's wishes, the major networks obliged. Still, many Americans later heard Hamer's testimony on the evening news. Johnson subsequently demanded that the MFDP accept a "compromise," whereby the Democrats would seat two at-large MFDP delegates, in exchange for which the regular Mississippi delegation would swear its loyalty to the national ticket and the party would promise to enact reforms by the next convention. To ensure acceptance of this compromise, LBJ used all the political skills and tricks at his disposal, as well as the FBI, which spied on the MFDP. Important delegates were threatened with the loss of federal patronage or promised rewards if they promoted the compromise. Johnson even warned that he would not nominate Hubert Humphrey, a darling of the liberal wing of the party for nearly two decades, for vice president if liberals in the party did not line up behind the compromise. Walter Reuther, a Humphrey backer and the president of the United Automobile Workers, threatened Joe Rauh with the loss of his job if he did not moderate his stance.

The MFDP, however, refused to budge, terming the suggested compromise tokenism and comparing Johnson's strong-arm tactics to the type of treatment they received back home. As Hamer, the moral symbol of the delegation, put it, "We didn't come all this way for that mess again." When the credentials committee bowed to the wishes of President Johnson, refusing even to allow a roll-call vote on the challenge, MFDP and SNCC leaders exploded with anger. The usually soft-spoken Robert Moses informed reporters that he would "have nothing to do with the political system any longer." Cleveland Sellers, SNCC's future chair, observed after the convention, "Things could never be the same. . . . Never again were we bullied into believing that our task was exposing injustices so that 'good' people of America could eliminate them." On the contrary, said Sellers, "We left Atlantic City with the knowledge that the movement had turned into something else. After Atlantic City, our struggle was not for civil rights, but for liberation."[11]

BLACK POWER AND THE LEGACY
OF THE MOVEMENT

Freedom Summer stood as a crucial moment in the history of the nation; it had a deep impact on the civil rights movement and on other aspects of American life. In some ways it made the sixties the sixties, an era of rebellion and turmoil rather than consensus. Many of the volunteers returned to their respective colleges and communities politically radicalized, soured on President Johnson and liberalism. Mario Savio, for example, a summer volunteer, returned to the University of California at Berkeley, where he led the first white student movement of the decade, the free speech movement. Staughton Lynd, Norma Becker, Sandra Addickes, Dennis Sweeny, and Mandy Samstein were just a handful of summer volunteers who became active participants in the budding anti–Vietnam War movement. Mary King and Casey Hayden, both of whom had been active in the civil rights movement prior to 1964, played key roles in forging the women's movement. Marshall Ganz, Mike Miller, and several others went to work for the United Farm Workers.

As Sellers's comments suggest, Freedom Summer had at least as dramatic an impact on SNCC and CORE. In the wake of the summer, both organizations increasingly challenged several of the basic tenets of the early civil rights movement. The call for coalition with liberals, already weakened by what SNCC and CORE members saw as the inadequacy of federal intervention in the South, suffered an even deeper blow from the fiasco at Atlantic City. The sheer number of deaths, beatings, and threats received in the summer, coming on top of years of repression, mocked the principle of nonviolence and convinced many SNCC and CORE activists to adopt new tactics and openly to advocate self-defense. For some activists, this did not represent a radical shift in views, as they had never held a deep philosophical attachment to nonviolence. For SNCC and CORE as a whole, however, both of which had been established on the principle of nonviolence, the repudiation of nonviolence represented a dramatic change.

At the same time, integration as a primary goal suffered a setback, partly because of petty jealousies that developed over the formation of interracial couples, more substantively due to the ways in which an influx of whites reinforced the old problem of black dependency. Nationwide, integration, which in practice often translated into token desegregation of all-white institutions rather than the transformation of traditionally all-white institutions into truly multicultural entities, came under increasing attack. Freedom Summer also left many veteran Mississippi activists emotionally and physically exhausted. Fearing that he was becoming too prominent, Robert Moses changed his name to Robert Parris (his middle name) and withdrew from the movement. This allowed for the ascendancy of more militant leaders within SNCC, most notably Stokely Carmichael, Cleveland Sellers, and H. Rap Brown, none of whom had ever held a deep philosophical commitment to nonviolence.

Proof of SNCC's and CORE's shifting vision came with their open advocacy of black power, a term Carmichael popularized in Greenwood, Mississippi, in 1966, during the March Against Fear. The march was James Meredith's idea. Following his return from Africa, he vowed to walk over two hundred and fifty miles across the state. Less than twenty miles into his journey, however, Meredith was shot and left for dead. While Meredith had not been a member of SNCC, CORE, or SCLC, they vowed to carry on his crusade. As the marchers approached Greenwood, the mood grew more militant. Confrontations took place between the police and civil rights activists, leading to the arrest of Stokely Carmichael, SNCC's new leader. After police released him from jail, Carmichael spoke at a nighttime rally: "This is the twenty-seventh time I have been arrested, and I ain't going to jail no more!" Carmichael declared: "The only way we gonna stop them white men from whuppin' us is to take over. We been saying freedom for six years—and we ain't got nothin'. What we gonna start saying now is 'Black Power!' "[12] Carmichael's colleague Willie Ricks immediately picked up on Carmichael's words, chanting, "What do you want?," to which the crowd responded (with Ricks still in the lead), "Black Power! Black Power! Black Power!"

Freedom Summer had a complex and in some ways paradoxical impact on local activists in Mississippi. Put simply, black power both became and did not become the goal of those who remained in Mississippi. Building on SNCC's efforts in the state, the Freedom Schools, and the MFDP, the civil rights movement kept plowing ahead after Atlantic City. In 1965 local activists challenged the seating of Mississippi's congressional delegation. Although their challenge was rejected, they maintained an interest in politics. Especially after the passage of the Voting Rights Act of 1965, civil rights forces in Mississippi focused much of their attention on first registering and then getting out the black vote. Whites threw up one barrier to political empowerment after another, from redrawing district lines to moving toward the election of representatives on an at-large basis to dilute the black vote. Local activists, nonetheless, were not deterred. Over the next two decades, they remained committed to attaining black political power by organizing voter registration drives county by county and encouraging blacks to stand for office. As a result, Mississippi, which in 1964 had the lowest percentage of registered black voters of all eleven states of the old Confederacy, by the mid-1980s had the highest percentage of registered black voters and the greatest number of black officials of any state in the nation. In 1964, 6.7 percent of the black voting-age population was registered. By 1980 that number had risen to 64.1 percent. In 1964 Mississippi had no black elected officials, but as of 1993 there were 751 black officeholders, including a justice of the state supreme court, forty-two state legislators (about one-fourth of the entire body), and one congressman. In communities where they once had been shot for trying to register to vote, blacks became mayors, city council members, and sheriffs during the 1980s and 1990s. Unita Blackwell, for example, one of the first local people to join Moses's efforts in Mayersville, Mississippi, became its mayor. In the political realm, blacks in Mississippi gained power.

A bit more subtly, the language and style of politics in the state changed significantly. Public advocacy of white supremacy declined with the rise in the black vote. Racial demagoguery, once a mainstay of Mississippi politics and the political calling card of such famous race-baiters as Theodore Bilbo, John Rankin, and Ross Barnett, diminished to the point where few if any serious candidates for higher office campaigned as open segregationists. During the same time period, at a time when black power advocates questioned the value of integration, blacks pressured the state to desegregate. In 1969 the Supreme Court unanimously ruled in *Alexander* v. *Holmes County* that the time for "all deliberate speed" had come to an end. As a result, the state acceded to the desegregation of its schools without further resistance. True, many whites left public schools for private academies, but by 1980 blacks in Mississippi were much more likely to attend an integrated school than blacks in the Northeast, the Midwest, or the West.

This is not to suggest that racial inequality disappeared in Mississippi or that the civil rights movement achieved a golden age after Freedom Summer. After 1964 the movement in Mississippi tended to become divided between reformers or pragmatists such as Charles Evers, Medgar's brother, on the one hand, and more radical, grassroots-oriented activists like Fannie Lou Hamer and Hollis Watkins, on the other. The persistence of poverty among a large segment of blacks in the state, in a large part the legacy of Mississippi's racist history, tempered all gains, and at times reinforced these divisions. So too did the Vietnam War. Partly to gain more influence in Washington, D.C., which would produce more federal antipoverty dollars at home, the so-called practical reformers favored coalition with moderate whites, which meant supporting President Johnson's policies in Vietnam or at least not publicly voicing opposition to them. In contrast, more militant or radical activists, seeking an independent base of political power, disdained coalition, opposed the Vietnam War, and called for more radical antipoverty measures than those proffered by the War on Poverty.

One of the most profound by-products of the civil rights movement in Mississippi, as in the rest of the South, was the resurgence of the Republican Party. In 1972 two Mississippi Republicans, Thad Cochran and Trent Lott, were elected to the House of Representatives. Neither of them sounded at all like the Radical Republicans who had once attained power in the state during Reconstruction. Both were strong advocates of states' rights and a smaller federal government, and both opposed further federal civil rights measures, such as affirmative action. By the end of the 1980s Cochran and Lott had moved up to the U.S. Senate, with Lott becoming the majority leader in 1996. While Democrats remained strong in the state, many of them tended to share Lott's and Cochran's ultraconservative views.

Nonetheless, the emergence of the Republican Party as a player in Mississippi politics should not obscure the fact that Mississippi had become a much different place. In a state where Ross Barnett had once vowed "Never" and Senator James Eastland had linked every civil rights organization and advocate to the Communist Party, even conservative Republicans did not openly advocate white supremacy. Moreover, black feelings of inferiority died because of the movement. Amzie Moore once remarked that since whites had most of the good things in life and blacks were poor, he believed that was the way it was meant to be. White supremacists often defended segregation as the natural order of things, arguing that blacks as a group were innately inferior. With the freedom struggle, this changed. Blacks no longer accepted the view that whites were superior, and even arch-conservative politicians no longer proclaimed that African Americans were naturally inferior. This shift in attitudes and self-perception, as much as the political gains and desegregation that took place, attested to the impact of the civil rights movement.

One final way to measure the change that occurred in Mississippi is to imagine what would happen today if a black veteran sought to register to vote in his hometown. Would whites terrorize a black man wearing a uniform to prevent him from exercising his rights as a citizen, as they had done to Medgar Evers in the wake of World War II? And if, perchance, someone sought to stop a black veteran from voting today, how would whites in general and the veteran react? Evers dared not defy the white mob that kept him away from the polls in 1946 because he understood that it enjoyed public support. In turn, other blacks did not come to Evers's defense either because they were too afraid or because, to an extent, they shared the white supremacist view that they did not deserve the vote. As the twentieth century draws to a close, the majority of whites no longer sanction such violence, and they no longer seek to disfranchise blacks as a group, in part because they know that blacks themselves would fight to preserve their rights.

White supremacy is not dead but no longer dominates Mississippi politics and society. Evidence of its decline resurfaced recently during the retrial of Byron de la Beckwith, the man accused of murdering Medgar Evers in 1963. Beckwith was tried for murder twice in the 1960s, but both trials ended in hung juries. Throughout the mid-1960s, Beckwith championed white supremacy and publicly warned civil rights activists to stay out of the state. During this period, many whites treated him as a folk hero. One prominent Greenwood businessman commented that even if Beckwith had assassinated Evers, "he was doing it for the South." Less than twenty-four hours after Beckwith had first been arrested for the crime, the White Citizens' Council organized a legal defense fund on his behalf; it received tens of thousands of dollars, including a contribution from the Veterans of Foreign Wars. Fan mail poured into the Hinds County jail during Beckwith's internment there.

In contrast, during his retrial for murder in 1994, made possible by the discovery of new evidence by a white prosecutor, Beckwith was treated as an outcast and a pariah. He no longer garnered the support of prominent whites in the state. Nor did Beckwith enjoy the luxury of an all-white jury—one of the by-products of black enfranchisement. Even those who felt that Beckwith should not have to face a third trial saw him as a sordid symbol of the past, not an emblem of a revered way of life.

In sum, a half-century after Medgar Evers came home from the war to Jim Crow Mississippi, a visitor to Jackson can drive on Medgar Evers Road and view a life-size statue of the slain civil rights leader in front of the Medgar Evers Library. Beckwith, in contrast, not only has had no monuments erected in his memory, but will probably die in obscurity in a state penitentiary. Such a reality allowed Darrell Kenyatta Evers, Medgar's son, to observe on the day of Beckwith's conviction that "Medgar's life was not in vain," that the civil rights movement has had an impact on the way people live in the state.[13]

NOTES

1. Williams, *Eyes on the Prize*, 208; John Dittmer, *Local People: The Struggle for Civil Rights in Mississippi* (Urbana: University of Illinois Press, 1994), 1; James W. Silver, *Mississippi: The Closed Society* (New York: Harcourt, Brace & World, 1963).

2. Levy, *Let Freedom Ring*, 129–30.

3. Anne Moody, *Coming of Age in Mississippi* (Garden City, N.Y.: Doubleday, 1968), 121–38.

4. Dittmer, *Local People*, 68.

5. Silver, *Mississippi: The Closed Society*, 20.

6. Barnett quoted in Silver, *Mississippi: The Closed Society*, 119–20.

7. Quoted in Williams, *Eyes on the Prize*, 217.

8. Quoted in ibid., 220–21.

9. Quoted in ibid., 221.

10. Quoted in Dittmer, *Local People*, 261.

11. Sellers quoted in Sitkoff, *Struggle for Black Equality*, 171.

12. Quoted in Dittmer, *Local People*, 395.

13. Quoted in the *Baltimore Sun*, February 2, 1994, 1A.

African American sharecroppers in the South. National Archives

Thurgood Marshall (left) works on legal strategy for Donald Gaines Murray's (center) suit against the University of Maryland with Charles Houston (right). NAACP Collection, Library of Congress

Freedom riders met with violence in Anniston, Alabama. Copyright *The Birmingham News*. All rights reserved. Reprinted by permission

Boycotts in Birmingham prompt use of police dogs, 1963. Copyright *The Birmingham News.* All rights reserved. Reprinted by permission

Martin Luther King, Jr., and other civil rights leaders at March on Washington, 1963. National Archives

March on Washington, 1963. National Archives

President Lyndon B. Johnson signs Voting Rights Act, 1965. National Archives

Black Panther Party poster. Library of Congress

4

With All Deliberate Speed: The Fight for Legal Equality

During a recent debate on the 1996 presidential election, a well-intentioned college student proclaimed that affirmative action had been established in order to retaliate against white society for slavery. The student added the oft-accepted assertion that affirmative action represented reverse racism and contradicted Martin Luther King's dream of a color-blind society. When asked to substantiate this claim, the student could not. That he was unable to do so, however, did not disturb the audience; rather, it reflected the general lack of understanding of the origins of affirmative action in particular, and the history of the fight for legal equality more generally. Yet, without knowledge about the long-term fight for legal equality and the specific context in which affirmative action programs developed, is it possible to determine whether or not affirmative action represents a betrayal of the civil rights movement and the aims of Dr. Martin Luther King, Jr.? And is it possible to judge the purpose and merits of affirmative action without an understanding of the history of the struggle for legal equality that preceded its development? Based on the assumption that it is not possible to do so, this chapter will survey the fight for legal equality from colonial times to the present, with an emphasis on the modern era.

"NO RIGHTS WHICH ANY WHITE MAN IS BOUND TO RESPECT"

While the legal status of the first Africans who arrived in British America remained imprecise, by the mid-seventeenth century a variety of laws had made clear that black and white were not equal. Many Africans brought to North America before the 1670s labored in the fields side by side with white indentured servants, who outnumbered them. While some of these Africans received their freedom after a set number of years of service, they came to America as captives rather than of their own free will. In addition, early censuses listed men and women of African ancestry as Negroes, often without personal names, while those of English ancestry were listed by name without reference to their race. Moreover, by the 1640s some blacks and their offspring were in servitude for life.[1]

As the number of blacks in America increased, the colonies clarified their status as slaves. In 1661 Maryland defined slavery as lifelong and inheritable. A year later, Virginia declared that "all children born in this country shall be held bond or free according to the condition of their mother." In 1670 Virginia established that "all servants not being Christian" were slaves for life. A subsequent act made clear that conversion to Christianity did not free one's offspring from slavery. Even before these statutes were enacted, the rights of blacks, free and slave, to bear arms and travel had been limited. In addition, nearly every colony restricted intermarriage between blacks and whites.[2]

As the institution of slavery expanded in the South and disappeared in the North, the debate over slavery grew in intensity. The role of the national government in either encouraging or prohibiting the expansion of slavery into its territories only added to friction between those who favored and opposed slavery. Congress tried to avoid the question by enacting compromises and accepting such ideas as popular sovereignty. Yet all such efforts exacerbated tensions rather than resolved them. Into this fray stepped the Supreme Court. In 1857, in the case of *Dred Scott* v. *Sandford*, the Court ruled that Scott, a slave who had sued for his freedom based on the fact that he had been taken by his master to a free territory and a free state, was still a slave. In his own written decision, Chief Justice Roger Taney argued that blacks had "no rights which any white man was bound to respect." Not only did the decision leave Scott a slave, it struck down the Missouri Compromise (which, passed in 1820, had divided the land purchased from France into free and slave territories), much to the dismay of many northerners. Taney's decision, which distorted facts, history, and logic, today is looked upon as among the worst Supreme Court decisions in U.S. history, if not the very worst. Nonetheless, it stood as the law of the land.

Even if Scott had been granted his freedom, he would not have been treated as an equal citizen in the North. In the years preceding the *Dred Scott* decision, many northern states had stripped free blacks of rights they once enjoyed, or did not extend to them rights that were being granted to an even larger and larger number of whites—such as the right of men who did not own property to vote. "In virtually every phase of existence," historian Leon Litwack writes, "Negroes [in the North] found themselves systematically separated from whites. They were either excluded from railway cars, omnibuses, stagecoaches . . . [or] assigned to special 'Jim Crow' sections . . . they prayed in Negro pews, in white churches . . . [and] were often educated in segregated schools . . . nursed in segregated hospitals and buried in segregated cemeteries."[3]

THE CIVIL WAR, RECONSTRUCTION, AND THE ERA OF JIM CROW

The Emancipation Proclamation represented a momentous shift in the history of the nation. Issued during the Civil War, it showed that the Union was committed to "a new birth of freedom." The contribution of over 180,000 blacks to the Union army helped win the war and supported blacks' claim to citizenship. As Lincoln once observed, slavery died so that the Union might live. Nonetheless, the Civil War left unresolved the legal status of African Americans, who, according to *Dred Scott*, were still not considered citizens. Emancipation did not nullify state laws that restricted the rights of free blacks, nor did it define the meaning of freedom in the South.

In the immediate aftermath of the Civil War, the former Confederate states passed a number of "black codes," which collectively signified that African Americans, though freed, were not legally equal. Blacks were denied the right to vote, limited in the kind of work they could do and how much property they could own, blocked from testifying against whites in court, and constrained in their movement and ability to assemble. Some northern states followed suit, tightening old restrictions on free blacks. Yet, for a variety of reasons, the black codes and the restrictive legislation in the North did not last.

Building on the momentum that had led to the emancipation of the slaves, and gaining support from moderate Republicans who were appalled by the South's arrogance in the face of defeat, Radical Republicans in 1866 and 1867 pushed through Congress reforms that dramatically altered the legal status of African Americans. Grappling with civil rights for the first time, Congress passed the Civil Rights Act of 1866, which defined citizenship to include blacks and guaranteed basic civil rights. More far-reaching were three constitutional amendments intended to secure liberty. The Thirteenth Amendment, adopted in 1865, abolished slavery in all states and territories, and, in a potentially powerful clause, empowered Congress to pass all necessary measures to do so. The Fourteenth Amendment, proposed in 1866 and ratified in 1868, overturned the *Dred Scott* decision and nullified the black codes by establishing that all "persons born or naturalized in the United States" enjoyed the same citizenship rights of due process and equal protection under the laws. The Fifteenth Amendment (1870) explicitly protected the right of black males to vote. In 1870 and 1871, Congress passed the Ku Klux Klan Acts, which gave the federal government the power to break the back of organizations that resisted the implementation of the Fourteenth and Fifteenth Amendments. In 1875, in its last bow to Radical Reconstruction, Congress passed another civil rights act that guaranteed equal rights in public places, such as inns and theaters, without distinction of color, and forbade the exclusion of "Negroes" from juries. To enforce these laws, the federal government maintained a military presence in the South, although by 1875 the number of troops in the South had declined considerably from the immediate postwar years. As a result of the reforms of Reconstruction, many former slaves went to the polls and participated in the governing of the nation, although they never attained as much power as southern critics of Reconstruction asserted they did.

After the election of 1876, however, the tide turned. In the so-called Compromise of 1877, the result of a contested presidential election, the Republican president-elect, Rutherford Hayes, agreed to withdraw the last federal troops from the South. In their absence, white supremacists had free rein to strip African Americans of their rights, which they did over the course of the next twenty-five years. Even before the compromise, the Supreme Court, which had a majority of northern-born judges, had begun to narrow the reach of the Fourteenth Amendment. In the *Slaughterhouse* cases (1873), the majority of the Court ruled that the Fourteenth Amendment protected only federal citizenship rights, not those established by state laws. Since most citizenship rights were determined by state laws, this jeopardized nearly all of the gains of Reconstruction. Subsequent civil rights cases further eroded the reach of the Fourteenth Amendment and the civil rights laws of the Reconstruction era. This process culminated in 1896 with the *Plessy* decision, which stood as another watershed in the history of the nation.

In May 1896, the United States Supreme Court upheld a Louisiana law, enacted in 1890, which mandated the separation or segregation of white and black passengers on railway cars. This decision grew out of the arrest of Homer Plessy, a man who appeared white but was deemed legally black because his great-grandmother was black. Plessy had violated the 1890 separation law by seeking to ride on a car reserved for whites. The Court upheld Plessy's arrest and the constitutionality of the Louisiana law that he broke. Only Justice John Marshall Harlan dissented, writing: "In the view of the Constitution, in the eye of the law, there is in this county no superior ruling class of citizens. There is no caste here. Our Constitution is color-blind, and neither knows nor tolerates classes among citizens."

The majority of the Court thought otherwise, finding that state-created segregation did not violate the Fourteenth Amendment's equal protection clause, so long as state laws allowed for "separate but equal" treatment of both races. Writing for the majority, Massachusetts-born justice Henry Billings Brown declared that the framers of the amendment had not "intended to abolish distinctions based upon color, or to enforce social . . . equality, or a commingling of the two races." To support this opinion, Justice Brown cited the pre–Civil War case of *State* v. *Gibson*, in which the Court had upheld the right of the states to prohibit interracial marriages, a right even Plessy's attorney, S. F. Phillips, did not challenge.[4]

At the time, laws that segregated blacks and whites were few in number. Segregation had been unnecessary as long as slavery existed, and it developed relatively slowly after the Civil War. But following *Plessy* and the populist upheaval of the 1890s, which hinted at the need for an interracial alliance of poor blacks and whites, the number of Jim Crow laws rapidly proliferated. "In public transportation, sports, hospitals, orphanages, prisons, asylums, funeral homes, morgues, cemeteries," historian Lerone Bennett, Jr., writes, blacks and whites were segregated by force of law. As a sign of the absurd lengths to which southern states went to separate blacks from whites, Bennett adds, Birmingham, Alabama, even "forbade blacks and whites to play checkers together."[5] During the same period, southern states disenfranchised African Americans, nullifying the Fifteenth Amendment. They did so by implementing a wide variety of laws, from poll taxes and literacy tests to grandfather clauses. Extralegal measures, lynchings, and race "riots" solidified Jim Crow's presence in the South.

In the North segregation also occurred, but more by custom than by law. Furthermore, most whites in the North as well as the South either agreed with the *Plessy* decision and the relegation of blacks to second-class status, or acquiesced to these developments, if they thought about them at all. Perhaps more surprisingly, a number of southern black leaders, the most important of whom was Booker T. Washington, publicly bowed to white power. In his "Atlanta Compromise" address (1895), Washington called for blacks to accommodate themselves to the reality of segregation and, for the time being, political disfranchisement. Instead of agitating for political and legal equality, Washington suggested that African Americans concentrate on programs of self-help, which, he argued, would allow them to pull themselves up by their own bootstraps without antagonizing whites. In time, Washington contended, blacks would earn white respect and a share of political power. But it made no sense to speak in a militant voice given the realities of the time. In the North, in contrast, where blacks, though segregated, retained the right to vote, and where lynchings were a less frequent occurrence, Washington's approach found fewer adherents. On the contrary, the modern civil rights movement, which sought complete legal equality, took root there.

THE BIRTH AND GROWTH OF THE FIGHT FOR LEGAL EQUALITY

One of Washington's sharpest critics, and in many ways the father of the modern civil rights movement, was W.E.B. Du Bois. Born in 1868 in Great Barrington, Massachusetts, Du Bois received a baccalaureate degree from Fisk University, an all-black college in Nashville, Tennessee, and a Ph.D. from Harvard University. A gifted sociologist and historian, Du Bois criticized Washington's accommodationist views, arguing that African Americans, especially as a working-class people, ought not cede their political and civil rights; they had to insist upon their legal equality as a matter of right and as the best means to improve their condition. Along with several other like-minded northern black radicals, in 1905 Du Bois founded the Niagara Movement, which called for aggressive action to ensure universal manhood suffrage, equal economic opportunities, and full civil rights. While the Niagara Movement quickly fell upon hard times, several of its members, including Du Bois, along with a number of white reformers, most notably Oswald Garrison Villard, the grandson of the well-known abolitionist William Lloyd Garrison, founded the National Association for the Advancement of Colored People (NAACP).

During the first half of the twentieth century, the NAACP became the most important civil rights organization in the nation. Operating as an interracial organization, it gained legitimacy and support by fighting for the rights of blacks in the courts and by mounting public campaigns against lynching. Among the NAACP's early victories was *Nixon* v. *Herndon* (1927), in which the civil rights group convinced the Supreme Court to rule against the all-white primary in Texas.

A crucial turn in the NAACP's history came in the 1930s. Recognizing that Congress was unlikely to enact civil rights legislation and believing that the president's ability to foster racial reform was limited by political and constitutional realities, especially during the hard times of the Great Depression, it decided to focus even more of its energy on gaining equality through the courts. The organization explicitly spelled out this plan of attack in the "Marigold Report," a study written in 1933 by Nathan Ross Marigold, a white, Harvard-educated NAACP lawyer. Marigold argued that the NAACP should file a series of suits which, step by step, would show that southern states had not established "separate but equal" facilities, the legal standard the Supreme Court had set for squaring segregation with the Fourteenth Amendment. After making this case, Marigold recommended that the NAACP challenge the concept of separate but equal itself by claiming that it violated the equal protection clause of the amendment.

The two individuals most responsible for transforming Marigold's recommendations into reality were Charles H. Houston and Thurgood Marshall. Born in Washington, D.C., the year before the *Plessy* v. *Ferguson* decision, Houston, the son of a lawyer, graduated Phi Beta Kappa from Amherst College in 1915 and then enlisted in the army, where during World War I he rose to the rank of first lieutenant. At war's end, he enrolled at Harvard University Law School, where en route to a law degree he became the first black to serve on the editorial board of Harvard's law review. Shortly after graduating, he began teaching at Howard University. In time, Houston became dean of the law school. By training a core of black lawyers who would have the skills to fight for equality in the courts, he sought to use the university to the benefit of the black race.

In the mid-1930s, Houston left Howard University to head the NAACP's legal efforts. Among those Houston recruited to work for him was one of his former students, Thurgood Marshall. Marshall's first big case was *Murray* v. *Maryland*, in which he and Houston argued that Maryland had violated the Constitution by denying Donald Murray admission to the University of Maryland Law School because Murray was black. Marshall and Houston observed that Maryland did not offer blacks the opportunity to study law in the state, instead, giving scholarships to qualified blacks so that they could attend law school elsewhere. This policy, Marshall and Houston contended, did not meet the separate but equal requirement laid down by *Plessy*. A federal appeals court agreed and ordered the university to admit Murray. The ruling offered a degree of vindication for Marshall, who had been denied admission to the University of Maryland Law School years earlier.

Two years later, Houston argued a similar case, *Missouri ex rel. Gaines* v. *Canada* before the Supreme Court. Houston asserted that Missouri, which had no black law school, had violated the Constitution by denying Gaines the opportunity to study law. In addition, Houston contended that even if the state built a new law school at the site of its all-black college, which it promised to do, it would be in violation of the Constitution because such a school would not be truly equal, since it would be impossible for the state to replicate the educational experiences of students who attended the all-white law school. The Court ruled in Gaines's favor, setting a precedent for further attacks on segregation in education and other arenas of life.

In 1940 Houston resigned from the NAACP, leaving Thurgood Marshall in charge of the recently created NAACP Legal Defense and Educational Fund. By the early 1950s, this arm of the NAACP, staffed by one of the greatest teams of constitutional lawyers in American history, several of whom had been trained at Howard University, won a series of precedent-setting cases that paved the way for the *Brown* decision. Building on its decision in the *Gaines* case, the Supreme Court ruled in *Sweatt* v. *Painter* (1950) that a separate black law school, which the state of Texas had established to avoid the desegregation of its all-white law school, violated the equal protection clause of the Fourteenth Amendment. Simultaneously, in *McLaurin* v. *Oklahoma State Regents for Higher Education* (1950), the Court ruled that the state of Oklahoma had violated the constitutional rights of George McLaurin, a seventy-year-old black man. Even though the university had admitted McLaurin to a doctorate program in education, it required him to sit in the hallway rather than in the classroom, and denied him equal use of the library and dining hall. This, the Court declared, did not constitute an equal educational experience. But in this decision, as in other so-called equalization suits, the Court limited its ruling to the facts of the particular case. As yet, the Court was not prepared to review the separate but equal doctrine in principle.

Even before gaining favorable rulings in these precedent-setting cases, the NAACP had won several other pro–civil rights decisions. In *Smith* v. *Allright* (1944), the Supreme Court banned "all-white primaries," one of the mechanisms that southern states effectively used to disfranchise blacks. In *Patton* v. *Mississippi* (1947), the Supreme Court overturned the murder conviction of Eddie Patton, an African American, on the grounds that the state automatically eliminated blacks from jury service. And in *Morgan* v. *Commonwealth of Virginia* (1946), the Supreme Court overturned the conviction of Irene Morgan on the grounds that the Virginia law that required segregated public transportation, which she had violated, could not apply to vehicles involved in interstate transportation.

BROWN v. BOARD OF EDUCATION

Charles Houston died in late April 1950. Prior to his death, James Nabritt, one of the lawyers Houston had trained and recruited, informed his mentor that he intended to seek cases that would challenge *Plessy* itself. While Houston welcomed this development, he did not live long enough to see it bear fruit. Moving beyond the issue of inequality in colleges and graduate and professional schools, Nabritt and his colleagues sought suits that attacked segregation in public education, grades K–12, in a wide variety of venues. Ultimately, the legal defense team took on five separate desegregation suits, which they argued together under the title of *Brown* v. *Board of Education of Topeka, Kansas*. The four other cases were *Bolling* v. *Sharpe*, which pitted Spottswood Bolling, Jr., age twelve, against Melvin Sharpe, the president of the school board in the District of Columbia; *Briggs* v. *Elliot*, in which the NAACP represented black plaintiffs from Clarendon County, South Carolina; *Gebhart* v. *Belton*, involving a school district in Delaware; and *Davis* v. *Prince Edward County*, Virginia.

While Linda Brown's suit became the most famous of these cases, *Briggs* v. *Elliot* probably reveals more about the fight for legal equality. The case was an especially fitting one because early in his career Charles Houston had traveled to South Carolina to document, on film, the inequities between black and white education. At the time, Houston showed that expenditures for white and black schools were vastly different. Returning to the county years after Houston produced this film, the NAACP established that these wide disparities persisted. As of 1950, white schools, on average, received $179 per child, while black schools got only $43 per child. Based on these discrepancies, twenty parents, led by the Reverend J. A. DeLaine, filed a suit against the school board. Harry Briggs's name came first alphabetically, hence the case took his name.

The Briggs case displayed the degree to which the fight for legal equality depended on grassroots action as well as legal expertise from the top. Blacks who filed the suit quickly found themselves under attack from the white establishment. Some lost jobs; others were evicted from their homes; several had their lives threatened or were chased out of the state. As DeLaine exclaimed: "Is this the price that free men must pay in a free country for wanting their children trained as capable and respectable American citizens? . . . What some of us have suffered is nothing short of Nazi persecution."[6] If individual black men and women had proven unable to withstand such persecution, the NAACP's legal efforts well might have gone for naught, since the Supreme Court may not have entertained arguments in cases that lacked individual plaintiffs. Moreover, the Briggs case showed that the fight for legal equality was staged by the black masses in concert with the black elite, that the struggle against desegregation was not a middle-class fight alone.

State courts found nothing wrong with the segregationist practices of the schools in their jurisdictions, confirming the NAACP's view that federal courts provided it with its only avenue of legal redress. Since some southern states were rushing to close the dollar gap in school expenditures, to build new black schools or upgrade old ones to keep the separate but equal ruling alive, the NAACP's lawyers did not simply tally up the differences in expenditures. Instead, the NAACP contended that education had to be measured by more than bricks and mortar, that the values learned and the psychological effects of the learning environment had to be considered. To make this case, the NAACP employed a range of social scientists, from historians to psychologists, who demonstrated that segregation violated the equal protection clause of the Fourteenth Amendment. This included the famous doll tests conducted by black psychologists Kenneth and Mamie Clark, in which the Clarks showed that segregation had a deleterious impact on the self-esteem of young black children. As Kenneth Clark argued, "Segregation was, is, the way in which a society tells a group of human beings they are inferior to other groups of human beings in the society." Children, Clark continued, internalize this view. As a result, separate could never be equal.[7]

The NAACP team, led by Thurgood Marshall, made its appearance before the Supreme Court on December 9, 1952. John Davis, a veteran of 250 Supreme Court appearances and the onetime presidential nominee of the Democratic Party, served as the chief defense attorney. Several days after the oral arguments began, the Court issued a set of questions, largely regarding the Fourteenth Amendment. They called for the two sides to address these questions at a later date. Nine months later, before reargument, Chief Justice Fred Vinson died of a heart attack.

President Dwight D. Eisenhower nominated Earl Warren, the governor of California, to replace Vinson as Chief Justice. Warren had little legal experience, but Eisenhower appointed him anyway, partly for political reasons and partly because he hoped that Warren would prove a moderating influence on the Court, which had recently taken a liberal turn. While the Court was inclined to rule in favor of the NAACP prior to Vinson's death, it was not united in its sentiment. Felix Frankfurter, one of the most influential judges in American history, felt uneasy about overturning *Plessy*, and if he ruled against *Brown*, so too would at least one other justice.

With Warren presiding (even though his nomination had not yet been confirmed), the Court held a second set of oral hearings in December 1953. Between this hearing and the time it issued its decision, on May 17, 1954, Warren struggled to gain a unanimous decision. Using all of his political skills, he pressured upon Frankfurter to join the majority, figuring that the other likely dissenter, Stanley Reed, would not stand alone. To gain their support, Warren promised that the Court would call for gradual rather than immediate desegregation of public education.

The opinion in the *Brown* case, written by Warren (his first), was short, simple, and to the point. "Does segregation of children in public schools solely on the basis of race, even though the physical facilities and other 'tangible' factors may be equal, deprive the children of the minority group of equal education opportunities? We believe that it does." Given the importance of education in contemporary life, and considering the Court's rulings in previous cases, such as *Sweatt* v. *Painter* and *McLaurin* v. *Oklahoma*, Warren continued, the views expressed by the court in *Plessy* had to be rejected. "We conclude that in the field of public education the doctrine of 'separate but equal' has no place. Therefore, we hold that the plaintiffs and others similarly situated for whom the actions were brought are, by reason of the segregation complained of, deprived of equal protection of the laws guaranteed by the Fourteenth Amendment."

As noted above, Warren obtained a unanimous decision in the *Brown* case by agreeing to a gradual timetable for implementing it. The Supreme Court spelled out this position in *Brown II*, or its "Enforcement Decree," which it issued a year after overturning *Plessy*. *Brown II* called upon the lower federal courts, in conjunction with local school districts, to develop plans for the desegregation of schools. While the decree stated that the courts should do so "with all deliberate speed," such a procedure did not demand immediate compliance. Most likely Warren and the other justices believed that the unanimity of the decision, along with its measured remedy, would result in the relatively speedy and peaceful desegregation of education in the South. But the opposite proved true. Although some school districts in border states such as Delaware began to desegregate even before *Brown II*, or established plans for desegregation soon after, the vast majority of districts in the South did not. For over ten years the states of the former Confederacy resisted desegregating in every manner possible, from outright defiance of the law, in the case of Little Rock, Arkansas, in 1957, to putting forth legal ruses or obfuscation. As a result, in the decade that followed *Brown*, the NAACP had to spend an unprecedented amount of time and energy getting local school districts to comply with the decision.

While it pursued the implementation of *Brown*, the NAACP simultaneously sought to overturn Jim Crow elsewhere. Case by case the NAACP argued that if *Plessy* no longer applied to public education, it no longer applied to other facets of life. In *Mayor and City Council of Baltimore* v.

Dawson (1955), the Supreme Court upheld a lower court decision, based in part on *Brown*, that ruled that separate public beaches and bathhouses were unconstitutional. Subsequent court decisions outlawed the segregation of public golf courses, buses, libraries, and parks. In *Gayle* v. *Browder* (1956), a case that grew out of the arrest of Rosa Parks, the Supreme Court ruled unconstitutional a Montgomery, Alabama, ordinance that required segregated city buses. Simultaneously, the NAACP sought to win back political and other civil rights. Among its major victories in this arena was *Baker* v. *Carr* (1962), which limited racial gerrymandering and established the standard of "one man, one vote."

PRESIDENTIAL AND CONGRESSIONAL ACTION

When Nathan Marigold laid out the NAACP's plan for attacking Jim Crow in the 1930s, he assumed that neither Congress nor the president could be depended on to alter significantly the legal status of African Americans. Even if northern white moderates could be persuaded to push for racial reforms, Marigold and others reasoned, southern conservatives in Congress, who, because of their seniority controlled key committees, could block all efforts to enact racial reforms. Yet, in the 1950s and especially in the 1960s, for a wide variety of reasons, the congressional and executive deadlock on civil rights came to an end. In 1957 and 1960, Congress passed and President Eisenhower signed two civil rights bills. While southern congressional leaders watered down both of these laws, their passage suggested that Congress, like the courts, could be mobilized in support of legal equality. In contrast, even during the New Deal years, President Franklin D. Roosevelt had been unable to gain passage of an antilynching bill. The Civil Rights Act of 1957 established a civil rights division of the Justice Department and a federal Civil Rights Commission with the authority to investigate violations of civil rights and to make reports and recommendations to the president based on its findings. The Civil Rights Act of 1960 outlawed interference with federal court orders on school desegregation and gave judges the power to appoint referees to hear complaints against state election officials accused of denying persons the rights to register and vote.

Even before Congress acted, Presidents Roosevelt and Truman used their executive authority to eliminate discrimination in aspects of life under the purview of the federal government. In 1941, in response to a proposed mass march on Washington, Roosevelt desegregated defense industries, and Congress created a wartime Fair Employment Practice Committee (FEPC) to implement this order. Seven years later, President Harry Truman ordered all branches of the military to desegregate. While President Dwight Eisenhower did not issue any executive orders of similar magnitude, he sent troops to Little Rock, Arkansas, to make sure that the community complied with the *Brown* decision. All three of these presidents appointed African Americans as well as whites who fostered racial equality to posts within the federal government. William Hastie, a prominent black NAACP leader, became a member of the Department of the Interior under Roosevelt and was elevated to the position of justice of the U.S. Court of Appeals by Truman. Ralph Bunche served as an advisor to the U.S. delegation that drafted the United Nations Charter and as a mediator for the State Department. While Eisenhower appointed few blacks to high posts, he had a very good record for nominating judges to the federal bench who ultimately proved invaluable allies to the cause of racial equality. In 1957, for example, Eisenhower nominated John Minor Wisdom, a native of New Orleans, to a position on the U.S. First Circuit Court of Appeals. For the rest of the 1950s and 1960s, Wisdom issued one opinion after another that upheld and expanded upon *Brown*. Often his decisions overturned those of state courts led by men who were committed to maintaining Jim Crow.

Congress's most significant actions came with the enactment of the Civil Rights Act of 1964 and the Voting Rights Act of 1965. The passage of these racial reforms demonstrated the power of the civil rights movement. Together they represented a watershed in the fight for legal equality. The Civil Rights Act of 1964 prohibited discrimination in public accommodations, in employment, and in programs that received federal funding (including education); it also provided increased federal protection for the civil rights of African Americans. The Voting Rights Act of 1965 banned laws that sought to keep African Americans from voting, such as those requiring literacy tests, and allowed the federal government to send registrars to states with a history of discriminating against black registrants. Broad interpretations of the Voting Rights Act allowed for the redrawing of congressional and legislative districts to the benefit of minority candidates. The ratification in 1964 of the Twenty-Fourth Amendment to the Constitution, which banned poll taxes, removed one other significant barrier to voting. In 1968 Congress passed a civil rights bill prohibiting discrimination in housing.

Certainly, Congress never would have passed these laws and the president would not have pursued or signed them if not for the rise of a massive civil rights movement. Protests from Birmingham and Selma, Alabama, to Jackson and Greenwood, Mississippi, put unprecedented pressure on the executive and legislative branches to act. Martin Luther King, Jr., the SCLC, SNCC, CORE, and independent activists all deserve credit for the crucial role they played in awakening the nation from its torpor over the denial of equal rights and the need for strong federal legislation to enforce and implement the ideals of the Declaration of Independence. Yet the full story of the fight for legal equality also must take into account the role played by those who struggled behind the scenes, in the corridors of Congress, lobbying politicians to enact meaningful rather than watered-down legislation. Without their efforts, the Civil Rights Act of 1964, in particular, would have been eviscerated by crafty congressmen, if passed at all.

At the center of this behind-the-scenes fight was the Leadership Conference on Civil Rights (LCCR), an umbrella organization that coordinated the lobbying efforts of over sixty groups, including the AFL-CIO, the Americans for Democratic Action, the National Urban League, SNCC, CORE, the SCLC, and the NAACP. LCCR kept a steady stream of telegrams, letters, and constituents pouring into the offices of congressmen and senators in support of strong civil rights legislation. LCCR, labor, religious, and civil rights leaders testified before congressional committees, made speeches, and issued press releases on behalf of civil rights legislation. On a daily basis, LCCR churned out the *Bipartisan Civil Rights Newsletter*, which it distributed to senators to keep them abreast of the latest details of the debate.

One example of LCCR's power came in spring 1964, when a Senate filibuster threatened to derail the Civil Rights Act of 1964. As the Senate's vote on cloture to stop the filibuster approached, LCCR initiated around-the-clock interdenominational prayer sessions, themselves the outgrowth of a long-term LCCR campaign aimed at cultivating organized religion's support for civil rights at the grassroots level. Testimony to the effectiveness of LCCR's efforts came from Senator Richard Russell of Georgia, one of the bill's chief opponents. Much to his chagrin, he observed, "There never has been as effective lobbying maintained in the city of Washington as there is today."[8]

LCCR's leading lobbyist was Clarence Mitchell. While he never achieved the same recognition as Martin Luther King, Jr., Thurgood Marshall, or Malcolm X, he had a profound impact on the struggle for legal equality. By the mid-1960s, Mitchell had twenty years of experience in Washington, D.C. After working for the Fair Employment Practice Committee during World War II, he took charge of the Emergency Civil Rights Mobilization, which lobbied for a permanent FEPC at war's end. Although he was unsuccessful in this struggle, Mitchell gained invaluable experience and numerous allies. He became so well known on Capitol Hill that he was dubbed "the 101st Senator." Perhaps Mitchell's most important accomplishment was his successful courting of Everett Dirksen, the Republican leader in the Senate. Without Dirksen's support, the Civil Rights Act would have been defeated or diluted. Mitchell made sure never to speak badly of Dirksen. For example, on *Meet the Press*, a popular weekend televised news show, Mitchell praised him as "a great Senator and a great American." Mitchell met regularly with Dirksen in his office and over drinks and meals, appealing to his sense of history and justice. In the end, partly due to Mitchell's efforts, Dirksen threw his support behind the Civil Rights Act of 1964, breaking the back of southern opposition to the bill.

Thurgood Marshall's appointment to the Supreme Court in 1967 symbolized the distance that blacks had traveled in the middle years of the twentieth century. Born in 1908 during the heyday of Jim Crow, Marshall had struggled much of his life to attain legal equality for all Americans. In the face of death threats, he had served as the lead attorney in many of the most important civil rights cases of the century. In explaining his nomination of Marshall to the press, President Lyndon Johnson declared, "It is the right thing to do, the right time to do it, the right man, and the right place." Johnson also observed in Marshall's favor that he had argued numerous cases before the Supreme Court, had served as chief council for the NAACP and as solicitor general, and had experience on the federal judiciary. In spite of these qualifications, all five southern Democratic senators on the Judiciary Committee voted against confirming his nomination, demonstrating that they had not come to accept the notion that African Americans should be treated equally before the law. Even without their support, Marshall was confirmed by the Senate, becoming the first African American Supreme Court justice in United States history.

LEVELING THE PLAYING FIELD: AFFIRMATIVE ACTION AND THE DILEMMA OF LEGAL EQUALITY

When Congress drafted the Civil Rights Act of 1964, it explicitly banned discrimination in all employment against individuals because of their race or color (or sex). In the words of Senator Hubert Humphrey, one of the bill's chief sponsors, the law prohibited the Equal Employment Opportunity Commission from requiring the "hiring, firing or the promotion of employees in order to meet a racial 'quota' or to achieve a certain racial balance." Furthermore, the act explicitly allowed employers to administer "bona fide qualification tests," even if members of one group tended to perform better than members of another group on these tests. Indeed, in order to gain its passage, proponents of the Civil Rights Act of 1964 had to assure northern Republicans, especially Senate Minority Leader Everett Dirksen, that all distinctions based on race were prohibited by the law, that the bill would not lead to preferential treatment of one group over another, and that the act protected individuals, not groups.[9]

About a year after he signed the Civil Rights Act of 1964, however, in a graduation address to students at Howard University, President Johnson suggested that full equality demanded more than color blindness. "You do not wipe away the scars of centuries by saying: Now you are free to . . . do as you desire," the president reasoned. "You do not take a person who for years has been hobbled by chains and liberate him, bring him up to the starting line of a race and then say, 'You are free to compete with all the others,' and still justly believe you have been completely fair." On the contrary, Johnson declared, to make the playing field more level, "we need not just freedom but opportunity . . . not just equality as a right and a theory but equality as a fact and as a *result*."[10]

To an extent, the views that LBJ expressed in his Howard University speech grew out of his earlier experiences in the field of civil rights, most specifically his work while vice president as the chair of the President's Committee on Equal Employment Opportunity (PCEEO). Unwilling to risk alienating southern Democrats by proposing civil rights legislation, President John F. Kennedy initially turned to improving the federal government's own record. To this end, he established the PCEEO. Headed by Vice President Johnson, the committee was charged with administering Executive Order 10925, which required "equal opportunity to Federal Government employees and applicants without restrictions based on race, creed, color or national origin." Cursory examinations of federal agencies revealed that the government had not complied with this regulation. As a result, blacks were severely underrepresented in federal jobs, especially in skilled positions.

Nine months after President Kennedy established it, the PCEEO issued its interim report, which confirmed the severity of the problem. As of 1961, only 1 percent of the positions from GS-12 through GS-18 were held by blacks, while 72 percent of all black federal employees were concentrated in the lower-level GS-1 through GS-4 categories.[11] In the State Department, for example, African Americans were clustered in the low grades, GS-1 through GS-8, primarily in custodial positions. Very few African Americans were found in the higher grades, in positions that involved the diplomatic mission of the department. To rectify such bias, the report declared that "affirmative" steps had to be taken to remedy past discrimination.

Acting on the PCEEO's recommendations, Johnson's team held a series of meetings with black leaders and the heads of various federal departments. At these meetings, the committee pushed for increased minority recruitment. For example, the State Department was prodded to develop a plan to "achieve a more representative service." This included encouraging blacks to take the Foreign Service examination and having State Department officers and visitors increase their contacts with black students, for example by recruiting at traditionally all-black colleges. Such affirmative steps, the PCEEO insisted, did not involve lowering or changing standards. On the contrary, the recruitment of minorities was considered wise policy that would improve the ability of the State Department to achieve its mission. The lack of African American foreign service officers, for example, hampered the United States ability to foster positive relations with many African nations.

The PCEEO also convened meetings with companies that received large federal contracts, most notably with the fifty largest defense contracting firms. In these meetings, corporate executives were strongly encouraged to develop "Plans for Progress," aimed at increasing minority employment. Johnson's committee also reported that "programs of affirmative action" similar to and patterned after the Plans for Progress in industry were being developed with labor unions.[12]

Nonetheless, these affirmative steps remained very limited in scope. Defense contractors were not required to increase minority employment. The government did little to convince firms to alter long-standing practices of maintaining segregated or nearly segregated work forces, which in unionized shops often would have involved abrogating seniority rights and establishing new or alternative apprenticeship programs. Nor did the Kennedy administration compel other federal contractors, for example those involved in the construction of public projects, to implement affirmative action programs.

The urban riots of the mid-1960s and the emergence of black power, paradoxically, made such affirmative measures both paramount and more difficult to achieve. The riots confirmed that the early civil rights movement had little impact on blacks outside the South, for whom Jim Crow in accommodations had never been a major issue. They lent a sense of urgency to rectifying past discrimination, especially as it pertained to economic inequality. At the same time, the riots and the calls for black power shattered the coalition that had developed around civil rights, making modification of the Civil Rights Act of 1964 or passage of further legislation explicitly calling for affirmative measures very unlikely.

Studies of employment conducted by the Equal Employment Opportunity Commission (EEOC), the government agency created by the Civil Rights of 1964 to enforce Title VII of the act, which prohibited racial and sexual discrimination in employment, lent further weight to the idea of affirmative action. These studies documented that African Americans did not enjoy equal opportunity in fact. In Kansas City, for example, the EEOC showed that although blacks comprised over 11.2 percent of the population, they held only 2.1 percent of the white-collar jobs. In Chicago, which contained the single largest black community in the nation, blacks held only 4.7 percent of all white-collar jobs, and 80 percent of these were on the lower end of the pay scale. Based on these studies, the EEOC concluded that it needed to combat institutional racism, defined as a "phenomenon that victimized *classes*, not just individuals, through accumulated historical wrongs."[13]

Put differently, in the latter half of the 1960s, the EEOC, other federal policy-making agencies involved with civil rights, and the courts came to the conclusion that discrimination meant not simply the blatant denial of employment and access to education to individuals because of their race, color, or sex. Rather, they began to argue that discrimination could also be measured in terms of outcomes, especially, but not always, if such outcomes were effected by historical discrimination against minorities. At roughly the same time, government agencies and the courts enlarged the number of groups that enjoyed protection. In the case of women, this shift did not demand a rereading of the law but rather a newfound determination to enforce the Civil Rights Act's explicit prohibition on sexual discrimination. In the case of other racial minorities, such as Hispanics and Native Americans, it is debatable whether government agencies and the courts added new groups or simply adopted a more inclusive definition of the terms "race" and "color."

While Kennedy and Johnson initiated affirmative action programs, not until Richard Nixon became president did affirmative action emerge full blown as a policy of the federal government. In fall 1969, Secretary of Labor George Shultz announced that the federal government had drawn up what was known as the Philadelphia Plan, aimed at increasing the hiring of minority workers in the construction industry. The plan grew out of long-standing discrimination against minorities in the building trades. In 1967 alone, the federal government spent about $30 billion on construction projects nationwide, directly or indirectly employing 20 million workers. In fiscal year 1968, Philadelphia received about $250 million in federal funds for projects ranging from the construction of libraries and college dormitories to a new U.S. mint. Surveys showed that minorities were vastly underrepresented in many of the construction trades in these projects and were barely found at all in a number of unions.

What followed from such reports of discrimination was the Philadelphia Plan, which required those bidding on contracts to submit plans that suggested numerical goals for minority employment on the project up for bid. While the blueprints for the Philadelphia Plan had been developed during Johnson's presidency, for a variety of reasons it did not become official federal policy until 1969. Partly because he could not resist setting two chief components of the Democratic coalition, labor and blacks, against one another, Nixon gave the plan his blessing. As Secretary of Labor Shultz informed a Senate subcommittee, the revised Philadelphia Plan established "ranges for minority manpower utilization on Federally-involved construction projects" for six specific trades that had a history of discriminatory practices. The plan did not, Shultz insisted, set quotas. Rather, it sought to "overcome the effects of past discrimination" through the establishment of goals. Contractors would only have to show that they made "a good faith" effort to meet these goals to be declared in compliance with their bid.[14]

During the latter half of 1969, Labor Department officials issued additional statements and briefs in support of the plan. On June 27, 1969, in his official remarks to the press, Assistant Secretary of Labor Arthur Fletcher proclaimed that the Constitution "guaranteed . . . the right to equal participation in the economic process of our society." Since this freedom had been denied to minorities, Fletcher continued, the federal government had the "obligation to see that every citizen has an equal chance at . . . the right to succeed." Nixon's attorney general, John Mitchell, cited the Supreme Court's decision in *Gaston County* v. *United States* (1969) case to justify the Philadelphia Plan. In this case the Court allowed for group relief to rectify the denial of voting rights to minorities. Early Labor Department communications made clear that the government intended to use the Philadelphia Plan as a model for affirmative action programs to increase minority hiring in work paid for by federal contracts in the construction and other industries, even those that had not been found to have had a history of specific discrimination.

In the same time period, busing came into being. Unlike affirmative action, busing grew out of explicit defiance of earlier court orders. Although *Brown II* called for the elimination of segregation in public education "with all deliberate speed," as of the mid-1960s only a token member of districts in the South had desegregated. In 1966 Judge Minor Wisdom ruled in *United States* v. *Jefferson County Board of Education* that the city of New Orleans had to produce racially balanced schools. Only by doing so, Wisdom determined, could the school district undo the discriminatory effects of de jure and de facto discrimination. Building on this case and others, in *Swann* v. *Mecklenburg* (1971), the Supreme Court, headed by Justice Warren Burger, whom Nixon had appointed to reverse the leftward drift of the

Warren Court, unanimously upheld a lower court decision that had ordered busing as the mechanism for achieving racial balance. Writing for the Court, Burger held that Title IV of the Civil Rights Act of 1964, which prohibited the courts from issuing any order "to achieve racial balance in any school by requiring transportation of pupils or students from one school to another," applied only to segregation outside of the South. Not long afterwards, in *Griggs* v. *Duke Power Co.*, which involved the use of tests that kept blacks from attaining skilled posts at the Duke Power Company, the Supreme Court provided further justification for group-based remedies.

Although Nixon appointees on the Court upheld busing, and even though busing increased during his tenure in office, Nixon spoke out strongly against it. Building on white backlash, which George Wallace had effectively tapped during the 1968 presidential election, Nixon aggressively pursued the political allegiance and votes of two of the Democratic Party's core constituencies, southern whites and blue-collar urban ethnics. Put differently, Nixon and other Republicans effectively used busing and affirmative action as wedge issues, severing large chunks of the Democratic Party and adding them to the Republican fold. On the local level as well, anti-busing sentiment, at times combined with anti–affirmative action views, became a mainstay of politics. In Boston, Massachusetts, for example, heretofore considered a bastion of liberalism and pro–civil rights attitudes, anti-busing fervor produced some of the most vocal and violent opposition to racial reform in the nation, particularly in Irish Catholic South Boston, where anti-busing riots took place.

Despite growing public disapproval, in 1978, in the *University of California Regents* v. *Bakke*, the Supreme Court sanctioned affirmative action. The Court declared unconstitutional the specific admission formula used at the University of California at Davis Medical School, which established quotas that kept Bakke, a white applicant, from being admitted; but it simultaneously ruled that the university could consider race as a factor in making admissions, in effect confirming that affirmative action was constitutional. Throughout the 1980s the high court continued to uphold the constitutionality of affirmative action. Yet, more recently, in the cases of *City of Richmond* v. *J. R. Croson Co.* (1989), *Wards Cove* v. *Antonio* (1989), and *Adarand Constructors* v. *Peña* (1995), the courts have significantly narrowed the reach of affirmative action, setting higher standards for proving discrimination and demanding more narrowly tailored remedies. Moreover, in 1996, voters in California passed Proposition 209, an initiative that bans affirmative action in state-based education and employment.

THE LEGACY

All along, critics of affirmative action have contended that it was the product of a liberal cabal, forced on the nation by a bunch of unelected bureaucrats who shared a certain agenda. They add that it represents a betrayal of Martin Luther King, Jr.'s dream of establishing a color-blind society. The fact that King endorsed affirmative steps to rectify past discrimination and that the Philadelphia Plan was implemented by the Nixon administration, with George Shultz, one of the most prominent Republicans of the twentieth century, in the lead, suggests otherwise. Recent opponents of affirmative action and busing also tend to downplay or overlook the context in which these policies arose. For years, southern school districts refused to comply with the *Brown* decision. For an even longer period of time, as Nixon's assistant secretary of labor, Arthur Fletcher, observed, de jure and de facto segregation set limits or boundaries on minorities to the benefit of whites as a group. These boundaries underlay the economic and educational gap between whites and blacks in America at the time the Civil Rights Act of 1964 was enacted; they created an uneven playing field that no law could eradicate overnight. In other words, if school districts, trade unions, and other organizations had, on their own, treated people as individuals rather than as members of a group, then busing and affirmative action would have been unnecessary. But since they had not, the courts and other federal agencies charged with implementing the civil rights reforms of the mid-1960s determined that affirmative action was consistent with the goal of establishing a color-blind society.

This said, the assumptions on which affirmative action and busing were based and the way they were implemented ensured that public support for them would never be strong. In the case of affirmative action, Labor Department officials insisted that efforts to increase the hiring of minority workers would not displace white workers. A September 1969 Labor Department memo estimated that there would be a 7.5 percent increase in "new job openings each year without any growth" in each of the specific building trades, and more job openings than that with economic expansion. This assertion was based on estimates of economic growth that proved incorrect. While the economy had grown at a steady clip in the twenty-five years before the implementation of the Philadelphia Plan, it did not continue to grow at the same rate in the quarter-century that followed. On the contrary, most trades experienced a decline in job opportunities in the 1970s and 1980s. As a result, affirmative action programs pitted minority workers against white workers in a shrinking job market. Busing too was based on rosy demographic assumptions that predicted it would be relatively easy to achieve racial balance in urban districts. Yet the reality proved otherwise; the number of minorities within most urban districts continued to grow, while the number of whites declined rapidly in the 1970s, 1980s, and 1990s.

Furthermore, civil rights groups hurt their own cause by justifying affirmative action as a temporary measure that would lead to a color-blind society. As time passed and the reach of affirmative action increased to include other minorities, from women and Hispanics to gays and lesbians, this defense became one of affirmative action's weakest aspects. One might even suggest that the implementation of affirmative action tended to reverse the momentum that civil rights forces had enjoyed for years. Rather than portraying themselves as defenders of a universal principle, such as color blindness, they took on the role of defenders of a policy that never enjoyed widespread support and had never been fully explained or articulated to the public, and whose efficacy was suspect. This allowed conservatives, in many cases the heirs of those who had fought tooth and nail against all racial reforms, to present themselves as the advocates of equality before the law, an assertion that was problematic.

John Marshall Harlan, if he were to return today, might be confused by the present debate. In *Plessy*, Harlan stood alone in defense of the notion that the Constitution was color-blind. Many argue that he would oppose affirmative action today based on the notion that the Constitution should still know no groups. Yet it would be wise, if possible, to introduce Harlan to Justice Thurgood Marshall, who, while he built on Harlan's dissent to topple *Plessy*, recognized that the failure of the nation to abide by Harlan's understanding of the Constitution had had a tremendous impact. As Marshall put it in his opinion in the *Bakke* case, "It is because of a legacy of unequal treatment that we must now permit the institutions of this society to give consideration to race." Yet even Marshall would have to acknowledge that the status of African Americans before the law has undergone a dramatic shift over the course of the twentieth century. Although de facto equality has not been achieved, de jure inequality, a large part of the basis of current racial inequality, has been largely eliminated. Put differently, to a large degree because of Marshall's efforts, Taney's assertion that blacks have no rights which the white men need respect no longer stands.

NOTES

1. Winthrop Jordan, *The White Man's Burden: The Historical Origins of Racism* (New York: Oxford University Press, 1974), 32–33, 39–42.

2. Thomas Morris, *Southern Slavery and the Law* (Charlotte: University of North Carolina Press, 1996).

3. Leon Litwack, *North of Slavery: The Negro in the Free States, 1790–1860* (Chicago: University of Chicago Press, 1961), introduction, 207.

4. Brown's majority opinion and Harlan's dissent can be found in Otto Olsen, *The Thin Disguise; Turning Point in Negro History; Plessy v. Ferguson: A Documentary Presentation* (New York: Humanities Press, 1967).

5. Lerone Bennett, Jr., *Before the Mayflower*, 5th ed. (New York: Penguin, 1982), 268.

6. Kluger, *Simple Justice*, 25.

7. Williams, *Eyes on the Prize*, 20–21.

8. Charles Whalen and Barbara Whalen, *The Longest Debate* (New York: Mentor, 1985), 168.

9. Humphrey and the law quoted in Hugh Davis Graham, *Civil Rights and the Presidency* (New York: Oxford University Press, 1992), 85–86.

10. Quoted in ibid., 98. Emphasis added.

11. President's Committee on Equal Opportunity, "Report: The First Nine Months," January 15, 1962.

12. Ibid.

13. Graham, *Civil Rights and the Presidency*, 119

14. Statement of Secretary of Labor George Shultz, October 28, 1969, Philadelphia Plan Documents, No. 20, Department of Labor Library.

5

Sisterhood Is Powerful: Women and the Civil Rights Movement

While the public memory of the civil rights years retains the names and images of a handful of women, from Rosa Parks to Coretta Scott King, the civil rights movement commonly has been portrayed and recollected as a male-led movement. Contemporary coverage highlighted the activities of James Farmer, Stokely Carmichael, Huey Newton, Roy Wilkins, Thurgood Marshall, and Whitney Young, leaders of CORE, SNCC, the Black Panther Party, the NAACP, and the National Urban League, respectively. Other black men, ranging from the young radicals H. Rap Brown, Eldridge Cleaver, and Bobby Seale to moderate figures like James Meredith, Medgar Evers, and Jackie Robinson, dominated the news. Polls showed that Muhammad Ali was the best known person in the world, and not just because he was the heavyweight boxing champion. Then and now, Martin Luther King, Jr., and Malcolm X dominate our sense of the struggle for racial equality. Only rarely did women receive much attention. Yet is it true that women only played a minor role in the civil rights movement? Were only a handful of women civil rights leaders? And if so, by implication, was the movement fought largely for the liberation of men, not women?

The answers to these questions are not simple and depend in part on how we define the civil rights movement and leadership itself. If the civil rights movement is defined as a national movement made up of national organizations led by national spokespersons who delivered the official policies of national groups, then we will find that it was dominated by men. But if we look more closely at the movement, if we zoom in and examine specific communities where struggles for racial equality erupted during the 1950s and 1960s, and if we define the movement in broad terms, as one that aimed to allow individuals to reach their fullest potential, then we will find that women played a very prominent role. Women served as official representatives of local civil rights organizations and as behind-the-scenes consultants and strategists. Often they comprised the bulk of the army of boycotters, demonstrators, and organizers. Even when women did not make the headlines or receive recognition as the leaders of national organizations, they often inspired others who did. And by their participation in the movement for racial equality, women also learned how to—and the need to—organize against sexual inequality. That the women's rights movement in significant ways emanated from the civil rights movement says much about both in terms of goals and tactics.

ESTHER BROWN, BARBARA JOHNS, MAMIE CLARK, AND THE LINDA BROWN DECISION

Most studies of the civil rights years take as their starting point one of two well-known events, the Supreme Court's ruling in the case of *Brown* v. *Board of Education* or the Montgomery bus boycott. Except for the fact that Rosa Parks sparked the latter, treatments of both events have tended to reinforce the perspective that men played the key roles. After all, it was a court of nine men, listening to the arguments of a number of other men, who handed down the *Brown* decision, and it was Martin Luther King, Jr., and his colleague the Reverend Ralph Abernathy who led the Montgomery bus boycott. Yet, who was Brown, and where and how did this seminal case originate and get carried to the top court of the land? And whence did King and Abernathy derive their power? Did they single-handedly convince blacks to abstain from riding Montgomery's buses for nearly a year?

The *Brown* case had multiple origins, including a desegregation suit filed on the behalf of Linda Brown against the Board of Education of Topeka, Kansas, which itself grew out of a similar suit initiated by Esther Brown (no relation to Linda), a white Jewish woman from a suburb of Kansas City. Outraged by the inferior education that blacks received in her community, Esther Brown demanded that this inequity be addressed by her local school board. For standing up for equal educational opportunities, she was met with catcalls and declarations such as "Well, let me tell you that no nigger will get into South Park school as long as I live."[1] Undeterred, Esther Brown prodded the Kansas City NAACP to file a suit to equalize education, which it did and subsequently won. Inspired by this victory, the NAACP set out to file suits in other border-state communities, including Topeka, whose schools were entirely segregated. To pursue these cases, the NAACP needed to recruit actual plaintiffs. Much of this task ultimately fell to Lucinda Todd, the secretary of the Topeka NAACP, who had unsuccessfully sought to enroll her own daughter, Nancy, at the all-white Lowman Hill Elementary School. The best-known plaintiff recruited by Todd was Linda Brown.

The broad assault on segregated public education became known as the *Brown* case simply because, among the Topeka plaintiffs, Linda Brown's name was first in alphabetical order. By the time the Supreme Court heard *Brown* v. *Board of Education of Topeka, Kansas*, the case had been joined to four other similar suits. One of these, *Griffin* v. *Prince Edward School Board*, grew out of a student protest against unequal education organized by sixteen-year-old Barbara Johns. In April 1951, Johns, a junior at Moton High School in Prince Edward County, Virginia, fooled the principal, Boyd Jones, into leaving the school. After he left, Johns organized a schoolwide assembly, informing the teachers that it was Jones's idea. No sooner had the student body and the faculty come together than Johns declared that "it was time for the students to do something about" their inferior education. "They were going to march out of school then and there and they were going to stay out until the white community responded properly." Shortly after the students rallied behind Johns's plea, the NAACP was called in to defend their action—not knowing that it had been organized by a student without the principal's fore-knowledge.[2]

In each one of these suits, male NAACP lawyers, the most well known being Thurgood Marshall, played crucial roles. (Constance Baker Motley, a woman, was also a member of the NAACP team that fought for desegregated education.) Pathbreaking research by another man, Kenneth Clark, on the impact of segregation on the psychological development of young school children proved vital to the Supreme Court's decision to overturn *Plessy* v. *Ferguson*. Without the support of black male ministers, several of these suits probably would have been dropped before they reached the Supreme Court. Yet it is not coincidental that several of the plaintiffs were girls, for whom education was very important within the African American community. At mid-century, black females on average attended school longer than black males, in part because they were the ones who served as teachers in all-black schools. In contrast, black males were less likely to pursue higher education because of widespread discrimination in the labor market, which blocked them from employment in a wide range of jobs even if they had a good education. Similarly, it was not coincidental that many of those who initiated the suits and helped sustain them were women, as women held a disproportionately large number of key positions within various volunteer organizations, ranging from the YWCA to the NAACP. Moreover, Mamie Clark, not Kenneth Clark, initiated the study of the impact of segregation on schoolchildren. After she married Kenneth Clark, her teacher at Howard University, the two jointly pursued this investigation via the so-called doll tests. Together they published their findings in several scholarly journals. Impressed by their findings, NAACP lawyers made the Clarks' analysis a central part of their argument, although Kenneth Clark, probably because he had a doctorate and was a man, received most of the credit.

Given the limitations placed on women in the legal arena, it would be inaccurate to suggest that they could have played as important a role as men in the legal struggle against discrimination. At the time, women had very limited opportunity to influence the courts. Very few women went to law school, even fewer practiced law, and yet fewer were judges or had the right to argue a case before the Supreme Court. However, once the struggle for civil rights moved into the streets, women faced fewer limitations.

ROSA PARKS, JO ANN ROBINSON, AND THE WOMEN OF THE MONTGOMERY BUS BOYCOTT

The Montgomery bus boycott was sparked by a woman and to a large extent organized, conducted, and carried on by women. While many view Rosa Parks's role in catalyzing the movement as an accident of history, this was hardly the case. Parks served as the secretary of the Montgomery NAACP. Not long before she refused to give up her seat, she had attended a human relations workshop at the Highlander Folk School, where, among other things, she learned the tune "We Shall Overcome," the school's official anthem, and an assortment of other freedom songs, most of them collected by Zilphia Horton, the wife of Myles Horton, Highlander's director. Montgomery's black community rallied around Rosa Parks in part because of the respect she engendered. It is likely that if a black man had refused to give up his seat, the African American community would not have been as enraged. But blacks, like whites, shared a belief that women should be treated as "ladies," that they deserved respect and certain courtesies. Ironically, the earlier arrest of Claudette Colvin by Montgomery authorities for similarly refusing to give up her seat had not sparked a boycott, because activists feared that the fact that she was an out-of-wedlock mother might become the issue rather than the fact that she had been denied a seat because of her race.

Following her arrest, Parks turned to E. D. Nixon, the head of the local NAACP and an officer with the Brotherhood of Sleeping Car Porters, to bail her out of jail. It was Nixon who first suggested that Montgomerians use Parks's arrest to call for a boycott. But it fell to the Women's Political Council (WPC), led by Jo Ann Gibson Robinson, an English professor at Alabama State College, to organize it. Over the course of a few days the Women's Political Council, which had already entertained the idea of staging a bus boycott, distributed thousands of leaflets and made hundreds of phone calls requesting that blacks stay off the buses. One leaflet written by Robinson began: "Another Negro *woman* [emphasis added] has been arrested and thrown in jail because she refused to get out of her seat. . . . The next time it could be you, or your daughter, or mother. This woman's case will come up on Monday. We are, therefore, asking every Negro to stay off the buses . . . in protest." Only after this one-day boycott took place, with nearly every black Montgomerian participating, did Martin Luther King, Jr., enter the picture, agreeing to head the newly formed Montgomery Improvement Association.[3]

King's role as the inspiring leader of the Montgomery bus boycott should not be underestimated, but the boycott itself depended on the dedication and energy of those who walked to work or organized carpools and attended the mass meetings that kept the movement going for over a year. Disproportionately, these individuals were women. As King himself wrote, "One day the South will recognize its real heroes . . . symbolized in a 72-year-old woman of Montgomery, Alabama, who rose up with a sense of dignity and with her people decided not to ride the segregated buses, and responded to one who inquired about her tiredness with ungrammatical profundity: 'My feet is tired, but my soul is rested.' "[4]

White women also played a role in the bus boycott. Even if only a handful of white women openly endorsed this challenge to segregation, their unwillingness to follow the commands of white men undercut the city's attempt to defeat the boycott. As Virginia Durr recalls, Mayor Tacky Gayle insisted that Montgomery "could break the boycott if white women would stop taking their black maids home, or even stop hiring them." Durr continued, "Well, you never heard such a roar of indignation in your life as came from the white women of Montgomery. They were just furious with Tacky Gayle. They said, okay, if Tacky Gayle wants to come out here and do my washing and ironing and cleaning and cooking and look after my children, he can do it, but unless he does, I'm going to get Mary or Sally or Suzy."[5] And they did.

DAISY BATES AND THE LITTLE ROCK CRISIS

After the Montgomery bus boycott, the next major development in the struggle for equality took place in Little Rock, Arkansas, spearheaded by another heroine of the movement, Daisy Bates. Bates and her husband, L. C. Bates, bought the *Arkansas State Press* in 1941 to promote the fight for equal rights. To a large degree because of their efforts, Little Rock desegregated its police force, libraries, parks, and public buses. After becoming president of the Little Rock chapter of the NAACP, Bates pursued the desegregation of the city's public schools. Shortly after the *Brown* decision, Virgil T. Blossom, the superintendent of Little Rock's schools, developed a plan for enrolling nine black students, six of whom were female, at Central High School in the fall of 1957. Before the school year began, however, public sentiment turned against the plan, as a rock hurled through Bates's window, made evident. Attached to the rock was the message "Stone this time. Dynamite next." Governor Orval Faubus, the leader of the anti-desegregationists, helped organize a Mothers' League of Little Rock Central High, which filed for an injunction to block implementation of the plan. Women were lining up on both sides of the struggle. Bates, however, refused to back down. She obtained an injunction ordering the schools to desegregate and carefully prepared the Little Rock Nine for their first day of school. In turn, a mob attack on Elizabeth Eckford, one of the nine students, along with Orval Faubus's refusal to provide protection for her or the other eight, prompted President Eisenhower to intervene.

After Eisenhower sent troops to Little Rock to enforce court orders to maintain public order, Bates met with the black students daily, rallying their spirits and conducting regular press conferences that kept the Little Rock story before the eyes of the world. Bates's hard work helped the students withstand extraordinary pressure. One of them, Minniejean Brown, cracked, dumping a bowl of chili on the head of a white classmate who had harassed her while on the cafeteria line, an act that led to her suspension. The others, among them Melba Pattillo Beals and Eckford, drew on a reservoir of inner strength to persevere until the end of the school year.

SEPTIMA CLARK AND ELLA BAKER: THE MOTHERS OF THE MOVEMENT

While Bates and the Little Rock Nine brought the struggle for civil rights before the nation, Septima Clark, whom Martin Luther King, Jr., described as the "Mother of the Movement," labored outside of the limelight to develop a grassroots struggle for racial equality. In the mid-1950s, Clark served as Highlander Folk School's director of education. Building on Highlander's ideal of developing community-based leaders, Clark established citizenship schools throughout the rural South. (After Highlander was red-baited virtually to death, these schools were operated under the SCLC banner, with Clark serving as their director.) The first of the schools was established in the back of a cooperative store on the Sea Islands of South Carolina in January 1957. Clark described a typical first day. "The teacher wrote 'citizen' on the blackboard. Then she wrote 'Constitution' and 'Amendment.' Then she turned to her class of 30 adult students. 'What do these mean, students?' She received a variety of answers, and when the discussion died down, the teacher was able to make a generalization. 'This is the reason we know we are citizens: Because it's written in an amendment to the Constitution.' "6

Clark's co-teachers on the Sea Islands and elsewhere included Bernice Robinson, Dorothy Cotton, and Ethel Grimball. None of these women became household names, yet their work had a long-lasting impact on the people and communities they encountered. As Bernice Robinson observed, "The Citizenship School Program became the basis for the civil rights movement because it was through these classes that people learned about their rights and *why* they should vote."7 In community after community, individuals who attended citizenship schools led grassroots campaigns to register blacks to vote and demanded that federal legislation that outlawed discrimination be enforced. They also promoted improvements in education, such as changes in the curriculum, and, later, the organization of Head Start programs.

The sit-ins that began in Greensboro, North Carolina, on February 1, 1960, signaled a new phase in the black freedom struggle. By the fall of 1961 sit-ins had taken place in over one hundred communities, in nearly every southern and border state. Over seventy thousand individuals participated; still more donated money to bail demonstrators out of jail or wrote letters of sympathy. Out of these protests emerged a new organization, the Student Nonviolent Coordinating Committee (SNCC), the cutting edge of the movement for most of the decade. Perhaps the crucial moment in SNCC's history came at its first meeting, when Ella Baker convinced students who gathered in Raleigh, North Carolina, to remain independent of adult organizations, namely the NAACP and the SCLC. Baker, who was a former organizer with the NAACP and who at the time was working as the acting executive director of the SCLC—until it hired a full-time male director—was the moving force behind the conference in the first place. At Raleigh she delivered one of the key addresses, "Bigger than a Hamburger."

Capturing the attention of the students, Baker proclaimed that the civil rights movement sought more than the desegregation of lunch counters, that it sought to "rid America of the scourge of racial discrimination . . . in every aspect of life." Julian Bond, one of the founders of SNCC, expressed the sentiment of many who were present, calling the speech an eye-opener. Baker warned against entanglements with adult, almost always male, leaders and prompted the students to define their goals in broad terms.[8]

James Forman, SNCC's executive director through most of the 1960s, observed that without Baker "there would be no story of the Student Nonviolent Coordinating Committee." Howard Zinn, an activist scholar who wrote the first study on SNCC, stated that Baker was "more responsible than any single individual for the birth of the new abolitionists [SNCC] as an organization."[9] In the years that followed, Baker continued to play a key role. She mediated disputes within SNCC, such as one that developed following the freedom rides over whether to focus on direct action or voter registration—Baker convinced SNCC it could do both; she helped connect inexperienced activists with seasoned local leaders whom she had met throughout her career as an organizer; and she served as a mentor to numerous young men and women.

To some extent, the civil rights movement, especially SNCC, adopted a female style and vision of leadership during the early 1960s embodied by Septima Clark and Ella Baker. Clark and Baker focused on organizing a broad-based, decentralized, grassroots movement led by ordinary people. They emphasized the goal of empowering individuals and communities as opposed to obtaining federal legislation. Arguably, in the latter half of the 1960s, as the civil rights movement grew more militant, Baker's and Clark's vision and style declined in significance. The tendency of the media to seek out men rather than women and to focus on sensational actions rather than quiet leadership reinforced this shift. Yet even the Black Panther Party, which to many symbolized a macho style of leadership, had its female side, most notably its community breakfast and educational programs and its emphasis on empowering ordinary men and women.

THREE STALWARTS: DIANE NASH, FANNIE LOU HAMER, AND GLORIA RICHARDSON

One of SNCC's defining moments occurred during the spring of 1961 when it came to the rescue of the freedom rides. Organized by CORE, the rides were put on the verge of extinction by white supremacists who brutally assaulted freedom riders in Alabama. As much as the original riders wanted to continue, they were physically unable to do so. Diane Nash, a veteran of the Nashville sit-ins and one of the co-founders of SNCC, however, refused to allow the freedom rides to perish. "If the Freedom Riders had been stopped as a result of violence," Nash recalled, "I strongly felt that the future of the movement was going to be cut short. The impression would have been that whenever a movement starts, all [you have to do] is attack it with massive violence and the blacks [will] stop."[10] Nash put out a call for SNCC to come to the rescue and quickly organized a group of SNCC members who rushed to Birmingham. In turn, they kept the freedom rides and the momentum of the civil rights movement going.

A year before, Nash had taken the lead at an equally pivotal moment in the movement's history. Along with James Lawson and John Lewis, she helped organize the Nashville Student Movement. The students prepared themselves in the techniques and philosophy of nonviolence, and then staged sit-ins involving approximately two hundred men and women at the city's department stores. After a first wave of students was attacked by white hoodlums and placed under arrest for disorderly conduct, more students came forth to take their place. Enraged white supremacists reacted by planting a bomb at the home of Alexander Looby, a prominent black attorney and a supporter of the Nashville Student Movement. Maintaining its commitment to nonviolence, the student movement, joined by much of the adult community, responded by staging a freedom march to City Hall. There, Diane Nash confronted Mayor Ben West. "Do you feel it is wrong to discriminate against a person solely on the basis of their race or color?" Nash inquired. With television cameras capturing his words, West replied that he personally felt it was wrong to do so. His comment and the determination and dignity of the protesters convinced merchants to desegregate their businesses, one of the first victories for the movement.[11]

Fannie Lou Hamer gained a reputation as an even more imposing figure in the movement than Nash. Put simply, nearly all who came to know her held her in awe. Hamer, who was born in Montgomery County, Mississippi, in 1917, was working as a timekeeper on a Sunflower County plantation when SNCC activists spread out across the Delta in 1962. For attending a SNCC-run voter education program and attempting to register to vote, Hamer was brutally beaten by police, fired from her job, and evicted from her home. Such acts by Mississippi white supremacists had crippled efforts to attain equality in the past. But Hamer, whose inner strength was legendary within civil rights circles, was not to be denied. Rather than acquiesce to white commands that she retreat from activism, she became a field secretary for SNCC and a leader of the Mississippi Freedom Democratic Party. After capturing the nation's attention with her breathtaking testimony to the Democratic Party's credentials committee, Hamer stood in the forefront of the MFDP's refusal to accept only token representation at the Democratic national convention. Some have credited Hamer's testimony, or more precisely the Mississippi Freedom Democratic Party's challenge to the Democratic Party, with splitting black radicals from white liberals in the second half of the 1960s and with contributing to major reforms within the Democratic Party.

Hamer's significance also lay in one of the means that, like many other women, from Bernice Reagon to Mahalia Jackson, she used to rally blacks around the struggle for equality. A strong orator, Hamer was an even more powerful singer. Frequently, she led activists in song at mass meetings and at public demonstrations. She would sing old spirituals like "This Little Light of Mine" as well as freedom songs, themselves often drawn from old spirituals. As Mary King, a white SNCC activist and author of *Freedom Song*, an autobiographical account of the movement, writes: "The Freedom songs uplifted us, bound us together, exalted us, and pointed the way, and, in a real sense, freed us from the shackles of psychological bondage. . . . Song leading became an organizing tool, helping to mobilize the dedicated or to motivate the reticent."[12]

Gloria Richardson, the middle-aged leader of the civil rights movement in Cambridge, Maryland, forged one of the most militant and vibrant local movements in the nation using the more traditional leadership techniques used by men. The granddaughter of H. Maydanair St. Clair, the former black representative on the town council (for nearly fifty years), Richardson was working in her family's drugstore when freedom riders first arrived in Cambridge in early 1962. She quickly assumed leadership of the Cambridge Nonviolent Action Committee (CNAC), the only adult-led affiliate of SNCC, winning broad-based support from blacks, most notably from youths and the working poor. In the spring of 1963, with Richardson in the lead, CNAC staged a series of protests that climaxed in one of the first urban riots of the decade. After the National Guard was called in to Cambridge to restore order, she personally negotiated a deal with local officials and Attorney General Robert F. Kennedy. Still, she drew the ire of many liberals and nearly all conservatives for refusing to support a local public accommodations measure, arguing that civil rights were human rights, which could not be left to the whim of the white majority.

THE WOMEN OF MISSISSIPPI

In addition to Hamer, studies of the Mississippi movement have identified many other leading women in the cause, including Annie Devine, Victoria Gray, June Johnson, Annelle Ponder, Winson Hudson, Unita Blackwell, Euvester Simpson, Rosemary Freeman, and Anne Moody. Of these, only Moody's story is known except by the smallest circle of civil rights scholars, and then only because she wrote one of the first memoirs of the movement, *Coming of Age in Mississippi*. These women, along with a number of equally obscure local men, were the backbone of the Mississippi movement. They provided SNCC activists with the safe harbor and resources they needed to build the movement into a mass phenomenon in the first place. During Freedom Summer, the best-known aspect of the movement in the state, hundreds of black women opened their homes to summer volunteers, attended mass meetings, circulated petitions, and rallied behind MFDP and the Freedom Schools. Even if men often led these efforts, as historian Charles Payne observes, "women organized."[13]

A fuller appreciation of the contributions that women made to the struggle for racial equality can be gleaned by examining the role played by Laura McGhee, of Greenwood, Mississippi. McGhee's involvement began in 1955, shortly after her brother, Gus Courts, a member of the local NAACP, was shot. While others might have recoiled from activism in the face of such raw violence, McGhee sought ways to make Mississippi a better place. In 1962, when SNCC organizers arrived in the Delta, she was one of the first persons to respond to their initiatives. After attempting to register to vote, she encouraged other blacks in Greenwood to do the same. Her home served as an unofficial meeting place and as a refuge for sharecroppers who were kicked off the land because of their civil rights activities. In addition, she used her property as collateral to bail SNCC representatives out of jail. Upon being warned by the FBI to stop her boys from shooting at nightriders who attacked their home, she replied, "Okay," because in the future she would do all of the shooting herself.

McGhee instilled a sense of fearlessness in her children and many of those around her, including seasoned SNCC activists. During Freedom Summer, shortly after the Civil Rights Act of 1964 was enacted, her sons sought to integrate the local movie theater, something no one else dared to do, fearing the wrath of Greenwood's whites, federal legislation notwithstanding. One evening, after sitting in the previously all-white section of the theater, the McGhee boys were attacked by a mob. During this time shots were routinely fired into their home. After arguing with a police officer, Silas McGhee was shot in the head. At the hospital, police bragged that Silas had finally gotten his. Several days later, Silas's brother, Jake, was arrested. When Laura McGhee went down to the police station to try to get Jake out of jail, the police refused to allow her to see him. Undeterred, she forced her way into the station, smacked a police officer in the eye, and demanded to see her son. Bob Zellner recalls:

She says, "I come down here to get my son, Jake." He [the police officer] says, "You can't go in there" and she says "Boppp!" Hit him in the eye, right in the eye as hard as I've ever seen anybody hit in my life. I remember it just like a movie. . . . I remember his eye swelling up and I remember thinking to myself "God, I didn't know you could *see* something swell up. . . . " And he's losing consciousness, sliding down the door. Meanwhile, Mrs. McGhee is following him on the way down. She's not missing a lick—boom, boom, boom!—and every time she hits him, his head hits the door. Meantime . . . he's going for his gun reflexively, but the man is practically knocked out. . . . The chief is going, "What the hell's going on?" Every time the chief would try to open the door it would hit the man—whomp—in the head again.

Although Laura McGhee was arrested for assaulting a police officer, she was never tried, apparently because it was too embarrassing for a white man to admit in court that he had been beaten up by a black woman. For Zellner, this episode reflected one of the major accomplishments of the era. "A new day is coming when a Black woman can just whip the yard-dog shit out of a white cop and not have to account for it."[14]

Charles Payne has speculated on why women played such an important role in Mississippi. Some joined the movement because their children or other family members did. Lula Belle Johnson, for instance, became involved after her daughter, June, was arrested and beaten. The shooting of her brother prompted Laura McGhee to get involved, and the attacks on her sons reinforced her commitment to struggle for equality. Religion, or perhaps more precisely faith in God, also played a role. This is not to argue that family and religion did not affect men, but in general these concerns animated women more. They had a greater investment in kin networks and tended to be more faithful in attending church regularly and organizing church affairs than men. SNCC's emphasis on developing nontraditional sources of leadership helps account for the number of women who became active in Mississippi as well.[15]

A LONG TRADITION OF LEADERSHIP

Paula Giddings and other scholars of race and gender have observed that women have a long tradition of leadership within the African American community. Steeled by a society that discriminated against them because of their race and gender, black women have exhibited much strength and wisdom in their battle to transcend both forms of discrimination. Sojourner Truth, the legendary black female abolitionist, and Harriet Tubman, the foremost "conductor" on the Underground Railroad, personified this image. During the era of Jim Crow, Mary Church Terrell, Ida Wells Barnett, and Mary McLeod Bethune fought tirelessly against the oppression and degradation of black men and women by white society. These women left a legacy of struggle upon which many unnamed others built.

Yet, Giddings's work reminds us that all black women are not cast in the same mold. Gloria Richardson, of Cambridge, Maryland, is an example of one type of female activist. Generally contemptuous of Martin Luther King, Jr., she gained the admiration of Malcolm X and Stokely Carmichael. She was a very strong woman whom some compared to Joan of Arc. Ironically, in 1964, at the peak of her fame, she went to live in New York with her new husband, Frank Dandridge, a *New York Times* photographer, whom she met during the heat of the struggle.

Amelia Platts Boynton is an example of another type of activist. In the late 1950s and early 1960s she and a core of other activists forged a voter education project in Dallas County, Alabama. Like Hamer and Nash, she faced constant physical threats and violence. In part because she was an independent businesswoman, Boynton was able to withstand economic pressures that blacks who depended on whites for work could not. As became evident with Freedom Day, a protest whereby over three hundred hundred blacks tried to register to vote in Selma in October 1963, her efforts began to pay off. Still, she worked in relative anonymity. Not until 1965, when Martin Luther King, Jr., came to Selma to mount a massive voter registration campaign, did the national media take notice of her efforts, and even then they gave King most of the credit for the success of the campaign.

Coretta Scott King, Martin Luther King, Jr.'s wife, represents still another type of female activist. She often appeared extremely reserved and refined, almost aloof. She gave up a career as a classical musician to serve as King's dutiful wife, raising their children and withstanding death threats and other forms of harassment that followed her husband. She also quietly put up with his marital infidelity. Yet, in her own way Coretta Scott King played an instrumental role in the struggle for racial equality. Through her dignity and persona she won support for the civil rights movement. And after her husband's death she took on a more active role, most notably by joining hands with female hospital workers who sought to organize a union in Charleston, South Carolina, in 1969, and later by insisting that the memorialization of her martyred husband be used as a reminder of how much remained to be done to achieve a just society.

THE CIVIL RIGHTS MOVEMENT
AND THE WOMEN'S MOVEMENT

While Gloria Richardson, Amelia Platts Boynton, and Coretta Scott King did not publicly identify themselves as feminists—at least during the early 1960s—the civil rights movement in general, and black and white female civil rights activists in particular, played a key role in fomenting the rebirth of feminism. On the broadest level, by challenging the racial caste system, the civil rights movement encouraged women to consider ways in which they, as women, faced caste restrictions. As Mary King and Casey Hayden, two white female members of SNCC, observed in their "Memo" to other women in the movement, "There seem to be many parallels that can be drawn between the treatment of Negroes and the treatment of women in our society as a whole." More specifically, King and Hayden declared, women "seem to be caught in a common-law caste system that operates, sometimes subtly, forcing them to work around or outside hierarchical structures of power which may exclude them."[16] In other words, they faced a caste system very much like the caste system blacks faced in the South during the age of Jim Crow.

Middle-aged black women helped launch the women's movement in another way, by serving as important role models. Women like Fannie Lou Hamer and Ella Baker stood in sharp contrast to the cult of domesticity that predominated at the time. They were working women who involved themselves actively in public affairs; they were strong women who defied the notion that assertive women were not real women. Put simply, they inspired Mary King, Casey Hayden, and countless others to redefine women's roles in America.

The civil rights movement also gave many women space and opportunity to grow as individuals. While participating in mass meetings and demonstrations and challenging southern authorities, many young women first discovered their own voice and gained a sense of their own power as individuals, capable of making history. Bernice Reagon, who joined the civil rights movement in her hometown of Albany, Georgia, noted that even while in jail "there was a sense of power, in a place where you didn't feel you had any power. There was a sense of confronting things that terrified you, like jail, police, walking in the street. . . . So you were saying in some basic ways, 'I'll never again stay inside these boundaries.' . . . in terms of what happened to me, and what happened to other people I know about, it was a change in my concept of myself and how I stood. . . . The Civil Rights Movement gave me the power to challenge *any* line that limits me."[17]

Ironically, the inability of numerous men within the civil rights movement to accept the claim that women were exploited, symbolized by Stokely

Carmichael's joke that the "only place for women in the movement was prone," provided further impetus for the women's movement. Claims by male leftists that calls for women's liberation were divisive and counterproductive backfired, convincing many women that they had to forge their own movement because men still did not take their concerns seriously. The rise of black power, which led to the exclusion of whites from SNCC and CORE, added further impetus to the women's movement.[18]

Even if women rarely won public notice for their efforts and had to tolerate male chauvinism within the civil rights movement, they learned valuable skills during the fight against racial inequality which they subsequently made use of in the fight for sexual equality. Put differently, they attended the best possible training school for social activism. They learned how to organize demonstrations, communicate with the mass media, and build up locally based leadership. In addition, many feminists absorbed the language and theories of the black freedom struggle, which they then adapted to their own uses. A notion prominent during the second half of the 1960s, that blacks sought not just equal rights but liberation, for example, dovetailed with the call for women's liberation held by many female veterans of the southern freedom movement during the same time period. Such transference of skills and language helps explain the speed with which the women's movement blossomed in the late 1960s and early 1970s.

Lastly, without the civil rights movement the United States might never have enacted legislation prohibiting sexual discrimination. In a desperate attempt to derail the Civil Rights Act of 1964, Representative Howard K. Smith of Virginia offered an amendment making sexual as well as racial discrimination illegal. Smith proposed this amendment not because he was a closet feminist but in the belief that it would make the bill more unpalatable to many members of Congress. At the time, there was no widespread call for legislation against sexual discrimination, and some women's organizations actually sought to kill Smith's amendment lest they be blamed for the defeat of the Civil Rights Act. Only because Congresswoman Edith Green of Oregon and a handful of other men and women fought to pass the civil rights bill with Smith's amendment intact did Title VII of the Civil Right Act of 1964, which prohibits sexual discrimination, become law.

After President Johnson signed the Civil Rights Act of 1964, the unwillingness of the EEOC, the agency charged with enforcing it, to take complaints of sexual discrimination seriously prodded the National Organization for Women (NOW), heretofore a relatively moderate organization, to seek passage of the Equal Rights Amendment (ERA). Many of the same forces that had coalesced around civil rights ultimately came together around the ERA, getting Congress and just short of the necessary two-thirds of the states to ratify this amendment. Its failure to become part of the Constitution signaled the resurgence of a conservative movement that took aim at reforms fostered by both the civil and women's rights movements. Nonetheless, even without the ERA, women enjoyed far greater legal protection than they had in the past due to the Civil Rights Act of 1964 and the courts' interpretation of it.

In spite of these links between the women's movement and the civil rights movement, tensions also existed between black and white women during the late 1960s and early 1970s. Many black women felt torn between their loyalty to the cause of racial equality and their desire to fight against sexual discrimination. They felt that the women's movement, comprised largely of white middle-class women, focused on issues that appeared unrelated to the concerns of the mass of black women. As Michele Wallace observed, "When I first became a feminist, my Black friends used to cast pitying eyes upon me and say, 'That's whitey's thing.' " "In *Ebony*, *Jet*, and *Encore* and even in the *New York Times*," Wallace continued, "various Black writers cautioned Black women to be wary of smiling white feminists. The women's movement enlists the support of Black women only to lend credibility to an essentially middle-class, irrelevant movement, they asserted."[19]

Over time, these tensions tended to subside. Many of the best-known women's rights leaders during the 1980s and 1990s have been African Americans, from writers and poets such as Toni Morrison, Maya Angelou, and Alice Walker to politicians such as Barbara Jordan, Shirley Chisholm, and Carol Moseley Braun. Similarly, it was not coincidental that Anita Hill, a black law professor, became a cause célèbre for the women's movement in the early 1990s, although, as polls showed, the black community still felt a bit torn in its allegiances, between Hill, a black woman who alleged that she had been sexually harassed by Clarence Thomas, a black man, and Thomas himself, whose nomination to the Supreme Court was placed in jeopardy by Hill's accusations.

In sum, although the collective public memory of the civil rights years tends to downplay the role women played, in reality, they played a leading part. In virtually every community that scholars of the civil rights movement have examined, women constituted the backbone of the movement and in many cases served as its leaders. Furthermore, by prompting society at large to make connections between racial and sexual discrimination, women who participated in the civil rights movement broadened its impact. They encouraged people all over the world, regardless of their race, color, gender, sexual preference, or religion to demand that they be allowed to participate as full and equal citizens.

NOTES

1. Kluger, *Simple Justice*, 389.

2. Ibid., 468–69.

3. David J. Garrow, ed., *The Montgomery Bus Boycott and the Women Who Started It: The Memoir of Jo Ann Gibson Robinson* (Knoxville: University of Tennessee Press, 1987), 19–52.

4. Martin Luther King, Jr., "Letter from [a] Birmingham Jail," in Levy, *Let Freedom Ring*, 1.

5. Hollinger F. Barnard, ed., *Outside the Magic Circle: The Autobiography of Virginia Foster Durr* (Tuscaloosa: University of Alabama Press, 1985), 274–85.

6. Septima Clark, *Echo in My Soul* (New York: E. P. Dutton, 1962), 131–33. Emphasis added.

7. Quoted in Susan B. Oldendorf, "The South Carolina Sea Island Citizenship Schools, 1957–1961," in Crawford, Rouse, and Woods, *Women in the Civil Rights Movement*, 180.

8. Ella Baker, "Bigger than a Hamburger," in Levy, *Let Freedom Ring*, 70–71.

9. Forman quoted in Hampton and Fayer, *Voices of Freedom*, 67; Howard Zinn, *SNCC: The New Abolitionists* (Boston: Beacon Press, 1964).

10. Quoted in *Hampton and Fayer, Voices of Freedom*, 82.

11. Williams, *Eyes on the Prize*, 138–39.

12. Mary King, *Freedom Song: A Personal Story of the 1960s Civil Rights Movement* (New York: William Morrow, 1987), 23–24.

13. Charles Payne, "Men Led, but Women Organized: Movement Participation of Women in the Mississippi Delta," in Crawford, Rouse, and Woods, *Women in the Civil Rights Movement*.

14. All of these quotes come from Payne, *I've Got the Light of Freedom*, 208–218.

15. Ibid., especially chap 9.

16. Casey Hayden and Mary King, "A Kind of Memo . . . to a Number of Other Women in the Peace and Freedom Movements," reprinted in Mary King, *Freedom Song*.

17. Bernice Reagon, "Interview," in Levy, *Let Freedom Ring*, 98–99.

18. Carmichael quoted in Sara Evans, *Personal Politics: The Roots of Women's Liberation in the Civil Rights Movement and the New Left* (New York: Vintage, 1980), 87. Mary King, who knew Carmichael well, understood that he made this remark in jest. Yet others who did not share King's insight and heard of the remark took it as indicative of the male-led movement.

19. Michele Wallace, "A Black Feminist's Search for Sisterhood," in Levy, *Let Freedom Ring*, 199–200 (originally published in the *Village Voice*, 1975).

6

A Second Redemption?

The end of Reconstruction in the 1870s undid much of the progress that had been made toward achieving racial equality. Indeed, an era nearly as repressive as the one that preceded the Civil War came into being. While the Fourteenth and Fifteenth Amendments were not repealed, they were virtually ignored by the white majority, circumscribed by narrow Court rulings, and undermined by segregation laws and black disfranchisement. To make matters worse, science and popular culture were sometimes enlisted to bolster racism. Biological "evidence" purported to prove that whites as a "race" were genetically superior to blacks. *Birth of a Nation* (1915), the first great full-length film, reinforced and spread racist views, such as that slavery had been relatively benign, that Reconstruction had been the worst period in American history, and that groups like the Ku Klux Klan had saved the nation from racial suicide.

Recent developments have led many to wonder if history is repeating itself. Is the Second Reconstruction, the term often used to identify the modern civil rights movement, giving way to a second reversal? One can muster much evidence to support the notion that it is. In 1996 California voters passed Proposition 209, which banned affirmative action in state-run programs. Over the past decade numerous court decisions have constrained aspects of affirmative action. For example, in the cases of *City of Richmond v. J. R. Croson Co.* (1989) and *Adarand Constructors v. Peña* (1995), the Supreme Court disallowed set-aside plans that required a specific percent of public contracts to be awarded to minority firms, and it demanded "strict scrutiny" in establishing racial classifications and narrowly tailored remedies for past discrimination. Similarly, in several recent voting rights cases, the Supreme Court has ruled that the use of race as a "predominant factor" in drawing election districts is unconstitutional, forcing several states to redraw majority-black districts that had sent African American representatives to Congress. In the field of education, the cry for integration has not only died out in many places, but has given way to resignation to the fact that de facto segregation is and will remain a way of life for millions of African American schoolchildren.

Meanwhile, the litany of social ills plaguing black Americans, particularly in urban areas, from extremely high homicide rates among black males to unprecedented rates of out-of-wedlock births by teenage black women, adds to the image of a people in crisis. When these problems are coupled with public apathy toward combating them—in contrast to the spirit of the 1960s, when the federal government championed programs to eradicate poverty and create a "great society"—it seems to some social critics that Jim Crow has returned, now by way of customs and indifference rather than laws.

The reemergence of white supremacist groups, symbolized by the recent wave of burnings of African American churches, the publication of works such as *The Bell Curve* by Richard J. Herrnstein and Charles Murray, which contends that African Americans as a whole are intellectually inferior to whites, and public opinion surveys that show increasing distrust and anger between whites and blacks add to the ominous sense that the civil rights movement was for naught. The ascendancy of white conservative Republicans, most notably the election of southern conservative Republicans as Speaker of the House and Senate Majority Leader, respectively, gives little comfort to those who feel that things are worse for blacks in the 1990s than they have been for a long time.

Yet, ultimately, the notion that history is repeating itself misrepresents reality by underestimating the magnitude and durability of the change Americans experienced during the civil rights years. Most obviously, the basic legal reforms of the civil rights era have not been reversed. In 1895 Booker T. Washington argued that blacks should accommodate themselves to their disfranchisement. About a half-century later, brave African Americans in the South like Medgar Evers attempted to vote but were turned back from the polls by white mobs. At the time, Evers and most blacks had little hope that they would attain equal citizenship rights in the near future. Yet as the twentieth century draws to a close, every legal barrier and most extralegal barriers to voting have been removed. In no other arena did the civil rights movement have a greater impact.

Since the mid-1960s, black participation in the political process has skyrocketed. At the end of World War II only a handful of African Americans held elective office. In the South, black politicians were almost unheard of; when Michigan congressman Charles Diggs, a black man, visited the courtroom in Mississippi where Emmett Till's murderers were being tried in 1955, local authorities could not even believe there was such a thing as a black congressman. In contrast, as of 1993, there were over eight thousand black elected officials, and Mississippi had more blacks in office than any other state in the nation. Blacks have served as mayors of America's largest cities, as justices on the Supreme Court and on other high courts, as members of presidential cabinets, and even as governor of a former state of the Confederacy. As of 1997, even the county where Emmett Till was lynched is represented in Congress by an African American.

In Congress and state legislatures, at the conventions of the Democratic and Republican parties, and in government agencies, black elected officials and appointees participate in the making and implementation of public policy and act as a bulwark against a return to the past. Just as important, so too do prominent black figures such as the former head of the Joint Chiefs of Staff, Colin Powell. True, much black political power has been localized, and it is sometimes more apparent than real. Black mayors often come to power in cities experiencing "white flight" of people and jobs to the suburbs. Urban political muscle in national politics has been declining, while largely white suburban political power has been rising. As a result, minorities do not enjoy an equal share of power in society. Still, they are no longer politically powerless, as they essentially were during the era of Jim Crow, and the fact that they are beginning to win the support of white voters suggests that their power is growing.

Similarly, while affirmative action and the Voting Rights Act of 1965 have been narrowed in scope by recent Supreme Court decisions, the Civil Rights Act of 1964, which bans discrimination in public accommodations and employment, and the Voting Rights Act, which protects the right of African Americans to register and vote, stand firmly in place. It took the assassination of John F. Kennedy, brutal assaults against nonviolent protesters in Birmingham, Selma, and elsewhere, and a massive lobbying effort to gain passage of these laws. But today, even the sharpest critics of affirmative action champion the ideal of a color-blind society and the right of all citizens to vote, and there has been no movement to reinstate Jim Crow laws or to disfranchise blacks.

A further example of the nation's shift came in 1996. One hundred years after *Plessy* v. *Ferguson*, an unusual coalition of congressmen, headed by southern Republicans, brought to a vote the Adoption Promotion and Stability Act, which sought to foster interracial adoption. One of the bill's chief sponsors, Bill Archer, a conservative Republican from Texas, declared, "It's simply not right to deny a child the opportunity to grow up in a loving family because the child's parents . . . are of a different race." The bill, which was part of the "Contract with America," the Republican Party's conservative agenda, gained overwhelming support, 392–12, in the House of Representatives. Its passage illustrated the breadth and depth of the impact of the civil rights years. A century earlier, even Homer Plessy's attorney, S. F. Phillips, had accepted the constitutionality and desirability of laws that prohibited interracial marriage. In *An American Dilemma*, his classic study of race relations conducted at mid-century, Gunnar Myrdal observed that Americans were most insistent on preserving separation of the races in their personal or private lives. Yet, in combination with the Supreme Court's ruling in *Loving* v. *Virginia* (1967), the Adoption Act removed any and all legal obstacles to the formation of interracial families. And 1990 census figures revealed a growing pattern of interracial marriages—so much so that children of such unions have lobbied for a new census classification, other than black or white or Hispanic, to reflect the "new American" of many backgrounds.

Perhaps the only way to assess truly the legacy of the civil rights movement is to return to the years immediately following World War II, when Jim Crow still presided as a way of life in the South and de facto segregation in housing and employment characterized much of the North. During World War II black soldiers fought in a segregated army, and after the war they returned to southern states that greeted their attempts to vote with mob violence. While President Truman and many newspapers condemned these acts of violence, Congress did not even entertain the idea of enacting voting rights legislation at the time. On the contrary, the most important racial reform of the World War II period, the creation of the Fair Employment Practice Committee, was killed by a coalition of southern Democrats and Republicans after the war. Nor should we forget that in the wake of *Brown* nearly every southern politician denounced the Supreme Court for overturning *Plessy* v. *Ferguson* and the principle of desegregation, and some suggested that integration was a communist plot. Still more joined White Citizens' Councils in an attempt to maintain Jim Crow by any means.

Not only did the modern civil rights movement successfully overcome this opposition, it altered the climate and the terrain of race relations in the United States. Although inequities in the justice system remain and a handful of openly white supremacist politicians hold public office, Americans live in a vastly different world today than that of the late 1940s or early 1950s. White murderers or lynchers are no longer routinely acquitted by all-white juries. Politicians who openly defend white supremacy and use straightforward appeals to racial hatred rarely get elected to office. Even in the realm of economics, blacks have made tremendous progress. While poverty grips tens of thousands of African Americans who appear trapped in inner-city ghettos across America or in rural enclaves in the deep South, blacks as a whole are better off economically than they were a half-century ago. In 1939 over 80 percent of all African Americans lived below the poverty line. By 1969 about one-third did, a proportion that has held fairly firm ever since. In 1940 only about 2 percent of all blacks ages twenty-five to twenty-nine graduated from college. By the mid-1980s, between 10 and 15 percent did, and black high school graduation rates had jumped from 1 in 5 to 8 out of 10 students. In the same time frame, median family income for blacks, adjusted for inflation, more than doubled. At the end of World War II, black professionals were a rarity and almost wholly confined to serving a black clientele in segregated settings, whereas in 1997 a substantial number of blacks can be found in every profession, living in both integrated and predominantly black middle-class neighborhoods. True, the greatest economic gains took place between 1950 and 1975, but these gains have held relatively steady ever since.

Of course, the skeptic might counter, if so much has changed, why has so much pessimism about race relations and minority progress marked the 1990s? Why do public opinion polls reveal such a high level of racial tension? One reason for this is that we have romanticized or forgotten about the realities of the past. The pre–civil rights years have too often been cast as an era of peace, tranquility, and order. Those who yearn to go back to these mythical golden years share a collective amnesia about the realities of race relations in the United States of America. They downplay the number of lynchings and disregard the everyday indignities that the system of segration compelled blacks to endure. They forget about the extent of the poverty that plagued the vast majority of African Americans. Perhaps by promoting a utopian vision of a color-blind society, of "black and white together," the civil rights movement contibuted to the letdown that followed by creating expectations that could not be met. Yet the fact that the dreams of Martin Luther King, Jr., and others were not achieved should not blind us to the accomplishments of one of the most important historic events of the twentieth century.

Biographies: The Personalities Behind the Civil Rights Movement

Ralph David Abernathy (1926–1990)

Ralph Abernathy was one of Martin Luther King, Jr.'s closest friends and associates and one of the most prominent civil rights leaders during the 1950s and 1960s. He played a pivotal role in the Montgomery bus boycott and the protests in Birmingham, Alabama, in 1963 and became the leader of the Southern Christian Leadership Conference (SCLC) following King's assassination.

Abernathy was born in the rural community of Linden, Alabama, on March 11, 1926. His father, William L. Abernathy, was a Baptist deacon and the owner of 500 acres of prime farm land. Ordained as a Baptist minister in 1948, Abernathy earned his B.S. from Alabama State University (1950) and his M.A. in sociology from Atlanta University (1951). In 1951 he accepted a post as the dean of men at Alabama State and took over as pastor of the First Baptist Church, both in Montgomery, Alabama. During the early 1950s he became close friends with the Reverend Vernon Johns, the charismatic minister of the Dexter Avenue Baptist Church. In 1955, when Johns left Montgomery, Abernathy befriended his replacement, Martin Luther King, Jr.

When Rosa Parks was arrested for refusing to give up her seat on a bus, sparking the Montgomery bus boycott, King and Abernathy were chosen to head the Montgomery Improvement Association (MIA), which orchestrated the yearlong campaign to end segregation on the buses. Both King and Abernathy advocated nonviolence and withstood death threats during the boycott. In 1957 Abernathy helped King form the SCLC. King served as the organization's president; Abernathy was its secretary-treasurer. In 1960 King convinced Abernathy to accept a post as pastor of the West Hunter Street Baptist Church so that they could be together in Atlanta. Together they mounted nonviolent freedom struggles in Albany, Birmingham, St. Augustine, Selma, and other southern communities.

In 1968 Abernathy took over the Poor People's Campaign in Washington, D.C., which King had helped plan before his death. Under Abernathy's direction, protesters converged on the capital and built a makeshift shantytown, known as Resurrection City, to emphasize the plight of the poor in the United States. The failure of the campaign to achieve any significant reforms led many to compare Abernathy unfavorably to King. Abernathy remained a prominent civil rights activist for several years after King's assassination, organizing a successful strike of hospital workers in Charleston, South Carolina, in 1969 and running unsuccessfully for Congress in Georgia in 1977.

In the 1980s Abernathy surprisingly supported Ronald Reagan for president and established the Foundation for Economic Development. In 1989 he published his autobiography, *And the Walls Came Tumbling Down*, a moving account of his lifelong activism, which some criticized because it discussed Martin Luther King, Jr.'s marital infidelity. Abernathy died on April 17, 1990, in Atlanta, Georgia.

Ella Jo Baker (1903–1986)

Ella Baker was one of the least known but most influential figures in the fight for civil rights. Over the course of her career she worked for the NAACP and the SCLC and served as an unofficial advisor to SNCC.

Born in Norfolk, Virginia, on December 13, 1903, the granddaughter of slaves and the daughter of a waiter and a teacher, Baker graduated at the top of her class from Shaw University in Raleigh, North Carolina, in the 1920s. She then moved to New York City, where she embarked upon a career of activism. In the 1920s she headed the Young Negroes Cooperative League; in the 1930s she served as a labor and consumer educator for the Works Progress Administration (WPA). In 1940 she became a field secretary for the NAACP, traveling throughout the South to recruit new members. However, in 1946, after rising to the post of director of branches, she resigned from the NAACP because of philosophical differences with the organization, namely, her disapproval of its top-down approach to reform.

In the late 1940s and 1950s, Baker worked for various organizations, including the National Urban League, In Friendship, and the New York City branch of the NAACP. In 1957 she joined the newly formed Southern

Christian Leadership Conference, organizing the Crusade for Citizenship, a voter registration drive. She served for several years as the SCLC's acting executive director, until a man was hired as permanent director. In 1960 she played an instrumental role in the founding of the Student Nonviolent Coordinating Committee. After organizing the conference in Raleigh at which SNCC was formed, she delivered the keynote address, entitled "Bigger than a Hamburger." To a large degree because of her advice, SNCC decided to remain independent of the SCLC and the NAACP. In the early 1960s, Baker offered key counsel to SNCC's leaders, ironing out disagreements between different factions and providing contacts for the students with an older generation of activists.

Following her credo, "A life that is important is a life of service," Baker remained involved in the fight for human rights throughout her senior years. She often spoke in favor of the rights of women, minorities, and workers. Distrustful of highly centralized organizations, she personified the concept of the "beloved community," which animated many activists during the 1960s. At times referred to as the godmother of the movement, Baker died in New York City on December 13, 1986. The pallbearers at her funeral, who included Jamil Abdullah Al-Amin (H. Rap Brown), Julian Bond, Charles McDew, Reginald Robinson, Charles Sherrod, Kwame Toure (Stokely Carmichael), and Robert Zellner, showed the reverence in which many younger activists held her.

Stokely Carmichael [Kwame Toure] (1941–)

Stokely Carmichael, who changed his name to Kwame Toure in 1978— after Kwame Nkrumah, the revolutionary leader of Ghana, and Sekou Toure, the leader of Guinea—gained national fame in 1966 when he coined the slogan "Black Power!" Shortly before he popularized this slogan, Carmichael had been elected chairman of the Student Nonviolent Coordinating Committee (SNCC). Carmichael's ascendancy within SNCC represented the radicalization of the organization, its rejection of nonviolence and integration.

Carmichael was born in Port of Spain, Trinidad, on July 29, 1941. He migrated with his parents to New York City in the early 1950s. After graduating from Bronx High School of Science, he enrolled at Howard University, where he became a member of the Nonviolent Action Group, or NAG, an affiliate of SNCC. He was one of several NAG members who rushed south to join the freedom rides in the late spring of 1961, for which he was arrested and sentenced to a seven-week term in Parchman Penitentiary. Carmichael participated in various SNCC efforts, including Freedom

Summer and a voter education project in Lowndes County, Alabama. This latter effort led to the formation of the Lowndes County Freedom Organization, which took as its symbol a black panther.

Carmichael's radicalization grew out of his experiences in the movement, from the arrest, beating, and murder of many activists in the South to what he saw as the inadequate response of the federal government and liberals to repression and the needs of African Americans. Carmichael helped define the concept of black power in several works, the most important being *Black Power* (1967), which he co-wrote with Charles Hamilton, and "What We Want," which appeared in the *New York Review of Books*. Carmichael explained that advocates of black power sought to increase black political and economic power and to enhance black pride in their African American heritage. To his chagrin, as Carmichael acknowledged, most Americans perceived black power as a call to arms.

After serving a brief stint as prime minister of the Black Panther Party, the radical black national organization headquartered in Oakland, California, Carmichael moved to West Africa. While Carmichael makes Guinea his home and calls himself a revolutionary pan-Africanist, he spends much of his time on the lecture circuit in the United States, at times verbally clashing with some of his former SNCC colleagues.

Medgar Evers (1925–1963)

On June 11, 1963, Medgar Evers, the NAACP's energetic leader in Mississippi, was assassinated outside of his home by Byron de la Beckwith, a fervid white supremacist. De la Beckwith was tried for murder twice during the 1960s, but both trials ended in hung juries. In 1994, following the release of new evidence, Beckwith was retried and convicted.

Evers was born on July 25, 1925, in Decatur, Mississippi. His father, James, was a strong man who refused to surrender his dignity during the darkest days of Jim Crow in Mississippi, and Evers looked up to him as a role model. During World War II, Evers served in the army in France. Upon returning to his home state, he attempted to register to vote, only to be rebuffed by a white mob who made clear that black veterans would not be allowed to exercise their rights. After earning his B.A. from Alcorn Agricultural and Mechanical College, he applied to the University of Mississippi law school but was rejected because of his race. He then went to work as an insurance agent, traveling and getting to know blacks across the state.

In 1954 Evers became Mississippi's first NAACP field director, laboring tirelessly to organize local chapters in the face of massive resistance. In 1955 he gained national attention by highlighting the lynching of Emmett

Till, a fourteen-year-old boy from Chicago who had been killed in Mississippi for allegedly talking fresh to a white woman. An admirer of Jomo Kenyatta, the African freedom fighter, Evers named his first son Darrell Kenyatta Evers.

In the early 1960s Evers championed the cause of James Meredith, who became the first black to attend the University of Mississippi. Evers was in the midst of mounting a massive freedom campaign in Jackson, the state capital, to integrate public accommodations, register black voters, and increase black employment when he was assassinated. Evers was buried in Arlington Cemetery. In the 1990s his wife, Myrlie Evers, ascended to the national leadership of the NAACP. His brother, Charles Evers, succeeded Medgar as the head of the NAACP in Mississippi, but he was never as effective of a leader as Medgar.

James Farmer (1920–   )

As the director of the Congress of Racial Equality (CORE), James Farmer was one of the most important civil rights leaders of the 1960s. He organized the freedom rides and countless other nonviolent direct-action protests.

Born in Marshall, Texas, on January 12, 1920, the son of a minister and professor at Rust College, Farmer studied at Wiley College, in his hometown, before moving to Washington, D.C., where he earned his bachelor of divinity degree at Howard University (1941). Strongly influenced by Mahatma Gandhi, the nonviolent leader of India's independence movement, Farmer declared himself a pacifist and dedicated himself to the cause of racial equality during the 1940s. Exempted from service during World War II because of his religious beliefs, Farmer went to work for the Fellowship of Reconciliation (FOR). In 1942 he founded CORE. Even though it was dwarfed by the larger and better-known NAACP and National Urban League, CORE gained notoriety in 1947 by staging the Journey of Reconciliation, which aimed at desegregating transportation in the upper South. In the 1950s, as the mood of the country shifted in a conservative direction, CORE's membership dwindled and Farmer resigned as its leader to work as a labor organizer.

In 1960, in the wake of the sit-ins, Farmer rejoined CORE as its national director. The following year, CORE and Farmer gained national headlines by staging the freedom rides, which sought to desegregate transportation facilities in the deep South. During these rides, Farmer was arrested and sent to prison for forty days in Mississippi's Parchman Penitentiary. Farmer was a gifted speaker who lectured across the country on the cause of racial equality. Dedicated to the ideals of nonviolence and integration—he was married to a white woman, Lula Farmer—he served as one of the promoters of the 1963 Great March on Washington and took part in a famous debate with Malcolm X. While director of CORE, he pushed hard for greater job opportunities for African Americans in the North as well as in the South, calling for compensation for past discrimination by the government and the private sector. Farmer left CORE in the second half of the 1960s after it renounced its commitment to integration and nonviolence. He taught briefly at Lincoln University in Pennsylvania, and in 1968 ran for Congress in Brooklyn on a third-party ticket (he lost to Shirley Chisholm). Afterwards he accepted an offer to work in the Nixon administration as Assistant Secretary of Health, Education and Welfare (HEW). His participation in the Nixon administration earned Farmer much criticism from many of his former allies. In 1971 Farmer resigned from the Nixon administration and established a black think tank, the Council on Minority Planning and Strategy, which quickly collapsed due to lack of funding. Through most of the 1970s and 1980s Farmer supported himself by giving lectures and writing. His autobiography, *Lay Bare the Heart* (1985), remains one of the best first-person accounts of the civil rights movement.

Fannie Lou Hamer (Townsend) (1917–1977)

In the 1960s Fannie Lou Hamer personified the backbone and strength of the civil rights movement. A poor, middle-aged sharecropper, she played a leading role in toppling Jim Crow in Mississippi and gained national prominence during the 1964 Democratic convention in Atlantic City as a leader of the Mississippi Freedom Democratic Party.

Born on October 6, 1917, in Montgomery County, Mississippi, the youngest of twenty children, she resided in the heart of the Mississippi Delta for most of her life. From the time she was a child until the early 1960s, Hamer labored in the cotton fields alongside her parents and later her husband, Perry Hamer, whom she married in 1944. When SNCC began organizing in the region, she became one of its first recruits. In August 1962, along with seventeen other local blacks, she sought to register to vote. Not only did the registrar declare her ineligible, because, according to him, she failed the literacy test, but her boss threatened to fire her if she did not withdraw her voter application. When she refused to do so, he not only fired her but gave her less than twenty-four hours to leave the plantation where she had lived for nearly twenty years. She was subsequently shot at by nightriders and harassed by local authorities. In June 1963, after attending a citizenship program, she was taken off a bus, beaten, and sexually abused by police in Winona, Mississippi.

Nonetheless, Hamer persevered, recruiting more black Mississippians to the struggle for racial equality. As a leader and one of the sixty-eight delegates of the Mississippi Freedom Democratic Party, she journeyed to the Democratic convention in Atlantic City in 1964, where she delivered spellbinding testimony in favor of recognizing the MFDP as the only legitimate delegation from the state. Declaring, "I'm sick and tired of being sick and tired," she rebuffed President Johnson's attempt to get the MFDP to settle for two at-large seats at the convention and promises of future reforms. In 1965 Hamer led a challenge to the seating of five Mississippi congressmen (all white) by the U.S. House of Representatives. Even after this challenge failed, Hamer continued to push for more reforms. She helped bring a Head Start program to Ruleville, her hometown, attained a seat as a member of another insurgent delegation at the Democratic convention in 1968, and founded the Freedom Farm Corporation, a throwback to the populist movement of the latter part of the nineteenth century.

Throughout the 1960s and early 1970s Hamer continually inspired others. As Eleanor Holmes Norton, who helped craft the MFDP's legal challenge in 1964 and who later became one of the most prominent black female leaders in the country, observed in a July 1977 article for *Ms*, Hamer "had a singular capacity to impart courage and chase timidity. She was a mixture of strength, humor, love, and determined honesty. She did not know the meaning of self-pity."

Martin Luther King, Jr. (1929–1968)

Martin Luther King, Jr., was the most famous civil rights leader in modern history. An extraordinary orator and the leader of numerous civil rights demonstrations, King had his life cut short in 1968, at age thirty-nine, by a bullet shot from a high-powered rifle by an escaped felon, James Earl Ray. Even though King had devoted his life to nonviolence, his assassination set off a paroxysm of rioting. Eighteen years after his death, a national holiday was established to honor him.

The son of Martin Luther King, Sr., pastor of Ebenezer Baptist Church in Atlanta, Georgia, King appeared destined to follow his father's and grandfather's footsteps from an early age. Born Michael King, Jr., in Atlanta on January 15, 1929, he changed his name to Martin Luther King, Jr., after the father of the Protestant reformation, in 1934. (His father also changed his name at the same time.) Yet it was not until late in his college career, at Morehouse College in Atlanta, where he came under the tutelage of its president, Benjamin E. Mays, that King finally determined to become a minister. After graduating from Morehouse, King attended Crozer Theological Seminary in Pennsylvania and earned his Ph.D. in theology at Boston University. In 1953, two years before receiving his doctoral degree, he married Coretta Scott, who at the time was studying at the New England Conservatory of Music.

In 1955 King accepted a position as minister of the Dexter Avenue Baptist Church in Montgomery, Alabama. Not long after his arrival, the arrest of Rosa Parks for refusing to give up her seat to a white person on a bus sparked the Montgomery bus boycott. In part because he was new to town and thus not affiliated with any of the different factions within the African American community, local black leaders asked him to head the newly formed Montgomery Improvement Association (MIA), which organized and carried out the boycott. King, who accepted this invitation, quickly gained national prominence. His call for nonviolent protest touched a responsive chord in the black community and won him the admiration of liberal and moderate whites nationwide. After the Supreme Court ruled in favor of the boycott, declaring segregated buses in Montgomery unconstitutional, he helped establish the Southern Christian Leadership Conference (SCLC).

In 1960 King relocated to his hometown of Atlanta, working at the Ebenezer Baptist Church and the SCLC's headquarters on Auburn Street. Between 1960 and 1965, King participated in numerous civil rights demonstrations. He took part in sit-ins sparked by SNCC activists in Atlanta in 1960. Some contend that his arrest and incarceration during these protests influenced a significant number of voters to back Kennedy rather than Nixon in 1960. He partook in a mass freedom campaign in Albany, Georgia, in 1961 and 1962, and in 1963 he organized protests in Birmingham, Alabama, that pitted nonviolent demonstrators against Sheriff Bull Connor, who had a reputation for violence. These protests garnered tremendous national attention and sympathy and helped convince President Kennedy to call for civil rights legislation. Later in 1963, King delivered his famous "I Have a Dream" speech at the March on Washington. After accepting the Nobel Peace Prize in 1964, King and the SCLC orchestrated another major campaign, this time in Selma, Alabama, in 1965, which helped produce the Voting Rights Act of 1965.

King experienced greater difficulty attracting support in the North in the late 1960s than he had in the South during the first half of the decade. Committed to showing that nonviolence could work, and determined to provide an alternative to black power, King and the SCLC staged protests in Chicago in 1966. After moving into the slums in Chicago and organizing rent strikes, King led open housing marches in all-white neighborhoods. Not until after his death, however, did the federal government enact open housing legislation. In addition, these protests displayed the fragility of the civil rights coalition that had formed in the first part of the decade. Many northern whites who had supported King in the early 1960s, such as Mayor Richard Daley of Chicago, distanced themselves from King this time around. King publicly proclaimed his opposition to the war in Vietnam in 1967. This also earned him the enmity of many former allies who felt he had no business criticizing President Lyndon Johnson in view of the latter's strong support for civil rights legislation and antipoverty programs.

During the late 1950s and the 1960s, King spent a good deal of his time traveling around the nation, delivering speeches, raising funds, and recruiting support for the cause of civil rights. He authored several books, including *Stride toward Freedom* (1958), the story of the Montgomery bus boycott, *Why We Can't Wait* (1964), which included his famous "Letter from a Birmingham Jail," and *Where Do We Go from Here?* (1967). In this final book and in speeches and interviews given before his death, King reiterated his commitment to nonviolence, while at the same time expressing sympathy for the black power goals of self-affirmation and economic and political power. He also suggested that the United States was in need of radical restructuring in order to overcome the legacy of racial inequality. King was busy aiding black sanitation workers, on strike in Memphis, Tennessee, whose struggle he saw as part of his larger Poor People's Campaign, when he was assassinated.

John Lewis (1940–   )

John Lewis played a prominent role in one chapter of the civil rights movement after another. The chairperson of SNCC until the mid-1960s, he was elected to the United States Congress in 1986, a post he still holds.

Born on February 21, 1940, in rural Pike County, Alabama, the son of two sharecroppers, Lewis was one of ten children. After earning his B.A. from the American Baptist Seminary of Nashville, Tennessee (1957), he helped organize the Nashville student movement, which staged some of the first sit-ins. He attended SNCC's founding conference in Raleigh, North Carolina, in 1960 and was one of the thirteen original freedom riders who set off from Washington, D.C., for New Orleans on May 4, 1961. Not long after the rides began, he was assaulted by white hoodlums in Rock Hill, South Carolina. Several days later he was beaten even more severely by a mob of whites in Montgomery, Alabama. Photographs of Lewis, bloodied by these attacks, were published worldwide, awakening many to the extremes to which the South would go in defense of Jim Crow. Lewis's courage in the face of these attacks and his devotion to using nonviolent means earned him the admiration of many. Members of the Student Nonviolent Coordinating Committee elected him as their chairman in 1963.

During the 1963 March on Washington, Lewis delivered the most militant address of the day, itself watered down at the last minute as part of a behind-the-scenes compromise in response to the concerns of several moderate clergymen who objected to Lewis's criticism of the Kennedy administration. In 1965 Lewis played a leading role in the Selma, Alabama, protests organized by Martin Luther King, Jr., and the SCLC. In 1966 Lewis was replaced as chairperson of SNCC by Stokely Carmichael, who, unlike Lewis, repudiated the organization's commitment to integration and non-violence. After leaving SNCC, Lewis remained active, speaking out against the Vietnam War, taking part in community organizing efforts, and directing a voter education project in Georgia.

In the the mid-1970s Lewis accepted a post in the Carter administration and then was elected to the Atlanta City Council. Ironically, in his 1986 bid for Congress, he defeated his longtime colleague, Julian Bond, another one of SNCC's earliest members. Since then he has become a powerful figure within the Democratic Party and one of the senior black politicians in the nation.

Malcolm X [El-Hajj Malik El-Shabazz] (1925–1965)

Malcolm X, America's most famous black radical, died by an assassin's bullet just before the rise of the black power movement in the United States. Long after his death, Malcolm X remained very influential as the guiding light of black nationalism and the most prominent symbol of black pride, anger, and defiance.

Born Malcolm Little in Omaha, Nebraska, on February 21, 1925, Malcolm X experienced many trials as a youth that shaped his later views. His father, the Reverend Earl Little, a follower of Marcus Garvey, was chased out of Omaha by the KKK. After the family moved to Michigan, his father was allegedly killed by the Black Legionnaires, another white supremacist group. Unable to support Malcolm and his seven brother and sisters, Malcolm's mother was forced to send him to live in a foster home in East Lansing, Michigan. While Malcolm initially excelled at school, he lost interest in education after his teacher informed him that it was unrealistic for a black man to strive to become a doctor, lawyer, or any other type of professional. As a teen, Malcolm moved to Boston to live with his sister, Ella, where he quickly got hooked on narcotics and the fast life of the streets.

After moving to Harlem, Malcolm rapidly earned a reputation as one of the toughest and craziest blacks in town. Constantly running from the law and from other dealers and numbers runners, he was arrested and convicted on burglary charges at age twenty-one.

While in jail, Malcolm transformed his life. Learning about Elijah Muhammad from his brother, he educated himself and joined Muhammad's Black Muslims. Following his release from prison, he became the minister of the Nation of Islam's temple, or mosque, in Harlem, building it into the largest in the nation. Malcolm converted hundreds to Islam and enthralled thousands more with fiery sermons that attacked whites as the devil. However, Malcolm's rise and his criticism of some of Elijah Muhammad's actions created tensions between the two. Following a trip to Mecca, Malcolm broke with his former mentor, contending that Elijah Muhammad's brand of antiwhite Islam was incorrect.

Malcolm X was often contrasted to Martin Luther King, Jr., although their differences were exaggerated by the press. After leaving the Nation of Islam, Malcolm focused his attention on forging a black nationalist movement without regard to religion. He established the Organization of Afro-American Unity, which demanded an investigation of racial affairs in the United States by the United Nations Commission on Human Rights. Claiming that blacks should use "any means necessary" to attain freedom, he advocated self-defense, political and economic self-determination, and black pride. A critic of U.S. foreign policy in general, and one of the earliest critics of America's involvement in Vietnam, Malcolm traveled to Africa, where he was warmly received.

On February 21, 1965, he was shot to death by two assassins in the Audubon Ballroom in Harlem, New York. While two members of the Nation of Islam were arrested and convicted of murdering him, many felt that the FBI and other government agencies shared complicity in his death. Not long after he was buried, *The Autobiography of Malcolm X* (which he had been working on with Alex Haley, the author of the popular book *Roots*) was published.

Thurgood Marshall (1908–1993)

Over the course of his long career, Thurgood Marshall served as the lead attorney for the National Association for the Advancement of Colored People (NAACP) during the heyday of its struggle against Jim Crow, as President Lyndon Johnson's solicitor general, defending the constitutionality of the most important civil rights legislation of the twentieth century, and as the first African American justice of the United States Supreme Court.

Marshall was born in Baltimore, Maryland, on July 2, 1908. His father worked as a steward at all-white boat clubs; his mother was employed as a teacher in the city's segregated schools. From early on, Marshall displayed a tendency toward rebellion. Not a particularly hard-working student as a youth, Marshall applied himself in college, graduating cum laude from Lincoln University in 1930, and at the top of his Howard University Law School class in 1933. At Howard, Marshall came under the tutelage of Charles Houston, who recruited him to work for the NAACP. For about twenty-five years, Marshall served as the director of the NAACP's Legal Defense and Educational Fund, arguing thirty-two cases before the U.S. Supreme Court, twenty-nine of which he won, including the path-breaking civil rights cases *Smith* v. *Allwright* (1944), *Morgan* v. *Virginia* (1946), *Sweatt* v. *Painter* (1950), and *Brown* v. *Board of Education* (1954), the latter of which overturned *Plessy* v. *Ferguson* (1896), the legal backbone of segregation.

In 1961, over the fierce objections of many southerners, some of whom termed him a communist, the U.S. Senate confirmed his nomination to the United States Court of Appeals. Four years later, he resigned from the bench to become President Johnson's solicitor general. In 1967 Marshall was appointed to the Supreme Court. During his twenty-five years on the bench, Marshall championed the rights of minorities and the downtrodden. A staunch civil libertarian, he supported the right of a woman to have an abortion and opposed capital punishment and restrictions on freedom of speech. Reviled by many conservatives for his liberal views, Marshall remained a combative defender of minorities and of individual rights through his final days on the Court. He died on January 24, 1993.

James Howard Meredith (1933–   )

In 1962 James Meredith, a native of Mississippi and a veteran of the Korean War, gained the national limelight when he attempted to become the first African American to enroll at the University of Mississippi. Following a confrontation between the federal government and Mississippi governor Ross Barnett, who sought to maintain segregation at Ole Miss, Meredith was allowed to enroll.

Meredith was born in Kosciusko, Mississippi, on June 25, 1933. After serving in the army during the Korean War, he attended Jackson State College between 1960 and 1962 before applying to the University of Mississippi. With the encouragement and support of Medgar Evers, who himself had been denied admission to Ole Miss because of his race, and from lawyers of the national offices of the NAACP, he contended that the university's refusal to admit him violated the Supreme Court's decision in

Brown v. *Board of Education* (1954), which had prohibited segregation in public education. In the case of *Meredith* v. *Fair* (1962), the United States Court of Appeals for the Fifth Judicial Circuit agreed. Governor Barnett, however, vowed to prevent Meredith from attending Ole Miss. This led to a showdown between Barnett and President John F. Kennedy that did not end until after Kennedy reluctantly sent U.S. marshals to the main campus in Oxford to put down a riot aimed at keeping Meredith from registering.

For over a year, Meredith, who remained the only black at Ole Miss, endured physical threats and the scorn of most of his fellow students. Often assuming a very stoical posture that earned him few friends, he graduated in 1963. Afterwards, he traveled to Africa, where he studied at Ibadan University in Nigeria. Upon his return to the United States, he enrolled at Columbia University Law School. Following the release of his autobiography, *Three Years in Mississippi* (1966), Meredith announced his plans to stage a solitary March Against Fear from Memphis, Tennessee, to Jackson, Mississippi. Less than two days into his trek, he was shot and left for dead at the side of the road. Infuriated by this assault, SNCC, CORE, and the SCLC joined together to complete Meredith's march. Along the way, Stokely Carmichael coined the term "black power," which became the rallying cry and symbol of the civil rights movement. While Meredith briefly rejoined the march and criticized nonviolence, he tended toward more individual pursuits.

In the late 1960s and early 1970s, Meredith initiated several business ventures. In 1972 he ran unsuccessfully for Congress. In 1989 Meredith joined the staff of Senator Jesse Helms, the arch-conservative from North Carolina who had initially gained fame by decrying the civil rights movement and attacking Martin Luther King, Jr., as a communist.

Clarence Maurice Mitchell, Jr. (1911–1984)

Although not as well known as Martin Luther King, Jr., Thurgood Marshall, Malcolm X, or a host of other civil rights activists, Clarence Mitchell had nearly as much impact on the fight for civil rights as any of them. As head of the Leadership Conference on Civil Rights (LCCR), the umbrella organization that coordinated the civil rights movement's lobbying efforts in Washington, D.C., he earned the admiration of even politicians who sought to block the racial reforms of the mid-1960s.

Mitchell, who was born on March 8, 1911, grew up in Baltimore, Maryland, the son of a chef. He earned his B.A. from Lincoln University of Pennsylvania in 1932. Following his graduation, he worked for several years for the *Baltimore Afro-American*, a prominent black-owned newspaper, reporting on the infamous trial of the Scottsboro Boys. After studying at the Atlanta School of Social Work, he worked for the Negro National Youth Administration, the National Urban League, and the Fair Employment Practice Committee. He married Juanita Jackson, herself a prominent civil rights leader.

After World War II, Mitchell joined the Washington, D.C., staff of the NAACP, heading up various efforts to maintain racial reforms gained during the war. In 1950 he helped form the Leadership Conference on Civil Rights. As the LCCR's legislative chairman, Mitchell worked the halls of Congress, drumming up support for one civil rights bill after another. He played an especially crucial role during the legislative battle over the Civil Rights Act of 1964, courting the support of key legislators, most notably Everett Dirksen, the Republican leader in the Senate. Senator Richard Russell of Georgia, an opponent of the Civil Rights Act of 1964, testified to Mitchell's political acumen, declaring that he had organized the most effective lobbying effort in the history of the nation. Mitchell passed down his political skills to his children, two of whom were elected to political office in Baltimore. His son, Parren Mitchell, was elected to Congress, becoming the first black congressman from Baltimore in its history. In 1975 President Gerald Ford appointed Mitchell to the U.S. delegation to the United Nations. President Jimmy Carter honored him with the Presidential Medal of Freedom in 1980. Four years later, on March 18, 1984, Mitchell died in Washington, D.C.

Robert Parris Moses (1935–   )

Robert Moses headed the Student Nonviolent Coordinating Committee's organizing efforts in Mississippi, including Freedom Summer. He was a soft-spoken and reflective individual whose influence was much greater than his fame. In 1965, fearing that he was gaining too much attention, he changed his last name to Parris, his mother's maiden name, and dropped out of the movement.

Moses was born in New York City on January 23, 1935. The grandson of a Baptist minister and the son of a janitor who struggled to hold on to his job throughout the Depression, Moses earned a B.A. from Hamilton College (1956) and an M.A. in philosophy from Harvard (1957). After being accepted to a Ph.D. program in mathematics at Harvard, however, Moses returned to New York City so that he could be with his ailing father.

While Moses was tending his father and working as a mathematics teacher at Horace Mann High School in New York City, the sit-ins erupted in the South. Moses was so moved by them that he journeyed to Atlanta to join the civil rights movement. He hooked up with SNCC and made a brief journey to Mississippi, where he made his contact with local activists. The following summer, after completing his teaching commitment in New York, he returned to Mississippi to establish a voter education campaign.

Moses was committed to organizing a grassroots movement that did not depend on a single charismatic leader. He led by example, earning tremendous admiration through his courage and bravery. Yet, after a couple years in the Mississippi Delta, he became convinced that it was necessary to mount a national crusade to overcome the extraordinary repression in the state. This led to Freedom Summer, whereby nearly one thousand volunteers, many of them white students from elite universities, came to Mississippi. Central to the summer's campaign was the Mississippi Freedom Democratic Party's attempt to be recognized as the legitimate representative of the state at the 1964 Democratic convention; however, the party's slate of delegates was rebuffed by President Johnson and his liberal allies in the party.

Moses was an early critic of the Vietnam War. He delivered one of the keynote addresses at the first national antiwar demonstration, sponsored by the Students for a Democratic Society in the spring of 1965. In spite of his growing disillusionment with liberalism, Moses did not join the cry for black power, which SNCC promoted in the late 1960s. After dropping out of the movement and traveling to Africa, Moses returned to the United States in 1976 to resume his graduate studies in mathematics. In 1980, with the help of grants from the MacArthur Foundation, he established the Algebra Project, which involved teaching mathematics to underprivileged youth. Like his work as a civil rights activist in the early 1960s, his work for the Algebra Project sought to empower individuals. In 1992 Moses set up the Delta Algebra Project in the same region of Mississippi where he had labored in the early 1960s.

Huey P. Newton (1942–1989)

Huey P. Newton was the co-founder and chairman of the Black Panther Party for Self-Defense. During the second half of the 1960s, the Panthers collectively, and Newton individually, personified the wave of black militancy that swept across the nation.

Born in Monroe, Louisiana, on February 17, 1942, Newton migrated with his parents to Oakland, California, a blue-collar industrial city across the bay from San Francisco, where he spent most of his youth. While studying at Merritt College, Newton and his college friend, Bobby Seale, established the Black Panther Party. The Panthers appealed primarily to young urban blacks who, like Newton and Seale, felt ignored by mainstream civil rights groups. They emphasized a machismo image and promoted programs that promised to address the needs of the urban black community. Most important, they armed themselves with guns and patrolled their neighborhoods to protect fellow citizens from police brutality and injustice. These patrols, however, inevitably led to confrontations with authorities. On October 28, 1967, following a shootout with police, Newton was arrested for murder.

The case quickly became a cause célèbre in radical circles, with student activists and many others proclaiming that Newton had acted in self-defense. "Free Huey" became nearly as popular a rallying cry as "Freedom Now" or "Make Love, Not War." In 1968 Newton was convicted of manslaughter. Two years later an appeals court overturned this decision on procedural grounds. After his release from prison, Newton sought to revive the Panthers, who had splintered into feuding factions. On one side stood those who identified with Eldridge Cleaver, a onetime convicted rapist and the cultural minister of the Black Panthers, who called for an international revolution. On the other side stood Newton, who advocated a more pragmatic approach, such as running candidates for local office and setting up free health clinics. In the face of external and internal opposition, Newton was unable to return the Panthers to their earlier prominence.

In the mid-1970s, after being charged with murdering a woman, Newton fled the United States, seeking exile in Cuba. Late in the decade, cleared of all charges, he returned to the United States. He earned his Ph.D. from the University of California and involved himself in a variety of political causes. (Newton's doctoral thesis was "War against the Panthers—A Study of Repression in America.") In the mid-1980s Newton was arrested for embezzlement and convicted of illegal possession of firearms. On August 22, 1989, he was killed by a drug dealer on the streets of Oakland.

Rosa Louise McCauley Parks (1913–   )

Rosa Parks, "Mother of the Civil Rights Movement," etched her name into the history books on December 1, 1955, when she refused to give up her seat to a white person on a Montgomery, Alabama, bus. She was arrested for violating a Montgomery law that mandated the segregation of public buses. This incident sparked the Montgomery bus boycott, the first great mass civil rights protest of the era.

Parks was born in Tuskegee, Alabama, home of Booker T. Washington, on February 4, 1913. In 1932, after graduating from high school and attending Alabama State College in Montgomery, she married Raymond Parks. She worked as a clerk, an insurance salesperson, and a tailor at a leading Montgomery department store. Parks was riding a bus home from work when she was arrested for refusing to give up her seat.

While many saw Parks merely as an accidental catalyst of the civil rights movement, she had in fact long been involved in quiet struggles to overcome racial inequality. She supported the Scottsboro Boys in the 1930s and joined the NAACP in Montgomery in 1943, serving as secretary to E. D. Nixon, the most important civil rights figure in the community at the time. She worked for the Montgomery Voters Registration League, which sought to register blacks to vote, and attended an integrated human rights workshop held by the Highlander Folk School in Tennessee in the summer of 1955. Even though Parks did not consciously precipitate a confrontation with white authorities on December 1, 1955, she immediately gave Nixon and other community activists permission to use her arrest as a rallying point for a boycott. Parks served on the executive committee of the Montgomery Improvement Association, the organization that led the bus boycott.

In 1957 Parks was fired from her job as a tailor. She and her husband then moved to Detroit, where she remained politically active. She belonged to the Southern Christian Leadership Conference and took part in a number of protests and rallies, including the 1963 March on Washington and the 1965 Selma-to-Montgomery march. In 1965 Parks became Congressman John Conyers's administrative assistant, a post she held until 1988. A year before she retired, she established the Rosa and Raymond Parks Institute for Self-Development, an organization devoted to cutting the number of school dropouts in Detroit. Parks has been showered with numerous awards and honorary degrees, including the NAACP's Spingarn Medal. Her autobiography, *Rosa Parks: My Story*, was published by Dial Press in 1992.

Gloria St. Clair Hayes Richardson (1922–   )

During the early 1960s, Gloria Richardson headed the Cambridge Nonviolent Action Committee (CNAC), an adult affiliate of SNCC that orchestrated some of the most militant protests in the nation. Lukewarm toward nonviolence and more concerned about attaining economic equality than integration, Richardson was notable for her independence and outspokenness in an era when most women remained behind the scenes.

Richardson was born in Baltimore, Maryland, on May 6, 1922. As a youth, she moved to Cambridge, on the Eastern Shore of Maryland, her mother's hometown. Richardson's grandfather, H. Maydanair St. Clair, a town councilman for over twenty-five years, was Cambridge's most prominent black leader. Nonetheless, even he and his family felt the sting of discrimination. In

1944 Richardson earned her B.A. from Howard University. Afterwards she married, had two daughters, divorced, and moved back to Cambridge.

In early 1962, SNCC and several other organizations staged freedom rides in Cambridge. These protests galvanized the black community and led to the creation of CNAC. In the summer of 1962 Richardson assumed leadership of CNAC, developing it into one of the most vibrant locally based and run movements in the nation. In the spring of 1963, daily protests against discrimination and the arrest of activists climaxed in a riot. Only the National Guard, which remained in Cambridge for about a year, and a special agreement brokered by Attorney General Robert F. Kennedy and signed by Richardson and local authorities restored order. In the fall of 1963, Richardson gained further notoriety when she urged blacks to boycott a vote over a special town ordinance on the integration of public facilities. Because of her stance, segregationists won the election. Liberals and conservatives, black and white, lambasted Richardson for taking this stance; some compared her to Joan of Arc, suggesting that she sought martyrdom and power, not real racial reform.

In the fall of 1964, after marrying Frank Dandridge, a black photographer who had covered the protests in Cambridge, Richardson moved to New York City. In subsequent years, Richardson visited Cambridge regularly, arranging for an appearance by H. Rap Brown, SNCC's fiery leader, in 1967, which precipitated another riot. Richardson participated in various civil rights protests in New York City during the 1960s. In the 1970s, she worked as the program director of the Manpower Development Office in New York City. In 1985 she accepted a top post with the city's Department of Aging.

Bayard Rustin (1912–1987)

Bayard Rustin was one of the most important strategists of the civil rights movement. He was a key advisor to Martin Luther King, Jr., an aide to A. Philip Randolph, and the person most responsible for the success of the 1963 March on Washington.

Rustin was born on March 17, 1912, in West Chester, Pennsylvania. Raised by his mother and grandmother in relatively well-off circumstances, Rustin displayed a penchant for activism from an early age. A Quaker and a pacifist, he joined the Young Communist League in Harlem during the 1930s. In 1941, after splitting with the communists, he went to work for A. Philip Randolph, who was busy organizing the March on Washington Movement, which successfully pressured President Franklin D. Roosevelt into desegregating the defense industries. At about the same time, Rustin worked with A. J. Muste, the radical founder of the Fellowship of Reconciliation (FOR), a pacifist organization dedicated to combating racial inequality. During the war, Rustin refused to join the military. As a result, he spent over two years in prison, during which time he befriended several other radical pacifists, some of whom became the founders of the Congress of Racial Equality.

In the late 1940s, Rustin helped organize the Journey of Reconciliation, a precursor to the freedom rides of the early 1960s, participated in regular workshops on nonviolent direct action, and pushed for the desegregation of the armed forces. In the early 1950s, he traveled to India and Africa, where he met prominent pacifists and anticolonialists, most notably Gandhi's sons. Shortly after the Montgomery bus boycott began, Rustin rushed to Alabama to give expert advice on nonviolence to Martin Luther King, Jr. While King met with Rustin and accepted his counsel, he kept his distance from him in public because of Rustin's previous affiliation with the communists and due to Rustin's homosexuality. In 1960, when Rustin sought to aid the sit-ins, he was spurned because young activists saw him as too radical.

In 1963 Rustin played a central role in organizing the March on Washington, attending to even the most minor details of the demonstration. Once again, however, Rustin's homosexuality and radical past forced him to remain outside the limelight. In the mid-1960s, he often clashed with black militants. Rustin's condemnation of black power and his advocacy of coalition with liberals, which he advanced in a seminal article, "From Protest to Politics," put him at odds with the Student Nonviolent Coordinating Committee and the Congress of Racial Equality, who characterized him as an apologist for the Vietnam War. Toward the tail end of the 1960s and in the early 1970s, Rustin spoke in favor of and supported the emerging gay rights movement. For about twenty years, until his death on August 24, 1987, Rustin headed the A. Philip Randolph Institute, a civil rights organization in New York City.

Roy Ottoway Wilkins (1901–1981)

In 1955 Roy Wilkins succeeded Walter White as the executive secretary of the National Association for the Advancement of Colored People (NAACP). He held this post during the organization's heyday until shortly before his death. During his tenure, the NAACP fought for and won implementation of the *Brown* decision, lobbied successfully for civil rights legislation, and sustained its reputation as the preeminent civil rights organization in the nation.

Roy Wilkins was born in St. Louis, Missouri, on August 30, 1901. Following the death of his mother in 1905, he moved to St. Paul, Minnesota, where he was raised by his aunt and uncle, Elizabeth and Sam Williams. After earning his B.A. from the University of Minnesota (1923) and working briefly as a journalist in St. Paul, he became the editor of the *Kansas City Call*, a black-run newspaper. Through this work and his active role in the affairs of the local NAACP, Wilkins caught the attention of Walter White, the organization's director. In 1931 White offered Wilkins a chance to work on the national staff of the NAACP in New York City, and Wilkins readily accepted. In 1934, NAACP co-founder W.E.B. Du Bois resigned as editor of its magazine, *The Crisis*. Wilkins assumed the post, and edited the magazine for fifteen years. In 1950, when Walter White's health began to fail, Wilkins became the NAACP's administrator. Five years later, upon White's death, Wilkins was elected the NAACP's executive secretary.

Between the mid-1950s and the early 1970s, the NAACP's membership expanded to over 400,000 and its treasury grew to nearly $4 million (up from about a half million dollars in 1955). Wilkins met with every president from Franklin D. Roosevelt to Jimmy Carter. Regularly interviewed by the press and reported on by the media, Wilkins earned the title "Mr. Civil Rights." Yet, Wilkins's dislike for direct-action protest, even when nonviolent, and his strong condemnation of black nationalism put him at odds with many younger black militants, and at times with Martin Luther King, Jr. His support for President Johnson's policy in Vietnam similarly earned him the condemnation of young radicals, black and white.

Paradoxically, Wilkins's tenure represented both the best of days for the NAACP and one of its most trying times. Although he was a very hard worker and a good administrator, Wilkins was not a particularly charismatic leader, and he was often overshadowed by King. Jealous of the attention King and others received, and feeling that the NAACP deserved more respect, at times Wilkins offered only grudging public support for their initiatives. Wilkins's dislike for direct action reinforced tensions between the NAACP and the SCLC, SNCC, and CORE. Nevertheless, at least until the rise of black power in the mid-1960s, Wilkins and the NAACP maintained a working alliance, albeit an uneasy one, with these groups. In the latter part of the decade, Wilkins sharply criticized black nationalism. The NAACP's ability to sustain itself through the tumult of the late 1960s, while SNCC, CORE, and the Black Panthers disintegrated, left Wilkins with a sense of vindication. Wilkins died in New York City on September 9, 1981. His autobiography, *Standing Fast* (1982), was published posthumously.

Whitney Moore Young, Jr. (1921–1971)

Whitney Young headed the National Urban League from 1961 until his untimely death in 1971. During his tenure as leader of the Urban League, which had been founded in 1911 to aid black migrants, he called for the government to enact a domestic version of the Marshall Plan, pushed for improved economic opportunities for blacks, and lobbied for equal political and civil rights. Business and governmental leaders often preferred to negotiate with Young rather than many younger black activists, seeing him as a more moderate and professional figure. In part due to his reputation, the Urban League garnered millions of dollars of outside support from the government, foundations, and private corporations, which it used to promote the economic advancement of African Americans.

Young was born on July 31, 1921, in Lincoln Ridge, Kentucky, the son of a teacher at Lincoln Institute, an all-black vocational high school. He earned a bachelor's degree from Kentucky State Industrial College in 1941. After serving in the U.S. Army during World War II, Young continued his studies, receiving a master's degree in social work from the University of Minnesota in 1947. During the late 1940s, he went to work for the Urban League, first in the twin cities of Minneapolis–St. Paul and then in Omaha, Nebraska. In 1954 Young became the dean of the School of Social Work at Atlanta University, where he joined various civil and human rights organizations. In the fall of 1961, he succeeded Lester Granger as head of the National Urban League.

Even though the Urban League disdained demonstrations in favor of quiet negotiations, Young publicly supported many protests and took part in the March on Washington in 1963. Under Young's leadership, the Urban League joined the Council for United Civil Rights Leadership (CUCRL), which coordinated fund-raising efforts, and the Leadership Conference on Civil Rights (LCCR), which orchestrated the civil rights movement's lobbying efforts in Washington, D.C. In the mid-1960s, the Urban League played an active role in the formulation of the War on Poverty and developed numerous job-training and placement programs. Young wrote a regular column, "To Be Equal" for the *Amsterdam News*, and published two books, *To Be Equal* (1964) and *Beyond Racism* (1969). He also served on the board of directors of numerous powerful institutions, including the Rockefeller Foundation and the Federal Reserve Bank of New York, and as president of the National Conference of Social Welfare (1967) and the National Association of Social Workers (1969). Young died while traveling in Lagos, Nigeria, on March 11, 1971.

Robert Zellner (1939–   )

Robert Zellner was one of the most important white civil rights activists. A southern native, he was one of the first and last white members of SNCC.

Born in southern Alabama, the son of an itinerant Methodist minister, Zellner came of age at a time when nearly all southern whites were rallying around Jim Crow. Zellner had relatives who belonged to the Ku Klux Klan, and he attended a segregated high school in Mobile and all-white Huntington College in Montgomery, Alabama. While in college, Zellner began to question the philosophy of white supremacy. During his senior year, he undertook a study of racial problems in Montgomery. This led him to attend the meetings of local civil rights groups, which in turn led to attacks on him by the local KKK, school administrators, and state authorities. For insisting on his right to interview Dr. Martin Luther King, Jr., Zellner was even accused of being a communist by the president of the college. Such hysterical intervention on the part of college and government officials backfired. Rather than being frightened away from interaction with civil rights groups, Zellner threw himself full force into the civil rights fight on the side of racial equality.

With the help of a grant from the Southern Christian Education Fund (SCEF), Zellner became SNCC's first white staff member in 1961, joining Robert Moses and a small core of activists in McComb, Mississippi. Throughout the early 1960s, Zellner distinguished himself through his courage and commitment. Perceiving him as a traitor to his race, white mobs often targeted him for attack. In McComb, during the first freedom march in the town's history, for instance, a mob of whites attacked Zellner on the steps of City Hall. Fortunately, Robert Moses and several others ripped him loose from his assailants and brought him inside City Hall, where Zellner, not his attackers, was placed under arrest for disturbing the peace. Zellner played a central role in SNCC's activities in Mississippi before, during, and after Mississippi Summer. He was the last white person to be purged from SNCC when it became an all-black organization in 1966.

Even in the wake of SNCC's turn to black power, Zellner remained committed to the struggle for racial equality. He and his wife, Dottie, another white SNCC veteran, established GROW (Grass Roots Organizing Committee), which sought to organize black and white workers into unions. He also protested against the war in Vietnam and worked with several other student and civil rights groups, such as the Southern Student Organizing Committee.

Primary Documents
of the Civil Rights Movement

Document 1
FROM PRESIDENT'S COMMITTEE ON CIVIL RIGHTS,
TO SECURE THESE RIGHTS (1947)

In 1946, in the wake of several brutal lynchings, including the murder of a black World War II veteran, President Harry S Truman established the President's Committee on Civil Rights to investigate race relations in the United States and to make recommendations based on its findings. Concerns over how racial incidents were affecting America's image abroad and its ability to contain communism prodded the commission to take an honest look at the subject. In 1947 the committee issued its report, entitled "To Secure These Rights" in which it delineated the basic rights and principles of a democratic society and detailed the many ways in which African-Americans were denied them. The report was the first of its kind and contained the strongest official condemnation of racial inequality since at least Reconstruction. Shortly after the committee issued its report, the President desegregated the armed forces. However, most of the committee's other recommendations were not implemented until the mid-1960s.

The Time Is Now

Twice before in American history the nation has found it necessary to review the state of its civil rights. The first time was during the 15 years between 1776 and 1791, from the drafting of the Declaration of Independence through the Articles of Confederation experiment to the writing of the Constitution and the Bill of Rights. It was then that the distinctively

American heritage was finally distilled from earlier views of liberty. The second time was when the Union was temporarily sundered over the question of whether it could exist "half-slave" and "half-free."

It is our profound conviction that we have come to a time for a third reexamination of the situation, and a sustained drive ahead. Our reasons for believing this are those of conscience, of self-interest, and of survival in a threatening world. Or to put it another way, we have a moral reason, an economic reason, and an international reason for believing that the time for action is now.

The Moral Reason

We have considered the American heritage of freedom at some length. We need no further justification for a broad and immediate program than the need to reaffirm our faith in the traditional American morality. The pervasive gap between our aims and what we actually do is creating a kind of moral dry rot which eats away at the emotional and rational bases of democratic beliefs. There are times when the difference between what we preach about civil rights and what we practice is shockingly illustrated by individual outrages. There are times when the whole structure of our ideology is made ridiculous by individual instances. And there are certain continuing, quiet, omnipresent practices which do irreparable damage to our beliefs.

As examples of "moral erosion" there are the consequences of suffrage limitations in the South. The fact that Negroes and many whites have not been allowed to vote in some states has actually sapped the morality underlying universal suffrage. Many men in public and private life do not believe that those who have been kept from voting are capable of self rule. They finally convince themselves that disfranchised people do not really have the right to vote.

Wartime segregation in the armed forces is another instance of how a social pattern may wreak moral havoc. Practically all white officers and enlisted men in all branches of service saw Negro military personnel performing only the most menial functions. They saw Negroes recruited for the common defense treated as men apart and distinct from themselves. As a result, men who might otherwise have maintained the equalitarian morality of their forebears were given reason to look down on their fellow citizens. This has been sharply illustrated by the Army study discussed previously, in which white servicemen expressed great surprise at the excellent performance of Negroes who joined them in the firing line. Even now, very few people know of the successful experiment with integrated combat units. Yet it is important in explaining why some Negro troops did not do well; it is proof that equal treatment can produce equal performance.

It is impossible to decide who suffers the greatest moral damage from our civil rights transgressions, because all of us are hurt. That is certainly true of those who are victimized. Their belief in the basic truth of the American promise is undermined. But they do have the realization, galling as it sometimes is, of being morally in the right. The damage to those who are responsible for these violations of our moral standards may well be greater. They, too, have been reared to honor the command of "free and equal." And all of us must share in the shame at the growth of hypocrisies like the "automatic" marble champion. All of us must endure the cynicism about democratic values which our failures breed.

The United States can no longer countenance these burdens on its common conscience, these inroads on its moral fiber.

The Economic Reason

One of the principal economic problems facing us and the rest of the world is achieving maximum production and continued prosperity. The loss of a huge, potential market for goods is a direct result of the economic discrimination which is practiced against many of our minority groups. A sort of vicious circle is produced. Discrimination depresses the wages and income of minority groups. As a result, their purchasing power is curtailed and markets are reduced. Reduced markets result in reduced production. This cuts down employment, which of course means lower wages and still fewer job opportunities. Rising fear, prejudice, and insecurity aggravate the very discrimination in employment which sets the vicious circle in motion.

Minority groups are not the sole victims of this economic waste; its impact is inevitably felt by the entire population.

Discrimination imposes a direct cost upon our economy through the wasteful duplication and many facilities and services required by the "separate but equal" policy. That the resources of the South are sorely strained by the burden of a double system of schools and other public services has already been indicated. Segregation is also economically wasteful for private business. Public transportation companies must often provide duplicate facilities to serve majority and minority groups separately. Places of public accommodation and recreation reject business when it comes in the form of unwanted persons. Stores reduce their sales by turning away minority customers. Factories must provide separate locker rooms, pay windows, drinking fountains, and washrooms for the different groups.

Similarly, the rates of disease, crime, and fires are disproportionately great in areas which are economically depressed as compared with wealthier areas. Many of the prominent American minorities are confined—by economic discrimination, by law, by restrictive covenants, and by social pressure—to the most dilapidated, undesirable locations. Property in these locations yields a smaller return in taxes, which is seldom sufficient to meet the inordinately high cost of public services in depressed areas. The majority pays a high price in taxes for the low status of minorities.

. . . It is not at all surprising that a people relegated to second-class citizenship should behave as second-class citizens. This is true, in varying degrees, of all of our minorities. What we have lost in money, production, invention, citizenship, and leadership as the price for damaged, thwarted personalities—these are beyond estimate.

The United States can no longer afford this heavy drain upon its human wealth, its national competence.

The International Reason

Our position in the postwar world is so vital to the future that our smallest actions have far-reaching effects. We have come to know that our own security in a highly interdependent world is inextricably tied to the security and well-being of all people and all countries. Our foreign policy is designed to make the United States an enormous, positive influence for peace and progress throughout the world. We have tried to let nothing, not even extreme political differences between ourselves and foreign nations, stand in the way of this goal. But our domestic civil rights shortcomings are a serious obstacle.

We cannot escape the fact that our civil rights record has been an issue in world politics. The world's press and radio are full of it. This Committee has seen a multitude of samples. We and our friends have been, and are, stressing our achievements. Those with competing philosophies have stressed—and are shamelessly distorting—our shortcomings. They have not only tried to create hostility toward us among specific nations, races, and religious groups. They have tried to prove our democracy an empty fraud, and our nation a consistent oppressor of underprivileged people. This may seem ludicrous to Americans, but it is sufficiently important to worry our friends.

. . . Our achievements in building and maintaining a state dedicated to the fundamentals of freedom have already served as a guide for those seeking the best road from chaos to liberty and prosperity. But it is not indelibly written that democracy will encompass the world. We are convinced that our way of life—the free way of life—holds a promise of hope for all people. We have what is perhaps the greatest responsibility ever placed upon a people to keep this promise alive. Only still greater achievements will do it.

The United States is not so strong, the final triumph of the democratic ideal is not so inevitable that we can ignore what the world thinks of us or our record.

Source: *To Secure These Rights: The Report of the President's Committee on Civil Rights* (Washington, D.C.: GPO, 1947).

Document 2
BROWN V. BOARD OF EDUCATION OF TOPEKA, KANSAS (1954) AND "ENFORCEMENT DECREE" [BROWN II] (1955)

On May 17, 1954, the Supreme Court handed down its momentous decision in the case of *Brown* v. *Board of Education of Topeka, Kansas.* Ruling unanimously in favor of the plaintiffs, the Court declared that segregation in public education was unconstitutional, overturning the 1896 Supreme Court decision in *Plessy* v. *Ferguson* in the process. The court case grew out of a series of suits initiated by the NAACP in the 1930s. Earl Warren, recently appointed Chief Justice, wrote the opinion for the Court in the *Brown* case in clear and simple language, agreeing with the NAACP's argument that segregation in public education violated the equal protection clause of the Fourteenth Amendment.

In order to win the support of all nine justices, however, Warren did not include in his opinion a remedy or penalty for the widespread violation of the Constitution. Instead, the Supreme Court waited a year before it issued its enforcement decree, known as *Brown II*. This part of the Court's ruling put lower federal courts in charge of implementing the *Brown* decision, adding that they should do so "with all deliberate speed." Warren hoped that the unanimity of the Court on *Brown* and the process for compliance spelled out by *Brown II would ensure peaceful acceptance of the end of Jim Crow in education. Much to his and the NAACP's dismay, southern compliance with Brown* was not forthcoming.

Warren, C. J. These cases come to us from the States of Kansas, South Carolina, Virginia, and Delaware. They are premised on different facts and different local conditions, but a common legal question justifies their consideration together in this consolidated opinion.

In each of the cases, minors of the Negro race, through their legal representatives, seek the aid of the courts in obtaining admission to the public schools of their community on a nonsegregated basis. In each instance, they have been denied admission to schools attended by white children under laws requiring or permitting segregation according to race. This segregation was alleged to deprive the plaintiffs of the equal protection of the laws under the Fourteenth Amendment. In each of the cases other than the Delaware case, a three-judge federal district court denied relief to the plaintiffs on the so-called "separate but equal" doctrine announced by this Court in *Plessy v. Ferguson*, 163 U.S. 537. Under that doctrine, equality of treatment is accorded when the races are provided substantially equal facilities, even though these facilities be separate. In the Delaware case, the Supreme Court of Delaware adhered to that doctrine, but ordered that the plaintiffs be admitted to the white schools because of their superiority to the Negro schools.

The plaintiffs contend that segregated public schools are not "equal" and cannot be made "equal," and that hence they are deprived of the equal protection of the laws. Because of the obvious importance of the question presented, the Court took jurisdiction. Argument was heard in the 1952 Term, and reargument was heard this Term on certain questions propounded by the Court.

Reargument was largely devoted to the circumstances surrounding the adoption of the Fourteenth Amendment in 1868. It covered exhaustively consideration of the Amendment in Congress, ratification by the states, then existing practices in racial segregation, and the views of proponents and opponents of the Amendment. This discussion and our own investigation convince us that, although these sources cast some light, it is not enough to resolve the problem with which we are faced. At best, they are inconclusive. The most avid proponents of the post-War Amendments undoubtedly intended them to remove all legal distinctions among "all persons born or naturalized in the United States." Their opponents, just as certainly, were antagonistic to both the letter and the spirit of the Amendments and wished them to have the most limited effect. What others in Congress and the state legislatures had in mind cannot be determined with any degree of certainty.

An additional reason for the inconclusive nature of the Amendment's history, with respect to segregated schools, is the status of public education at that time. In the south, the movement toward free common schools, supported by general taxation, had not yet taken hold. Education of white children was largely in the hands of private groups. Education of Negroes was almost nonexistent, and practically all of the race were illiterate. In fact, any education of Negroes was forbidden by law in some states. Today, in contrast, many Negroes have achieved outstanding success in the arts and sciences as well as in the business and professional world. It is true that public education had already advanced further in the North, but the effect of the Amendment on Northern States was generally ignored in the congressional debates. Even in the North, the conditions of public education did not approximate those existing today. The curriculum was usually rudimentary; ungraded schools were common in rural areas; the school term was but three months a year in many states; and compulsory school attendance was virtually unknown. As a consequence, it is not surprising that there should be so little in the history of the Fourteenth Amendment relating to its intended effect on public education.

In the first cases in this Court construing the Fourteenth Amendment, decided shortly after its adoption, the Court interpreted it as proscribing all state-imposed discriminations against the Negro race. The doctrine of "separate but equal" did not make its appearance in this Court until 1896 in the case of *Plessy v. Ferguson*, supra, involving not education but transportation. American courts have since labored with the doctrine for over half a century. In this Court, there have been six cases involving the "separate but equal" doctrine in the field of public education. In *Cumming v. Board of Education of Richmond County*, 175 U.S. 528, and *Gong Lum v. Rice*, 275 U.S. 78, the validity of the doctrine itself was not challenged. In more recent cases, all on the graduate school level, inequality was found in that specific benefits enjoyed by white students were denied to Negro students of the same educational qualifications. *State of Missouri ex rel. Gaines v. Canada*, 305 U.S. 337; *Sipuel v. Board of Regents of University of Oklahoma*, 332 U.S. 631; *Sweatt v. Painter*, 339 U.S. 629; *McLaurin v. Oklahoma State Regents*, 339 U.S. 637. In none of these cases was it necessary to reexamine the doctrine to grant relief to the Negro plaintiff. And in *Sweatt v. Painter*, supra, the Court expressly reserved decision on the question whether *Plessy v. Ferguson* should be held inapplicable to public education.

In the instant cases, that question is directly presented. Here, unlike *Sweatt v. Painter*, there are findings below that the Negro and white schools involved have been equalized, or are being equalized, with respect to buildings, curricula, qualifications and salaries of teachers, and other "tangible" factors. Our decision, therefore, cannot turn on merely a comparison of these tangible factors in the Negro and white schools involved in each of the cases. We must look instead to the effect of segregation itself on public education.

In approaching this problem, we cannot turn the clock back to 1868 when the Amendment was adopted, or even to 1896 when *Plessy v. Ferguson* was written. We must consider public education in the light of its full development and its present place in American life throughout the Nation. Only in this way can it be determined if segregation in public schools deprives these plaintiffs of the equal protection of the laws.

Today, education is perhaps the most important function of state and local governments. Compulsory school attendance laws and the great expenditures for education both demonstrate our recognition of the importance of education to our democratic society. It is required in the performance of our most basic public responsibilities, even service in the armed forces. It is the very foundation of good citizenship. Today it is a principal instrument in awakening the child to cultural values, in preparing him for later professional training, and in helping him to adjust normally to his environment. In these days, it is doubtful that any child may reasonably be expected to succeed in life if he is denied the opportunity of an education. Such an opportunity, where the state has undertaken to provide it, is a right which must be made available to all on equal terms.

We come then to the question presented: Does segregation of children in public schools solely on the basis of race, even though the physical facilities and other "tangible" factors may be equal, deprive the children of the minority group of equal educational opportunities? We believe that it does.

In *Sweatt v. Painter*, supra [339 U.S. 629, 70 S.Ct. 850], in finding that a segregated law school for Negroes could not provide them equal educational opportunities, this Court relied in large part on "those qualities which are incapable of objective measurement but which make for greatness in a law school." In *McLaurin v. Oklahoma State Regents*, supra [339 U.S. 637, 70 S.Ct. 853], the Court, in requiring that a Negro admitted to a white graduate school be treated like all other students, again resorted to intangible considerations: ". . . his ability to study, to engage in discussions and exchange views with other students, and, in general, to learn his profession." Such considerations apply with added force to children in grade and high schools. To separate them from others of similar age and qualifications solely because of their race generates a feeling of inferiority as to their status in the community that may affect their hearts and minds in a way unlikely ever to be undone. The effect of this separation on their educational opportunities was well stated by a finding in the Kansas case by a court which nevertheless felt compelled to rule against the Negro plaintiffs.

Segregation of white and colored children in public schools has a detrimental effect upon the colored children. The impact is greater when it has the sanction of the law; for the policy of separating the races is usually interpreted as denoting the inferiority of the Negro group. A sense of inferiority affects the motivation of a child to learn. Segregation with the sanction of law, therefore, has a tendency to retard the educational and mental development of Negro children and to deprive them of some of the benefits they would receive in a racially integrated school system.

Whatever may have been the extent of psychological knowledge at the time of *Plessy v. Ferguson*, this finding is amply supported by modern authority. Any language in *Plessy v. Ferguson* contrary to this finding is rejected.

We conclude that in the field of public education the doctrine of "separate but equal" has no place. Separate educational facilities are inherently unequal. Therefore, we hold that the plaintiffs and others similarly situated for whom the actions have been brought are, by reason of the segregation complained of, deprived of the equal protection of the laws guaranteed by the Fourteenth Amendment. This deposition makes unnecessary any discussion whether such segregation also violates the Due Process Clause of the Fourteenth Amendment.

Because these are class actions, because of the wide applicability of this decision, and because of the great variety of local conditions, the formulation of decrees in these cases presents problems of considerable complexity. On reargument, the consideration of appropriate relief was necessarily subordinated to the primary question—the constitutionality of segregation in public education. We have now announced that such segregation is a denial of the equal protection of the laws. In order that we may have the full assistance of the parties in formulating decrees, the cases will be restored to the docket, and the parties are requested to present further argument. . . . The Attorney General of the United States is again invited to participate. The Attorneys General of the states requiring or permitting segregation in public education will also be permitted to appear as *amici curiae* upon request to do so by September 15, 1954, and submission of briefs by October 1, 1954.

It is so ordered.

Source: Brown v. Board of Education of Topeka, Kansas, 347 U.S. 483 (1954).

"Enforcement Decree"

(Opinion delivered by Chief Justice Earl Warren.)

The cases were decided on May 17, 1954. The opinions of the date declaring the fundamental principle that racial discrimination in public education is unconstitutional, are incorporated herein by reference. All provisions of federal, state, or local law requiring or permitting such discrimination must yield to this principle. There remains for consideration the manner in which relief is to be accorded.

Because these cases arose under different local conditions and their disposition will involve a variety of local problems, we requested further argument on the question of relief. . . . The parties, the United States, and the States of Florida, North Carolina, Arkansas, Oklahoma, Maryland, and Texas filed briefs and participated in the oral arguments.

The presentations were informative and helpful to the Court in its consideration of the complexities arising from the transition to a system of public education freed of racial discrimination. The presentations also demonstrated that substantial steps to eliminate racial discrimination in public schools have already been taken, not only in some of the communities in which the cases arose, but in some of the states appearing as *amici curiae*, and in other states as well. Substantial progress has been made in the District of Columbia and in the communities in Kansas and Delaware involved in this litigation. The defendants in the cases coming to us from South Carolina and Virginia are awaiting the decision of the Court concerning relief.

Full implementation of these constitutional principles may require solution of varied local school problems. School authorities have the primary responsibility for elucidating, assessing, and solving these problems; courts will have to consider whether the action of school authorities constitutes good faith implementation of the governing constitutional principles. Because of their proximity to local conditions and the possible need for further hearings, the courts which originally heard these cases can best perform this judicial appraisal. Accordingly, we believe it appropriate to remand the cases to those courts.

In fashioning and effectuating the decrees, the courts will be guided by equitable principles. Traditionally, equity has been characterized by a practical flexibility in shaping its remedies and by a facility for adjusting and reconciling public and private needs. These cases call for the exercise of these traditional attributes of equity power. At stake is personal interest of the plaintiffs in admission to public schools as soon as practicable on a nondiscriminatory basis. To effectuate this interest may call for elimination of a variety of obstacles in making the transition to school systems operated in accordance with the constitutional principles set forth in our May 17, 1954, decision. Courts of equity may properly take into account the public interest in the elimination of such obstacles in a systematic and effective manner. But it should go without saying that the vitality of these constitutional principles cannot be allowed to yield simply because of disagreement with them.

While giving weight to these public and private considerations, the courts will require that the defendants make a prompt and reasonable start toward compliance with our May 17, 1954 ruling. Once such a start has been made, the courts may find that additional time is necessary to carry out the ruling in an effective manner. The burden rests upon the defendants to establish that such time is necessary in the public interest and is consistent with good faith compliance at the earliest practicable date. To that end, the courts may consider problems related to administration, arising from the physical condition of the school plant, the school transportation system, personnel, revision of school districts and attendance areas into compact units to achieve a system of determining admission to the public schools on a nonracial basis, and revision of local laws and regulations which may be necessary in solving the foregoing problems. They will also consider the adequacy of any plans the defendants may propose to meet these problems and to effectuate a transition to a racially nondiscriminatory school system. During this period of transition, the courts will retain jurisdiction of these cases.

The judgments below, except that in the Delaware case, are accordingly reversed, and the cases are remanded to the District Courts to take such proceedings and enter such orders and decrees consistent with this opinion as are necessary and proper to admit to public schools on a racially nondiscriminatory basis with all deliberate speed the parties to these cases. . . .

It is so ordered.

Source: *Brown* v. *Board of Education of Topeka, Kansas*, Enforcement Decree, 349 U.S. 294 (1955).

Document 3
FROM "THE SOUTHERN MANIFESTO: DECLARATION OF CONSTITUTIONAL PRINCIPLES" (1956)

In the wake of the *Brown* decision numerous southerners displayed their unwillingness to comply with the Supreme Court's order to desegregate their schools. In Mississippi, White Citizens' Councils were formed with the aim of maintaining segregation through economic and political pressure. These councils rapidly spread across the South. At the same time, the Ku Klux Klan enjoyed a revival, and arch-segregationist politicians won a series of victories over more moderate candidates.

The following document, "The Southern Manifesto," provides a sense of the breadth of southern resistance to desegregation. Largely the work of Senator Samuel J. Ervin, Jr., of North Carolina, the "Manifesto," which was read into the *Congressional Record*, was endorsed by nearly all of the South's leading citizens, including one hundred congressmen from eleven states of the old Confederacy. Even though the "Manifesto" called for using only lawful means to resist desegregation, some contend that it legitimated extralegal forms of resistance.

The unwarranted decision of the Supreme Court in the public school cases is now bearing the fruit always produced when men substitute naked power for established law.

The Founding Fathers gave us a Constitution of checks and balances because they realized the inescapable lesson of history that no man or group of men can be safely entrusted with unlimited power. They framed this Constitution with its provisions for change by amendment in order to secure the fundamentals of government against the dangers of temporary popular passion or the personal predilections of public office-holders.

We regard the decision of the Supreme Court in the school cases as a clear abuse of judicial power. It climaxes a trend in the Federal Judiciary undertaking to legislate, in derogation of the authority of Congress, and to encroach upon the reserved rights of the States and the people.

The original Constitution does not mention education. Neither does the 14th amendment nor any other amendment. The debates preceding the submission of the 14th amendment clearly show that there was no intent that it should affect the system of education maintained by the States. . . .

In the case *Plessy v. Ferguson* in 1896 the Supreme Court expressly declared that under the 14th amendment no person was denied any of his rights if the States provided separate but equal public facilities. This decision has been followed in many other cases. It is notable that the Supreme Court, speaking through Chief Justice Taft, a former President of the United States, unanimously declared in 1927 in *Lum v. Rice* that the "separate but equal" principle is "within the discretion of the State in regulating its public schools and does not conflict with the 14th amendment."

This interpretation, restated time and again, became a part of the life of the people of many of the States and confirmed their habits, customs, traditions, and way of life. It is founded on elemental humanity and common sense, for parents should not be deprived by Government of the right to direct the lives and education of their own children. . . .

This unwarranted exercise of power by the Court, contrary to the Constitution, is creating chaos and confusion in the States principally affected. It is destroying the amicable relations between the white and Negro races that have been created through 90 years of patient effort by the good people of both races. It has planted hatred and suspicion where there has been heretofore friendship and understanding.

Without regard to the consent of the governed, outside agitators are threatening immediate and revolutionary changes in our public-school systems. If done, this is certain to destroy the system of public education in some of the States.

With the gravest concern for the explosive and dangerous condition created by this decision and inflamed by outside meddlers:

We reaffirm our reliance on the Constitution as the fundamental law of the land.

We decry the Supreme Court's encroachments on the rights reserved to the States and to the people, contrary to established law, and to the Constitution.

We commend the motives of those States which have declared the intention to resist forced integration by any lawful means.

We appeal to the States and people who are not directly affected by these decisions to consider the constitutional principles involved against the time when they too, on issues vital to them, may be victims of judicial encroachment.

Even though we constitute a minority in the present Congress, we have full faith that a majority of the American people believe in the dual system of government which has enabled us to achieve our greatness and will in time demand that the reserved rights of the States and of the people be made secure against judicial usurpation.

We pledge ourselves to use all lawful means to bring about a reversal of this decision which is contrary to the Constitution and to prevent the use of force in its implementation.

In this trying period, as we all seek to right this wrong, we appeal to our people not to be provoked by the agitators and troublemakers invading our States and to scrupulously refrain from disorder and lawless acts.

Source: Congressional Record, 84th Congress, 2nd Session, March 12, 1956, 4460–64, 4515–16.

Document 4
FROM PRESIDENT DWIGHT D. EISENHOWER, RADIO AND TELEVISION "ADDRESS TO THE AMERICAN PEOPLE ON THE SITUATION IN LITTLE ROCK" (SEPTEMBER 24, 1957)

In response to the *Brown* decision, the school board in Little Rock, Arkansas, developed a plan for gradually desegregating its public schools, beginning with the enrollment of nine black students at Central High School. As the fall of 1957 approached, however, public opposition to the plan grew. Governor Orval Faubus, who sought to shore up his support among arch-segregationists, incited much of this opposition. On the first day of school, the National Guard, under Faubus's orders, blocked Elizabeth Eckford, one of the nine, from entering Central High and allowed a white mob to taunt, harass, and nearly lynch her.

This action, in combination with Faubus's defiance of a federal court order commanding that the school implement the desegregation plan, compelled President Eisenhower to act. Initially, Ike met with Faubus at the president's summer retreat in Newport, Rhode Island, where he negotiated what he thought was a peaceful resolution to the crisis. When Faubus reneged on his agreement to allow the desegregation of Central High—by withdrawing all troops from Little Rock, thus leaving the black students at the mercy of white mobs—Eisenhower determined he had to intervene. In a televised address, excerpted below, the president explained his decision to send federal troops to Little Rock. Observing that defiance of the law by white mobs was damaging America's image abroad, he declared that he had a constitutional obligation to maintain law and order. While the bulk of the forces were withdrawn shortly after the initial crisis, some federal troops remained in Little Rock for the entire school year.

My fellow citizens, . . . I must speak to you about the serious situation that has arisen in Little Rock. . . . In that city, under the leadership of demagogic extremists, disorderly mobs have deliberately prevented the carrying out of proper orders from a federal court. Local authorities have not eliminated that violent opposition and, under the law, I yesterday issued a proclamation calling upon the mob to disperse.

This morning the mob again gathered in front of the Central High School of Little Rock, obviously for the purpose of again preventing the carrying out of the court's order relating to the admission of Negro children to that school.

Whenever normal agencies prove inadequate to the task and it becomes necessary for the executive branch of the federal government to use its powers and authority to uphold federal courts, the President's responsibility is inescapable.

In accordance with that responsibility, I have today issued an Executive Order directing the use of troops under federal authority to aid in the execution of federal law at Little Rock, Arkansas. This became necessary when my Proclamation of yesterday was not observed, and the obstruction of justice still continues.

It is important that the reasons for my action be understood by all our citizens.

As you know, the Supreme Court of the United States has decided that separate public educational facilities for the races are inherently unequal and therefore compulsory school segregation laws are unconstitutional. . . .

During the past several years, many communities in our southern states have instituted public school plans for gradual progress in the enrollment and attendance of school children of all races in order to bring themselves into compliance with the law of the land.

They thus demonstrated to the world that we are a nation in which laws, not men, are supreme. . . .

Now let me make it very clear that federal troops are not being used to relieve local and state authorities of their primary duty to preserve the peace and order of the community. . . .

The proper use of the powers of the Executive Branch to enforce the orders of a federal court is limited to extraordinary and compelling circumstances. Manifestly, such an extreme situation has been created in Little Rock. This challenge must be met and with such measures as will preserve to the people as a whole their lawfully protected rights in a climate permitting their free and fair exercise.

The overwhelming majority of our people in every section of the country are united in their respect for observance of the law—even in those cases where they may disagree with that law. . . .

A foundation of our American way of life is our national respect for law.

In the South, as elsewhere, citizens are keenly aware of the tremendous disservice that has been done to the people of Arkansas in the eyes of the nation, and that has been done to the nation in the eyes of the world.

At a time when we face grave situations abroad because of the hatred that communism bears toward a system of government based on human rights, it would be difficult to exaggerate the harm that is being done to the prestige and influence, and indeed to the safety, of our nation and the world.

Our enemies are gloating over this incident and using it everywhere to misrepresent our whole nation. We are portrayed as a violator of those standards of conduct which the people of the world united to proclaim in the Charter of the United Nations. There they affirmed "faith in fundamental human rights" and "in the dignity and worth of the human person" and they did so "without distinction as to race, sex, language or religion."

And so, with deep confidence, I call upon the citizens of the State of Arkansas to assist in bringing an immediate end to all interference with the law and its processes. If resistance to the federal court orders ceases at once, the further presence of federal troops will be unnecessary and the City of Little Rock will return to its normal habits of peace and order and a blot upon the fair name and high honor of our nation in the world will be removed.

Thus will be restored the image of America and all its parts as one nation, indivisible, with liberty and justice for all.

Source: Public Papers of the Presidents of the United States, Dwight D. Eisenhower, 1957 (Washington, D.C.: GPO, 1958).

Document 5
JAMES M. LAWSON, JR.,
"FROM A LUNCH-COUNTER STOOL" (1960)

On February 1, 1960, four black college students sat down at a lunch counter in a Woolworth's drugstore in Greensboro, North Carolina, and ordered a cup of coffee and doughnuts. When the waitress refused to serve them because they were black (only whites were served at the lunch counter), they remained sitting until the store closed. Their "sit-in" sparked a wave of similar protests across the South, involving over one hundred communities and seventy thousand men and women, which took place against a backdrop of heightened but unfulfilled expectations.

To help coordinate and maintain the energy and momentum displayed by the sit-ins, student leaders from over thirty states held a conference at Shaw University in Raleigh, North Carolina, on Easter weekend, 1960. Even though the conference was sponsored by the Southern Christian Leadership Conference (SCLC), Martin Luther King, Jr.'s organization, the student leaders decided to form their own independent organization, the Student Nonviolent Coordinating Committee (SNCC). One of SNCC's founders and a keynote speaker at the conference was James Lawson, a leader of the Nashville Student Movement and a student of Gandhi's theory and practice of nonviolence. Lawson insisted that SNCC and the sit-ins were about much more than integrating the lunch counters of the South. His speech captured the spirit of many of those who assembled at Shaw University and reflected the early vision of the Student Nonviolent Coordinating Committee.

These are exciting moments in which to live. Reflect how over the last few weeks, the "sit-in" movement has leaped from campus to campus, until today hardly any campus remains unaffected. At the beginning of the decade, the student generation was "silent," "uncommitted," or "beatnik." But after only four months, these analogies largely used by adults appear as hasty clichés which should not have been used in the first place. The rapidity and drive of the movement indicates that all the while American students were simply waiting in suspension; waiting for the cause, that ideal, that event, that "actualizing of their faith" which would catapult their right to speak powerfully to their nation and world. . . .

But as so frequently happens, these are also enigmatic moments. Enigmatic, for like man in every age who cannot read the signs of the times, many of us are not able to see what appears before us, or hear what is spoken from lunch counter stools, or understand what has been cried behind jail cell bars.

Already the paralysis of talk, the disobedience of piety, the frustration of false ambition, and the insensitivity of an affluent society yearns to diffuse the meaning and flatten the thrust of America's first non-violent campaign.

One great university equates the movement to simply another student fad similar to a panty raid, or long black stockings. . . . Amid this welter of irrelevant and superficial reactions, the primary motifs of the movement, the essential message, the crucial issues raised are often completely missed. So the Christian student who has not yet given his support or mind to the movement might well want to know what the issue is all about. Is it just a lot of nonsense over a hamburger? Or is it far more?

To begin, let us note what the issue is not. . . .

Police partiality is not the issue. Nashville has been considered one of those "good" cities where racial violence has not been tolerated. Yet, on a Saturday in February, the mystique of yet another popular myth vanished. For only police permissiveness invited young white men to take over store after store in an effort to further intimidate or crush the "sit-in." Law enforcement agents accustomed to viewing crime, were able to mark well-dressed students waiting to make purchases, as loitering on the lunch-counter stools, but they were unable even to suspect and certainly not to see assault and battery. . . . Such partiality, however, is symptomatic of the diagnosis only—an inevitable by-product—another means of avoiding the encounter. But the "sit-in" does not intend to make such partiality the issue.

Already many well-meaning and notable voices are seeking to define the problem in purely legal terms. But if the students wanted a legal case, they had only to initiate a suit. But not a single sit-in began in this fashion. No one planned to be arrested or desired such. The legal battles which will be fought as a consequence of many arrests never once touch on the matter of eating where you normally shop, or on segregation *per se*. . . .

Let us admit readily that some of the major victories gained for social justice have come through the courts. . . . The Negro has been a law-abiding citizen as he has struggled for justice against many unlawful elements.

But the major defeats have occurred when we have been unable to convince the nation to support or implement the Constitution, when a court decision is ignored or nullified by local and state action. A democratic structure of law remains democratic, remains lawful only as the people are continuously persuaded to be democratic. Law is always nullified by practice and disdain unless the minds and hearts of a people sustain law. . . .

Eventually our society must abide by the Constitution and not permit any local law or custom to hinder freedom or justice. But such a society lives by more than law. In the same respect the sit-in movement is not trying to create a legal battle, but points to that which is more than law.

Finally, the issue is not integration. This is particularly true of the Christian oriented person. Certainly the students are asking in behalf of the entire Negro community and the nation that these eating counters become places of service for all persons. But it would be extremely short-sighted to assume that integration is the problem or the word of the "sit-in." To the extent to which the movement reflects deep Christian impulses, desegregation is a necessary next step. But it cannot be the end. If progress has not been at a genuine pace, it is often because the major groups seeking equal rights tactically made desegregation the end and not the means.

The Christian favors the breaking down of racial barriers because the redeemed community of which he is already a citizen recognizes no barriers dividing humanity. The Kingdom of God, as in heaven so on earth, is the distant goal of the Christian. That Kingdom is far more than the immediate need for integration. . . .

In the first instance, we who are demonstrators are trying to raise what we call the "moral issue." That is, we are pointing to the viciousness of racial segregation and prejudice and calling it evil or sin. The matter is not legal, sociological or racial, it is moral and spiritual. Until America (South and North) honestly accepts the sinful nature of racism, this cancerous disease will continue to rape all of us. . . .

In the second instance, the non-violent movement is asserting, "get moving." The pace of social change is too slow. At this rate it will be at least another generation before the major forms of segregation disappear. All of Africa will be free before the American Negro attains first-class citizenship. Most of us will be grandparents before we can live normal human lives.

The choice of the non-violent method, "the sit-in," symbolizes both judgment and promise. It is a judgment upon middle-class conventional, half-way efforts to deal with radical social evil. It is specifically a judgment upon contemporary civil rights attempts. As one high school student from

Chattanooga exclaimed, "We started because we were tired of waiting for you to act. . . ."

But the sit-in is likewise a sign of promise: God's promise that if radical Christian methods are adopted the rate of change can be vastly increased. Under Christian non-violence, Negro students reject the hardship of disobedient passivity and fear, but embrace the hardship (violence and jail) of obedience. Such non-violence strips the segregationalist power structure of its major weapon: the manipulation of law or law-enforcement to keep the Negro in his place.

Source: Student Nonviolent Coordinating Committee Papers, 1959–1972. Martin Luther King, Jr. Center for Nonviolent Social Change, Atlanta, GA.

Document 6
ROBERT MOSES, "LETTER FROM A MISSISSIPPI JAIL CELL" (1961)

When the sit-ins swept across the South in the spring of 1960, Robert Moses, a young black Harvard graduate, was teaching mathematics at a high school in New York City. Inspired by the protests, Moses determined to join the budding freedom movement in the South as soon as he could. In 1961, building on some initial contacts he had made in the summer of 1960, Moses established a SNCC-sponsored voter registration/education campaign in McComb County, Mississippi. With the help of several local activists, Moses recruited support for his campaign and convinced a few brave blacks to register to vote. The white community's response to these efforts was predictable. Authorities harassed Moses and blacks who dared challenge the racial status quo. Herbert Lee, one of the blacks who dared register, was shot to death in broad daylight by E. H. Hurst, a state legislator. When local black high school students rallied to SNCC's defense, staging a freedom march, a mob of whites attacked Moses and his colleagues. Nonetheless, the police placed Moses and other civil rights activists, not the white mob, under arrest for disturbing the peace. From his jail cell Moses penned the following letter, one of the classic texts of the movement.

We are smuggling this note from the drunk tank of the country jail in Magnolia, Mississippi. Twelve of us are here, sprawled out along the concrete bunker; Curtis Hayes, Hollis Watkins, Ike Lewis and Robert Talbert, four veterans of the bunker, are sitting up talking—mostly about girls; Charles McDew ("Tell the story") is curled into the concrete and the wall; Harold Robinson, Stephen Ashley, James Wells, Lee Chester, Vick, Leotus Eubanks, and Ivory Diggs lay cramped on the cold bunker; I'm sitting with smuggled pen and paper, thinking a little, writing a little; Myrtis Bennett and Janie Campbell are across the way wedded to a different icy cubicle.

Later on Hollis will lead out with a clear tenor into a freedom song; Talbert and Lewis will supply jokes; and McDew will discourse on the history of the black man and the Jew. McDew—a black by birth, a Jew by choice and a revolutionary by necessity—has taken on the deep hates and deep loves which America, and the world, reserve for those who dare to stand in a strong sun and cast a sharp shadow.

In the words of Judge Brumfield, who sentenced us, we are "cold calculators" who design to disrupt the racial harmony (harmonious since 1619) of McComb into racial strife and rioting; we, he said, are the leaders who are causing young children to be led like sheep to the pen to be slaughtered (in a legal manner). "Robert," he was addressing me, "haven't some of the people from your school been able to go down and register without violence here in Pike county?" I thought to myself that Southerners are most exposed when they boast.

It's mealtime now: we have rice and gravy in a flat pan, dry bread and a "big town cake"; we lack eating and drinking utensils. Water comes from a faucet and goes into a hole.

This is Mississippi, the middle of the iceberg. Hollis is leading off with his tenor, "Michael, row the boat ashore, Alleluia; Christian brothers don't be slow, Alleluia; Mississippi's next to go, Alleluia." This is a tremor in the middle of the iceberg—from a stone that the builders rejected.

Source: Peter B. Levy, ed., *Let Freedom Ring: A Documentary History of the Modern Civil Rights Movement* (Westport, Conn.: Praeger, 1992), 94–95.

Document 7
GEORGE C. WALLACE, "INAUGURAL ADDRESS" (1963)

In the 1960s, Alabama governor George C. Wallace gained the reputation as the most notorious defender of white supremacy in the nation. A fiery orator and a masterful politician, Wallace not only defended the southern way of life, he reached out to whites across the nation with subtle and not-so-subtle racist appeals. In 1964 he entered several presidential primaries, performing remarkably well in a handful of northern and border states. Four years later, he won a larger percentage of the vote for president than any third-party or independent candidate since Theodore Roosevelt in 1912. In 1972, running for the Democratic nomination, he strung together a series of primary victories, only to have his campaign cut short by a bullet in an attempted assassination that left him paralyzed and unable to complete his run for the White House.

Wallace's most famous words were delivered in his 1963 gubernatorial inaugural address, in which he pledged to defend segregation "forever." In the following months, he personally sought to stop the desegregation of the University of Alabama, an action that not only failed to stay the integration of the university but also helped convince President John F. Kennedy to call for sweeping civil rights legislation. Years later, Wallace met with Jesse Jackson, one of Martin Luther King, Jr.'s protégés and himself a presidential candidate. During their meeting, Wallace apologized for his earlier actions and words. Indeed, after similar apologies to blacks in Alabama, Wallace was elected governor, in part on the strength of black votes, in 1982.

Governor Patterson, Governor Barnett . . . fellow Alabamians:

. . . This is the day of my Inauguration as Governor of the State of Alabama. And on this day I feel a deep obligation to renew my pledges, my covenants with you . . . the people of this great state.

General Robert E. Lee said that "duty" is the sublimest word in the English language and I have come, increasingly, to realize what he meant. I SHALL do my duty to you, God helping . . . to every man, to every woman . . . yes, and to every child in this State. . . .

Today I have stood, where once Jefferson Davis stood, and took an oath to my people. It is very appropriate then that from this Cradle of the Confederacy, this very Heart of the Great Anglo-Saxon Southland, that today we sound the drum for freedom as have our generations of forebearers before us done, time and again down through history. Let us rise to the call of freedom-loving blood that is in us and send our answer to the tyranny that clanks its chains upon the South. In the name of the greatest people that ever trod the earth, I draw the line in the dust and toss the gauntlet before the feet of tyranny . . . and I say . . . segregation now . . . segregation tomorrow . . . segregation forever.

The Washington, D.C. school riot report is disgusting and revealing. We will not sacrifice our children to any such type of school system—and you can write that down. The federal troops in Mississippi could better be used guarding the safety of the citizens of Washington, D.C., where it is even unsafe to walk or go to a ball game—and that is the nation's capitol. I was safer in a B-29 bomber over Japan during the war in an air raid, than the people of Washington are walking in the White House neighborhood. A closer example is Atlanta. The city officials fawn for political reasons over school integration and THEN build barricades to stop residential integration—what hypocrisy!

Let us send this message back to Washington . . . that from this day we are standing up, and the heel of tyranny does not fit the neck of an upright man . . . that we intend to take the offensive and carry our fight for freedom across the nation, wielding the balance of power we know we possess in the Southland. . . . that WE, not the insipid bloc voters of some sections will determine in the next election who shall sit in the white House . . . that from this day, from this minute, we give the word of a race of honor that we will not tolerate their boot in our face no longer. . . .

Hear me, Southerners! You sons and daughters who have moved north and west throughout this nation. We call on you from your native soil to join with us in national support and vote and we know wherever you are, away from the hearths of the Southland, that you will respond, for though you may live in the farthest reaches of this vast country, your heart has never left Dixieland.

And you native sons and daughters of old New England's rock-ribbed patriotism, and you sturdy natives of the great Mid-West, and you descendants of the far West flaming spirit of pioneer freedom, we invite you to come and be with us, for you are of the Southern mind, and the Southern spirit, and the Southern philosophy. You are Southerners too and brothers with us in our fight. . . .

To realize our ambitions and to bring to fruition our dreams, we as Alabamians must take cognizance of the world about us. We must re-define our heritage, re-school our thoughts in the lessons our forefathers knew so well, first hand, in order to function and to grow and to prosper. We can no longer hide our head in the sand and tell ourselves that the ideology of our free fathers is not being attacked and is not being threatened by another idea, for it is. We are faced with an idea that if centralized government assumes enough authority, enough power over its people that it can provide a utopian life, that if given the power to dictate, to forbid, to require, to demand, to distribute, to edict and to judge what is best and enforce that will of judgment upon its citizens from unimpeachable authority, then it will produce only "good" and it shall be our father and our God. It is an idea of government that encourages our fears and destroys our faith, for where there is faith, there is no fear, and where there is fear, there is no faith. . . .

Not so long ago men stood in marvel and awe at the cities, the buildings, the schools, the autobahns that the government of Hitler's Germany had built . . . but it could not stand, for the system that built it had rotted the souls of the builders and in turn rotted the foundation of what God meant that God should be. Today that same system on an international scale is sweeping the world. It is the "changing world" of which we are told. It is now called "new" and "liberal." It is as old as the oldest dictator. It is degenerate and decadent. As the national racism of Hitler's Germany persecuted a national minority to the whim of a national majority so the international racism of liberals seeks to persecute the international white minority to the whim of the international colored majority, so that we are footballed about according to the favor of the Afro-Asian bloc. But the Belgian survivors of the Congo cannot present their case to the war crimes commission . . . nor the survivors of Castro, nor the citizens of Oxford, Mississippi.

It is this theory of international power politics that led a group of men on the Supreme Court for the first time in American history to issue an edict, based not on legal precedent, but upon a volume, the editor of which has said our Constitution is outdated and must be changed and the writers of which, some had admittedly belonged to as many as half a hundred communist front organizations. It is this theory that led this same group of men to briefly bare the ungodly core of the philosophy in forbidding little school children to say a prayer. . . .

This nation was never meant to be a unit of one but a unit of the many, that is the exact reason our freedom loving forefathers established the states, so as to divide the rights and powers among the many states, insuring that no central power could gain master control.

In united effort we were meant to live under this government, whether Baptist, Methodist . . . or whatever one's denomination or religious belief, each respecting the others right to a separate denomination. And so it was meant in our political lives . . . each . . . respecting the rights of others to be separate and work from within the political framework. . . .

And so it was meant in our racial lives, each race, within its own framework has the freedom to teach, to instruct, to develop, to ask for and receive deserved help from others of separate racial stations. This is the great freedom of our American founding fathers. But if we amalgamate into the one unit as advocated by the communist philosophers, then the enrichment of our lives, the freedom for our development, is gone forever. We become, therefore, a mongrel unit of one under a single all powerful government and we stand for everything and for nothing.

The true brotherhood of America, of respecting separateness of others and uniting in effort, has been so twisted and distorted from its original concept that there is small wonder that communism is winning the world.

We invite the negro citizen of Alabama to work with us from his separate racial station, as we will work with him, to develop, to grow. . . . But we warn those, of any group, who would follow the false doctrine of communistic amalgamation that we will not surrender our system of government, our freedom of race and religion, that freedom was won at a hard price and if it requires a hard price to retain it, we are able and quite willing to pay it. . . .

We remind all within hearing of the Southland that . . . Southerners played a most magnificent part in erecting this great divinely inspired system of freedom, and as God is our witness, Southerners will save it.

Let us, as Alabamians, grasp the hand of destiny and walk out of the shadow of fear and fill our divine destiny. Let us not simply defend but let us assume the leadership of the fight and carry our leadership across the nation. God has placed us here in this crisis. Let us not fail in this our most historical moment.

Source: Alabama Department of Archives and History, Montgomery, Alabama.

Document 8
FROM JOHN F. KENNEDY, "ADDRESS ON CIVIL RIGHTS" (JUNE 11, 1963)

John F. Kennedy's election to the presidency in 1960 and his reputation for political courage and vigor raised the hopes of millions of African Americans. Yet, for two years, President Kennedy let the African American community down. Not wanting to jeopardize the rest of his domestic and foreign policy agenda, which depended on white southern support, he neither proposed significant civil rights legislation nor spoke to the nation about its racial problems. Even when faced with crises such as the freedom rides and the University of Mississippi's refusal to enroll James Meredith, President Kennedy tended to equivocate.

Yet the civil rights struggle did not retreat from the streets, keeping the pressure on Kennedy to live up to his promise to promote civil rights and to desegregate public housing in particular. On the evening of June 11, 1963, he delivered a nationally televised speech, one of the most significant discussions of racial matters by a president in American history. In the speech, Kennedy demanded that the nation honor its moral principles and called for sweeping civil rights legislation. In November 1963, however, he was assassinated in Dallas, Texas, his proposed civil rights bill still bottled up in Congress.

Good evening my fellow citizens. This afternoon, following a series of threats and defiant statements, the presence of Alabama National Guardsmen was required on the campus of the University of Alabama to carry out the final and unequivocal order of the United States District Court of the Northern District of Alabama.

The order called for the admission of two clearly qualified young Alabama residents who happened to have been born Negro.

That they were admitted peacefully on the campus is due in good measure to the conduct of the students of the University of Alabama who met their responsibilities in a constructive way.

I hope that every American, regardless of where he lives, will stop and examine his conscience about this and other related incidents.

This nation was founded by men of many nations and backgrounds. It was founded on the principle that all men are created equal, and that the rights of every man are diminished when the rights of one man are threatened.

Today we are committed to a worldwide struggle to promote and protect the rights of all who wish to be free. And when Americans are sent to Vietnam or West Berlin we do not ask for whites only.

It ought to be possible, therefore, for American students of any color to attend any public institution they select without having to be backed up by troops. It ought to be possible for American consumers of any color to receive equal service in places of public accommodation, such as hotels and restaurants, and theaters and retail stores without being forced to resort to demonstrations in the street.

And it ought to be possible for American citizens of any color to register and to vote in a free election without interference or fear of reprisal.

It ought to be possible, in short, for every American to enjoy the privileges of being American without regard to his race or his color.

In short, every American ought to have the right to be treated as he would wish to be treated, as one would wish his children to be treated. But this is not the case.

The Negro baby born in America today, regardless of the section or the state in which he is born, has about one-half as much chance of completing high school as a white baby, born in the same place, on the same day . . . twice as much chance of becoming unemployed . . . a life expectancy which is seven years shorter. . . .

This is not a sectional issue. Difficulties over segregation and discrimination exist in almost every city . . . producing . . . a rising tide of discontent that threatens the public safety.

Nor is this a partisan issue. In a time of domestic crisis, men of goodwill and generosity should be able to unite regardless of party or politics.

This is not even a legal or legislative issue alone. It is better to settle these matters in the courts than on the streets, and new laws are needed at every level. But law alone cannot make men see right.

We are confronted primarily with a moral issue. It is as old as the Scriptures and is as clear as the American Constitution. The heart of the question is whether all Americans are to be afforded equal rights and equal opportunities; whether we are going to treat our fellow Americans as we want to be treated.

If an American, because his skin is dark, cannot eat lunch in a restaurant open to the public; if he cannot send his children to the best public school available; if he cannot vote for the public officials who represent him; if, in short, he cannot enjoy the full and free life which all of us want, then who among us would be content to have the color of his skin changed and stand in his place?

Who among us would then be content with the counsels of patience and delay. One hundred years of delay have passed since President Lincoln freed the slaves, yet their heirs, their grandsons, are not fully free. . . .

And this nation, for all its hopes and all its boasts, will not be fully free until all its citizens are free.

We preach freedom around the world, and we mean it. And we cherish our freedom here at home. But are we to say to the world—and more importantly to each other—that this is the land of the free, except for the Negroes. . . .

Now the time has come for this nation to fulfill its promise. The events in Birmingham and elsewhere have so increased the cries for equality that no city or state or legislative body can prudently choose to ignore them.

The fires of frustration and discord are burning in every city, North and South. Where legal remedies are not at hand, redress is sought in the streets in demonstrations, parades and protests, which create tensions and threaten violence—and threaten lives.

We face, therefore, a moral crisis as a country and a people. It cannot be met by repressive police action. It cannot be left to increased demonstrations in the streets. It cannot be quieted by token moves or talk. It is time to act in the Congress, in your state and local legislative body, in all of our daily lives.

It is not enough to pin the blame on others, to say this is a problem of one section of the country or another, or deplore the facts that we face. A great change is at hand, and our task, our obligation is to make that revolution, that change peaceful and constructive for all.

Those who do nothing are inviting shame as well as violence. Those who act boldly are recognizing right as well as reality.

Next week I shall ask the Congress of the United States to act, to make a commitment it has not fully made in this century to the proposition that race has no place in American life or law. . . .

But legislation, I repeat, cannot solve this problem alone. It must be solved in the homes of every American in every community across our country.

In this respect, I want to pay tribute to those citizens, North and South, who've been working in their communities to make life better for all. They are acting not out of a sense of legal duty but out of a sense of human decency. Like our soldiers and sailors in all parts of the world, they are meeting freedom's challenge on the firing line and I salute them for their honor—their courage. . . .

We have a right to expect that the Negro community will be responsible, will uphold the law. But they have a right to expect that the law will be fair, that the Constitution will be color blind, as Justice Harlan said at the turn of the century.

Source: Public Papers of the Presidents of the United States, John F. Kennedy, 1963 (Washington, D.C.: GPO, 1964).

Document 9
FROM MARTIN LUTHER KING, JR.,
"I HAVE A DREAM" (1963)

On August 28, 1963, over two hundred thousand men and women, black and white, young and old, staged the largest demonstration in the nation's history to date, the March on Washington for "jobs and freedom." The protest had been organized by a broad coalition of civil rights groups, headed by A. Philip Randolph, the dean of the movement, who in 1941 had prodded President Franklin D. Roosevelt to desegregate the defense industries by threatening to stage a similar protest. Even though the weather was hot and muggy, the mood at the 1963 demonstration was magical. After the crowd marched down the mall in Washington, D.C., it assembled around the Lincoln Memorial, where it listened to a series of performers and speakers, culminating with King's "I Have a Dream" address.

King was well known for his brilliant oratory, and the speech he gave that day was one of the greatest in American history. In contrast to his "Letter from a Birmingham Jail," which had a militant, even radical tone, his "I Have a Dream" speech had an idealistic and amiable feel. King poetically traced the nation's failure to live up to its ideals and sketched out his vision of a color-blind society in which all Americans would be judged by the content of their character rather than the color of their skin. In response to the crowd's enthusiasm, he broke from his prepared remarks, expanding on this dream and demanding that freedom be allowed to ring all across the nation. His speech, along with the march in general, garnered widespread support, including support from many who heretofore had felt that the civil rights movement had been pushing too fast and too hard.

Five score years ago, a great American, in whose symbolic shadow we stand, signed the Emancipation Proclamation. This momentous decree came as a great beacon of light of hope to millions of Negro slaves who had been seared in the flames of withering injustice. It came as a joyous daybreak to end the long night of captivity.

But one hundred years later, we must face the tragic fact that the Negro is still not free. One hundred years later, the life of the Negro is still sadly crippled by the manacles of segregation and the chains of discrimination. One hundred years later, the Negro lives on a lonely island of poverty in the midst of a vast ocean of material prosperity. . . . So we have come here today to dramatize an appalling condition.

In a sense we have come to our nation's Capital to cash a check. When the architects of our republic wrote the magnificent words of the Constitution and the Declaration of Independence, they were signing a promissory note to which every American was to fall heir. This note was a promise that all men would be guaranteed the unalienable rights of life, liberty, and the pursuit of happiness.

It is obvious today that America has defaulted on this promissory note insofar as her citizens of color are concerned. Instead of honoring this sacred obligation, America has given the Negro people a bad check; a check which has come back marked "insufficient funds." But we refuse to believe that the bank of justice is bankrupt. We refuse to believe that there are insufficient funds in the great vaults of opportunity of this nation. So we have come to cash this check. . . .

We have also come to this hallowed spot to remind America of the fierce urgency of now. This is no time to engage in the luxury of cooling off or to take a tranquilizing dose of gradualism. Now is the time to make real the promises of Democracy. Now is the time to rise from the dark and desolate valley of segregation to the sunlit path of racial justice. Now is the time to open the doors of opportunity to all of God's children. Now is the time to lift our nation from the quicksands of racial injustice to the solid rock of brotherhood.

It would be fatal for the nation to overlook the urgency of the moment and to underestimate the determination of the Negro. The sweltering summer of the Negro's legitimate discontent will not pass until there is an invigorating autumn of freedom and equality. 1963 is not an end, but a beginning. Those who hope that the Negro needed to blow off steam and will now be content will have a rude awakening if the Nation returns to business as usual. There will be neither rest nor tranquility in America until the Negro is granted his citizenship rights. The whirlwinds of revolt will continue to shake the foundations of our Nation until the bright day of justice emerges.

But there is something that I must say to my people who stand on the warm threshold which leads into the palace of justice. In the process of gaining our rightful place we must not be guilty of wrongful deeds. Let us not need to satisfy our thirst for freedom by drinking from the cup of bitterness and hatred. We must forever conduct our struggle on the high plane of dignity and discipline. . . . The marvelous new militancy which has engulfed the Negro community must not lead us to distrust white people, for many of our white brothers, as evidenced by their presence here today, have come to realize that their destiny is tied up with our destiny and their freedom is inextricably bound to our freedom. We cannot walk alone. . . .

There are those who are asking the devotees of civil rights, "When will you be satisfied?" We can never be satisfied as long as the Negro is the victim of the unspeakable horrors of police brutality. . . . We cannot be satisfied as long as the Negro's basic mobility is from a smaller ghetto to a larger one. We can never be satisfied as long as a Negro in Mississippi cannot vote and a Negro in New York believes he has nothing for which to vote. No, no we are not satisfied, and we will not be satisfied until justice rolls down like waters and righteousness like a mighty stream.

I am not unmindful that some of you have come here out of great trials and tribulations. Some of you have come fresh from narrow jail cells. Some of you have come from areas where your quest for freedom left you battered by the storms of persecution. You have been the veterans of creative suffering. Continue to work with the faith that unearned suffering is redemptive.

Go back to Mississippi, go back to Alabama, go back to South Carolina . . . go back to the slums and ghettos of our modern cities, knowing that somehow this situation can and will be changed. Let us not wallow in the valley of despair.

I say to you today, my friends, that in spite of the difficulties and frustrations of the moment I still have a dream. It is a dream deeply rooted in the American dream.

I have a dream that one day this nation will rise up and live out the true meaning of its creed: "We hold these truths to be self-evident; that all men are created equal."

I have a dream that one day on the red hills of Georgia the sons of former slaves and the sons of former slaveowners will be able to sit down together at the table of brotherhood.

I have a dream that one day even the state of Mississippi, a desert state sweltering with the heat of injustice and oppression, will be transformed into an oasis of freedom and justice.

I have a dream that my four children will one day live in a nation where they will not be judged by the color of their skin but by the content of their character.

I have a dream today.

I have a dream that one day the state of Alabama, whose governor's lips are presently dripping with the words of interposition and nullification, will be transformed into a situation where little black boys and black girls will be able to join hands with little white boys and white girls and walk together as sisters and brothers.

I have a dream today.

I have a dream that one day every valley shall be exalted, every hill and mountain shall be made low, the rough places will be made plains, and the crooked places will be made straight, and the glory of the Lord shall be revealed, and all flesh shall see it together.

This is our hope. This is the faith with which I return to the South. With this faith we will be able to hew out of the mountain of despair a stone of hope. With this faith we will be able to transform the jangling discords of our nation into a beautiful symphony of brotherhood. With this faith we will be able to work together, to pray together, to struggle together, to go to jail together, to stand up for freedom together, knowing that we will be free one day.

This will be the day when all God's children will be able to sing with new meaning "My country 'tis of thee, sweet land of liberty, of thee I sing. Land where my fathers died, land of the pilgrim's pride, from every mountainside, let freedom ring."

And if America is to be a great nation this must come to be true. So let freedom ring from the prodigious hilltops of New Hampshire. Let freedom ring from the mighty mountains of New York. Let freedom ring from the heightening Alleghenies of Pennsylvania!

. . . But not only that; let freedom ring from Stone Mountain of Georgia! Let freedom ring from Lookout Mountain, Tennessee! Let freedom ring from every hill and mole hill of Mississippi. From every mountainside, let freedom ring.

When we let freedom ring, when we let it ring from every village and every hamlet, from every state and every city, we will be able to speed up that day when all of God's children, black men and white men, Jews and Gentiles, Protestants and Catholics, will be able to join hands and sing in the words of the old Negro spiritual, "Free at last! Free at last! thank God almighty, we are free at last!"

Source: Peter B. Levy, ed., *Let Freedom Ring: A Documentary History of the Modern Civil Rights Movement* (Westport, Conn.: Praeger, 1992), 122–25.

Document 10
FROM FANNIE LOU HAMER, "TESTIMONY BEFORE THE CREDENTIALS COMMITTEE OF THE DEMOCRATIC NATIONAL CONVENTION," ATLANTIC CITY, NEW JERSEY (1964)

In early 1964, SNCC decided to undertake a major campaign in Mississippi known as Freedom Summer. Its coordinators put forth two main goals, the opening of Freedom Schools and the establishment of the Mississippi Freedom Democratic Party (MFDP). Encouraged by several prominent liberals, most notably Joe Rauh, counsel for the United Automobile Workers union and a leader of the Americans for Democratic Action, the MFDP decided to challenge the legitimacy of the "regular" Democratic Party's delegation from Mississippi at the Democratic national convention in Atlantic City in the summer of 1964. The MFDP's challenge climaxed with the testimony of Fannie Lou Hamer, a middle-aged Mississippi sharecropper and one of the leaders of the MFDP. Fearing that the MFDP's challenge would undermine his support among white southerners, President Lyndon B. Johnson pressured the credentials committee to offer the group a compromise of two at-large delegates at the 1964 convention. (There were sixty-eight members in the full Mississippi delegation.) While most moderates and liberals supported this offer, the MFDP rejected the plan, terming it tokenism. In the wake of this confrontation, many civil rights activists never fully trusted LBJ or his liberal allies again, and the liberal coalition that had prospered during the first half of the decade began to fall apart.

Mr. Chairman, and the Credentials Committee, my name is Mrs. Fannie Lou Hamer, and I live at 626 East Lafayette Street, Ruleville, Mississippi, Sunflower County, the home of Senator James O. Eastland, and Senator Stennis.

It was the 31st of August in 1962 that 18 of us traveled 26 miles to the county courthouse in Indianola to try to register to try to become first-class citizens. We was met in Indianola by Mississippi men, Highway Patrolmen and they allowed two of us to take the literacy test at the time. After we had taken the test and started back to Ruleville, we was held up by the City Police and the State Highway Patrolmen and carried back to Indianola where the bus driver was charged that day with driving a bus the wrong color.

After we paid the fine among us, we continued on to Ruleville, and Reverend Jeff Sunny carried me the four miles in the rural area where I had worked as a time-keeper and sharecropper for 18 years. I was met there by my children, who told me the plantation owner was angry because I had gone down to try to register.

After they told me, my husband came, and said the plantation owner was raising cain because I had tried to register and before he quit talking the plantation owner came, and said, "Fannie Lou, do you know—did Pap tell you what I said?" And I said, "Yes sir." He said, "I mean that. . . . If you don't go down and withdraw . . . well—you might have to go because we are not ready for that." . . .

And I addressed him and told him and said, "I didn't try to register for you. I tried to register for myself."

I had to leave that same night.

On the 10th of September, 1962, 16 bullets was fired into the home of Mr. and Mrs. Robert Tucker for me. That same night two girls were shot in Ruleville, Mississippi. Also Mr. Joe McDonald's house was shot in.

And in June, the 9th, 1963, I had attended a voter registration workshop, was returning back to Mississippi. Ten of us was traveling by the Continental Trailways bus. When we got to Winona, Mississippi, which is Montgomery County, four of the people got off to use the washroom. . . . I stepped off the bus to see what was happening and somebody screamed from the car that four workers was in and said, "Get that one there," and when I went to get in the car, when the man told me I was under arrest, he kicked me.

I was carried to the county jail and put in the holding room. They left some of the people in the booking room and began to place us in cells. I was placed in a cell with a young woman called Miss Euvester Simpson. After I was placed in the cell I began to hear sounds of licks and screams. I could hear the sounds of licks and horrible screams, and I could hear somebody say, "Can you say, yes, sir, nigger?" "Can you say yes, sir?"

And they would say horrible names. She would say, "Yes, I can say yes, sir." . . . They beat her, I don't know how long, and after a while she began to pray and asked God to have Mercy on those people. And it wasn't long before three white men came to my cell. One of these men was a State Highway Patrolmen and he asked me where I was from, and I told him Ruleville; he said, "We are going to check this."

And they left my cell and it wasn't too long before they came back. He said, "You are from Ruleville all right," and he used a curse word, he said, "We are going to beat you until you wish you was dead."

I was carried out of that cell into another cell where they had two Negro prisoners. The State Highway patrolmen ordered the first Negro to take the blackjack. The first Negro prisoner ordered me, by orders from the State

Highway Patrolmen, for me to lay down on a bunk bed on my face, and I laid on my face.

The first Negro began to beat, and I was beat by the first Negro until he was exhausted, and I was holding my hands behind at this time on my left side because I suffered polio when I was six years old. After the first Negro had beat until he was exhausted the state Highway Patrolman ordered the second Negro to take the blackjack. The second Negro began to beat and I began to work my feet, and the State Highway Patrolmen ordered the first Negro who had beat to set on my feet to keep me from working my feet. I began to scream and one white man got up and began to beat me in my head and tell me to hush.

One white man—my dress had worked up high, he walked over and pulled my dress down and he pulled my dress back, back up. . . .

All of this on account we want to register, to become first-class citizens, and if the Freedom Democratic Party is not seated now, I question America, is this America, the land of the free and the home of the brave where we have to sleep with our telephones off the hooks because our lives be threatened daily because we want to live as decent human beings, in America?

Source: Peter B. Levy, ed., *Let Freedom Ring: A Documentary History of the Modern Civil Rights Movement* (Westport, Conn.: Praeger, 1992), 139–41.

Document 11
LYNDON B. JOHNSON, "SPECIAL MESSAGE TO THE CONGRESS: THE AMERICAN PROMISE" (MARCH 15, 1965)

When President John F. Kennedy was assassinated in November 1963, most civil rights forces feared that his successor, Lyndon B. Johnson, a Texan with a poor record on civil rights, would hurt their efforts to attain racial reforms. Yet, from his first days in the White House, Johnson pleasantly surprised the civil rights movement. He marshaled the Civil Rights Act of 1964 through Congress and signed it into law. He developed numerous antipoverty programs that benefitted large numbers of African Americans. He appointed prominent blacks to top positions within his administration and to the courts, most notably Thurgood Marshall, the onetime head of the NAACP's Legal Defense and Educational Fund.

Moreover, in the face of mass demonstrations in Selma, Alabama, organized by Martin Luther King, Jr., Johnson rallied the nation behind voting rights legislation. In the following address, delivered to a joint session of Congress, he made probably the strongest statement on racial matters by a president in U.S. history. Johnson even invoked the motto of the movement, "We shall overcome." Not long afterwards, he signed into law the Voting Rights Act of 1965, which in a short period of time allowed millions of African Americans to register to vote and redrew the political map of the country.

I speak tonight for the dignity of man and the destiny of democracy. I urge every member of both parties, Americans of all religions and of all colors, from every section of this country, to join me in that cause.

At times history and fate meet at a single time in a single place to shape a turning point in man's unending search for freedom. So it was at Lexington and Concord. . . . So it was last week in Selma, Alabama. There, long-suffering men and women peacefully protested the denial of their rights as Americans. Many were brutally assaulted. One good man, a man of God, was killed. There is no cause for pride in what happened in Selma. There is no cause for self-satisfaction in the long denial of equal rights of millions of Americans. But there is cause for hope and for faith in our democracy in what is happening here tonight. For the cries of pain and the hymns and protests of oppressed people have summoned into convocation all the majesty of this great government of the greatest nation on earth.

Our mission is at once the oldest and the most basic of this country: to right wrong, to do justice, to serve man. . . . Rarely in any time does an issue lay bare the secret heart of America itself. Rarely are we met with a challenge, not to our growth or abundance, or our welfare or our security, but rather to the values and the purposes and the meaning of our beloved nation.

The issue of equal rights for American Negroes is such an issue. And should we defeat every enemy and should we double our wealth and conquer the stars and still be unequal to this issue, then we will have failed as a people and as a nation. For with a country as with a person, "What is a man profited, if he shall gain the whole world, and lose his own soul?"

There is no Negro problem. There is no Southern problem. There is no Northern problem. There is only an American problem. And we are met here tonight as Americans, not as Democrats or Republicans, we are met here as Americans to solve the problem.

This was the first nation in the history of the world to be founded with a purpose. The great phrases of that purpose still sound in every American heart, North and South: "All men are created equal"—"government by consent of the governed"—"give me liberty or give me death." Those are not just clever words. These are not just empty theories. In their name Americans have fought and died for two centuries, and tonight around the world they stand there as guardians of our liberty, risking their lives.

These words are a promise to every citizen that he shall share in the dignity of man. . . . It says that he shall share in freedom, he shall choose his leaders, educate his children, provide for his family according to his ability and his merits as a human being. To apply any other test—to deny a man his hopes because of his color or race, or his religion, or the place of his birth—is not only to do injustice, it is to deny America and to dishonor the dead who gave their lives for American freedom.

Our fathers believed that if this noble view of the rights of man was to flourish, it must be rooted in democracy. The most basic right of all was the right to choose your own leaders. The history of this country in large measure is the history of expansion of that right to all of our people.

Many of the issues of civil rights are very complex and most difficult. But about this there can and should be no argument. Every American citizen must have an equal right to vote. There is no reason which can excuse the denial of that right. There is no duty which weighs more heavily on us than the duty we have to ensure that right.

Yet the harsh fact is that in many places in this country men and women are kept from voting simply because they are Negroes. Every device of which human ingenuity is capable has been used to deny this right. . . .

The Constitution says that no person shall be kept from voting because of his race or his color. We have all sworn an oath before God to support and to defend that Constitution. We must now act in obedience to that oath.

Wednesday, I will send to congress a law designed to eliminate illegal barriers to the right to vote. . . . To those who seek to avoid action by their national government in their own communities, who want to and who seek to maintain purely local control over elections, the answer is simple. Open your polling places to all your people. Allow men and women to register and vote whatever the color of their skin. Extend the rights of citizenship to every citizen of this land. There is no constitutional issue here. The command of the Constitution is plain. There is no moral issue here. It is wrong to deny any of your fellow Americans the right to vote in this country. There is no issue of states rights or national rights. There is only the struggle for human rights. . . .

We cannot, we must not refuse to protect the right of every American to vote in every election that he may desire to participate in. And we ought not, we must not wait another eight months before we get a bill. We have already waited a hundred years and more and the time for waiting is gone. . . .

Even if we pass this bill, the battle will not be over. What happened in Selma is part of a far larger movement which reaches into every section and state of America. It is the effort of American Negroes to secure for themselves the full blessings of American life. Their cause is our cause too. Because it is not just Negroes, but really it is all of us, who must overcome the crippling legacy of bigotry and injustice. And, we shall overcome.

As a man whose roots go deeply into Southern soil I know how agonizing racial feelings are. I know how difficult it is to reshape attitudes and the structure of our society. But a century has passed, more than a hundred years, since the Negro was freed. And he is not fully free tonight. . . .

The time of justice has now come. I tell you that I believe sincerely that no force can hold it back. It is right in the eyes of man and God that it should come. And when it does, I think that the day will brighten the lives of every American. For Negroes are not the only victims. How many white children have gone uneducated, how many white families have lived in stark poverty, how many white lives have been scarred by fear because we wasted our energy and substance to maintain the barriers of hatred and terror?

So I say to all of you here and to all in the nation tonight, that those who appeal to you to hold on to the past do so at the cost of denying you your future. This great, rich, restless country can offer opportunity and education and hope to all—all black and white, all North and South, sharecropper, and city dweller. These are the enemies—poverty, ignorance, disease. They are enemies, not our fellow man, not our neighbor, and these enemies too . . . we shall overcome. . . .

This is one nation. What happens in Selma or in Cincinnati is a matter of legitimate concern to every American. But let each of us look within our hearts and our own communities, and let each of us put our shoulder to the wheel to root out injustice wherever it exists.

The real hero of this struggle is the American Negro. His actions and protests, his courage to risk safety and even to risk his life, have awakened the conscience of this nation. His demonstrations have been designed to call our attention to injustice, designed to provoke change, designed to stir reform. He has called upon us to make good the promise of America. And who among us can say that we would have made the same progress if not for his persistent bravery, and his faith in democracy.

Source: Public Papers of the Presidents of the United States, Lyndon B. Johnson, 1965 (Washington, D.C.: GPO, 1966).

Document 12
MALCOLM X, "ADDRESS TO A MEETING IN NEW YORK" (1964)

Malcolm X, the most prominent black nationalist in America in the post–World War II era, was born Malcolm Little in Omaha, Nebraska, in 1925. In 1965, just short of his fortieth birthday, he was assassinated at the Audubon Ballroom in Harlem. He lived a fascinating and turbulent life. When Malcolm was a child, his father was allegedly killed by the Black Legionnaires, a Michigan-based white supremacist group. In his teens, he got hooked on narcotics, zoot suits, and a life of crime. At age twenty-one he was arrested on burglary charges and sent to jail. While in prison, Malcolm X learned of Elijah Muhammad and the Nation of Islam, which he joined shortly thereafter. Following his release from jail, he became a minister in Elijah Muhammad's church, converting hundreds to Islam and enthralling thousands more with his powerful sermons. Following a trip to Mecca, however, Malcolm X broke with Elijah Muhammad, arguing that his mentor's brand of antiwhite Islam was incorrect. As the following speech suggests, however, Malcolm X continued to condemn white institutions and cultural domination and remained a militant critic of society. Even after his death, Malcolm X gained an ever-increasing following, especially among young northern blacks.

Friends and enemies, tonight I hope that we can have a little fireside chat with as few sparks as possible tossed around. Especially because of the very explosive condition that the world is in today. Sometimes, when a person's house is on fire and someone comes in yelling fire, instead of the person who is awakened by the yell being thankful, he makes the mistake of charging the one who awakened him with having set the fire. I hope that this little conversation tonight about the black revolution won't cause many of you to accuse us of igniting it when you find it at your doorstep.

I'm still a Muslim, that is, my religion is still Islam. I still believe that there is no god but Allah and that Mohammed is the apostle of Allah. That just happens to be my personal religion. But in the capacity which I am functioning in today, I have no intention of mixing my religion with the problems of 22,000,000 black people in this country. . . .

I'm still a Muslim, but I'm also a nationalist, meaning that my political philosophy is black nationalism, my economic philosophy is black nationalism, my social philosophy is black nationalism. And when I say that this philosophy is black nationalism, to me this means that the political philosophy for black nationalism is that which is designed to encourage our people, the black people, to gain complete control over the politics and the politicians of our own people.

Our economic philosophy is that we should gain economic control over the economy of our own community, the businesses and the other things which create employment so that we can provide jobs for our own people instead of having to picket and boycott and beg someone else for a job.

And, in short, our social philosophy means that we feel that it is time to get together among our own kind and eliminate the evils that are destroying the moral fiber of our society, like drug addiction, drunkenness, adultery that leads to an abundance of bastard children, welfare problems. We believe that we should lift the level or the standard of our own society to a higher level wherein we will be satisfied and then not inclined toward pushing ourselves into other societies where we are not wanted. . . .

Just as we can see that all over the world one of the main problems facing the West is race, likewise here in America today, most of your Negro leaders as well as the whites agree that 1964 itself appears to be one of the most explosive years yet in the history of America on the racial front, on the racial scene. Not only is the racial explosion probably to take place in America, but all of the ingredients for this racial explosion in America to blossom into a world-wide racial explosion present themselves right here in front of us. America's racial powder keg, in short, can actually fuse or ignite a world-wide powder keg.

And whites in this country who are still complacent when they see the possibilities of racial strife getting out of hand and you are complacent simply because you think you outnumber the racial minority in this country, what you have to bear in mind is wherein you might outnumber us in this country, you don't outnumber us all over the earth.

Any kind of racial explosion that takes place in this country today, in 1964, is not a racial explosion that can be confined to the shores of America. It is a racial explosion that can ignite the racial powder keg that exists all over the planet that we call the earth. Now I think that nobody would disagree that the dark masses of Africa and Asia and Latin America are already seething with bitterness, animosity, hostility, unrest, and impatience with the racial intolerance that they themselves have experienced at the hands of the white West.

And just as they themselves have the ingredients of hostility toward the West in general, here we also have 22,000,000 African-Americans, black, brown, red, and yellow people in this country who are also seething with bitterness and impatience and hostility and animosity at the racial intoler-ance not only of the white West but of white America in particular. . . .

1964 will be America's hottest year; her hottest year yet; a year of much racial violence and much racial bloodshed. But it won't be blood that's going to flow only on one side. The new generation of black people that have grown up in this country during recent years are already forming the opinion, and it's just opinion, that if there is to be bleeding, it should be reciprocal—bleeding on both sides. . . .

So today, when the black man starts reaching out for what America says are his rights, the black man feels that he is within his rights—when he becomes the victim of brutality by those who are depriving him of his rights—to do whatever [is] necessary to protect himself. . . .

There are 22,000,000 African-Americans who are ready to fight for independence right here. When I say fight for independence right here, I don't mean any non-violent fight, or turn-the-other-cheek fight. Those days are gone. Those days are over.

If George Washington didn't get independence for this country non-violently, and if Patrick Henry didn't come up with a non-violent statement, and you taught me to look upon them as patriots and heroes, then it's time for you to realize that I have studied your books well. . . .

Every time a black man gets ready to defend himself some Uncle Tom tries to tell us, how can you win? That's Tom talking. Don't listen to him. This is the first thing we hear: the odds are against you. You're dealing with black people who don't care anything about odds. . . .

Again I go back to the people who founded and secured the independence of this country from the colonial power of England. . . . They didn't care about the odds. . . .

Our people are becoming more politically mature. . . . The Negro can see that he holds the balance of power in this country politically. It is he who puts in office the one who gets in office. Yet when the Negro helps that person get in office the Negro gets nothing in return. . . .

The present administration, the Democratic administration, has been there for four years. Yet no meaningful legislation has been passed by them that proposes to benefit black people in this country, despite the fact that in the House they have 267 Democrats and only 177 Republicans. . . . In the Senate there are 67 Democrats and only 33 Republicans. The Democrats control two thirds of the government and it is the Negroes who put them in a position to control the government. Yet they give the Negroes nothing in return but a few handouts in the form of appointments that are only used as window-dressing to make it appear that the problem is being solved.

No, something is wrong. And when these black people wake up and find out for real the trickery and the treachery that has been heaped upon us you are going to have revolution. And when I say revolution I don't mean that stuff they were talking about last year about "We Shall Overcome." . . .

And the only way without bloodshed that this [revolution] can be brought about is that the black man has to be given full use of the ballot in every one of the 50 states. But if the black man doesn't get the ballot, then you are going to be faced with another man who forgets the ballot and starts using the bullet. . . .

So you have a people today who not only know what they want, but also know what they are supposed to have. And they themselves are clearing the way for another generation that is coming up that not only will know what it wants and know what it should have, but also will be ready and willing to do whatever is necessary to see what they should have materializes immediately. Thank you.

Source: Peter B. Levy, ed., *Let Freedom Ring: A Documentary History of the Modern Civil Rights Movement* (Westport, Conn.: Praeger, 1992), 174–77.

Document 13
FROM STOKELY CARMICHAEL,
"WHAT WE WANT" (1966)

In the second half of the 1960s a large segment of the civil rights movement, including SNCC, adopted a radical tone and endorsed the goal of "black power." Stokely Carmichael, a veteran of the freedom rides and as of 1966 the chair of SNCC, first popularized this term during the "Meredith" or "March Against Fear" protest in Mississippi in 1966. In a speech delivered in Greenwood, Mississippi, Carmichael asked the crowd, "What do we want?," to which they replied, following the lead of Carmichael and his colleague, Willie Ricks, "Black Power!" Almost overnight, this slogan, broadcast across the nation by the media, replaced "We Shall Overcome" and "Freedom Now" as the movement's motto.

Much of the press presumed that black power stood for violence and racial separatism. In *Black Power*, co-written with Charles Hamilton, and in the following article, published in the *New York Review of Books*, however, Carmichael presented a more nuanced definition of the term, arguing that black power advocates largely wanted the same things whites had and took for granted—namely, political and economic power and pride in their heritage. For example, just as Irish Americans historically had supported Irish American candidates for political office, Carmichael proposed that African Americans should support African American candidates. In spite of Carmichael's entreaties in these works, the public continued to associate black power with violence and reverse racism.

One of the tragedies of the struggle against racism is that up to now there has been no national organization which could speak to the growing militancy of young black people in the urban ghetto. There has been only a civil rights movement, whose tone of voice was adapted to an audience of liberal whites. It served as a sort of buffer zone between them and angry young blacks. None of its so-called leaders could go into a rioting community and be listened to. In a sense, I blame ourselves—together with the mass media—for what has happened in Watts, Harlem, Chicago, Cleveland and Omaha. Each time the people in those cities saw Martin Luther King get slapped, they became angry; when they saw four little black girls bombed to death, they were angrier; and when nothing happened, they were steaming. We had nothing to offer that they could see, except to go out and be beaten again. We helped to build their frustration. . . .

An organization which claims to speak for the needs of a community—as does the Student Nonviolent Coordinating Committee—must speak in the tone of that community, not as somebody else's buffer zone. This is the significance of black power as a slogan. For once, black people are going to use the words they want to use—not just the words whites want to hear. And they will do this no matter how often the press tries to stop the use of the slogan by equating it with racism or separatism. . . .

Black power can be clearly defined for those who do not attach the fears of white America to their questions about it. We should begin with the basic fact that black Americans have two problems: they are poor and they are black. All other problems arise from this two-sided reality: lack of education, the so-called apathy of black men. Any program to end racism must address itself to that double reality. . . .

The concept of "black power" is not a recent or isolated phenomenon: It has grown out of the ferment of agitation and activity by different people and organizations in many black communities over the years. Our last year of work in Alabama added a new concrete possibility. In Lowndes county, for example, black power will mean that if a Negro is elected sheriff, he can end police brutality. If a black man is elected tax assessor, he can collect and channel funds for the building of better roads and schools serving black people—thus advancing the move from political power into the economic arena. In such areas as Lowndes, where black men have a majority, they will attempt to exercise control. This is what they seek: control. Where Negroes lack a majority, black power means proper representation and sharing of control. It means the creation of power bases from which black people can work to change statewide or nationwide patterns of oppression through pressure from strength—instead of weakness. Politically, black power means what it has always meant to SNCC: the coming-together of black people to elect representatives and *to force those representatives to speak to their needs*. It does not mean merely putting black faces into office. A man or woman who is black and from the slums cannot be automatically expected to speak to the needs of black people. Most of the black politicians we see around the country today are not what SNCC means by black power. The power must be that of a community, and emanate from there. . . .

Ultimately, the economic foundations of this country must be shaken if black people are to control their lives. The colonies of the United States—and this includes the black ghettos within its borders, north and south—must be liberated. For a century, this nation has been like an octopus of exploitation, its tentacles stretching from Mississippi and Harlem to South America, the Middle East, southern Africa, and Vietnam; the form of exploitation varies from area to area but the essential result has been the same—a powerful few have been maintained and enriched at the expense of the poor and voiceless colored masses. This pattern must be broken. As its grip loosens here and there around the world, the hopes of black Americans become more realistic. For racism to die, a totally different America must be born.

This is what the white society does not wish to face; this is why the society prefers to talk about integration. But integration speaks not at all to the problem of poverty, only to the problem of blackness. Integration today means the man who "makes it," leaving his black brothers behind in the ghetto as fast as his new sports car will take him. It has no relevance to the Harlem wino or to the cotton-picker making three dollars a day. As a lady I know in Alabama once said, "the food that Ralph Bunche eats doesn't fill my stomach."

Integration, moreover, speaks to the problem of blackness in a despicable way. As a goal, it has been based on complete acceptance of the fact that *in order to have* a decent house or education, blacks must move into a white neighborhood or send their children to a white school. This reinforces, among both black and white, the idea that "white" is automatically better and "black" is by definition inferior. This is why integration is a subterfuge for the maintenance of white supremacy. It allows the nation to focus on a handful of Southern children who get into white schools, at great price, and to ignore the 94 per cent who are left behind in unimproved all-black schools. Such situations will not change until black people have power—to control their own school boards, in this case. Then Negroes become equal in a way that means something, and integration ceases to be a one-way street. Then integration doesn't mean draining skills and energies from the ghetto into white neighborhoods; then it can mean white people moving from Beverly Hills into Watts, white people joining the Lowndes County Freedom organization. Then integration becomes relevant. . . .

To most whites, black power seems to mean that the Mau Mau are coming to the suburbs at night. The Mau Mau are coming, and whites must stop them.

Articles appear about plots to "get Whitey," creating an atmosphere in which "law and order must be maintained." Once again, responsibility is shifted from the oppressor to the oppressed. Other whites chide, "Don't forget—you're only 10 per cent of the population: if you get too smart, we'll wipe you out." If they are liberals, they complain, "What about me?—don't you want my help any more?" These are people supposedly concerned about black Americans, but today they think first of themselves, of their feelings of rejection. Or they admonish, "You can't get anywhere without coalitions," when there is in fact no group at present with whom to form a coalition in which blacks will not be absorbed or betrayed. Or they accuse us of "polarizing the races" by our calls for black unity, when the true responsibility for polarization lies with whites who will not accept their responsibility as the majority power for making the democratic process work.

White America will not face the problem of color, the reality of it. The well-intended say: "We're all human, everybody is really decent, we must forget color." But color cannot be "forgotten" until its weight is recognized and dealt with. White America will not acknowledge that the ways in which this country sees itself are contradicted by being black—and always have been. Whereas most of the people who settled this country came here for freedom or for economic opportunity, blacks were brought here to be slaves. When the Lowndes County Freedom Organization chose the black panther as its symbol, it was christened by the press "the Black Panther Party"—but the Alabama Democratic Party, whose symbol is a rooster, has never been called the White Cock Party. No one ever talked about "white power" because power in this country *is* white. All this adds up to more than merely identifying a group phenomenon by some catchy name or adjective. The furor over the black panther reveals the problems that white America has with color and sex; the furor over "black power" reveals how deep racism runs and the great fear which is attached to it. . . .

From birth, black people are told a set of lies about themselves. We are told that we are lazy—yet I drive through the Delta area of Mississippi and watch black people picking cotton in the hot sun for fourteen hours. We are told, "If you work hard, you'll succeed"—but if that were true, black people would own this country. We are oppressed because we are black—not because we are ignorant, not because we are lazy, not because we're stupid (and got good rhythm), but because we're black. . . .

The need for psychological equality is the reason why SNCC today believes that blacks must organize in the black community. Only black people can convey the revolutionary idea that black people are able to do things themselves. Only they can help create in the community an aroused and continuing black consciousness that will provide the basis for political strength. In the past, white allies have furthered white supremacy without the whites involved realizing it—or wanting it, I think. Black people must do things for themselves; they must get poverty money they will control and spend themselves, they must conduct tutorial programs themselves so that black children can identify with black people. This is one reason Africa has such importance. The reality of black men ruling their own nations gives blacks elsewhere a sense of possibility, of power, which they do not now have.

This does not mean we don't welcome help, or friends. But we want the right to decide whether anyone is, in fact, our friend. In the past, black Americans have been almost the only people whom everybody and his momma could jump up and call their friends. We have been tokens, symbols, objects—as I was in high school to many young whites, who liked having "a Negro friend." We want to decide who is our friend. . . . We will not be isolated from any group or nation except by our own choice. We cannot have the oppressor telling the oppressed how to rid themselves of the oppressor. . . .

We hope to see, eventually, a coalition between poor blacks and poor whites. That is the only coalition which seems acceptable to us, and we see such a coalition as the major internal instrument of change in American society. . . . It is purely academic today to talk about bringing poor blacks and whites together, but the job of creating a poor-white community power block must be attempted. The main responsibility for it falls upon whites.

Source: *New York Review of Books*, September 26, 1966.

Document 14
FROM *REPORT OF THE NATIONAL ADVISORY COMMISSION ON CIVIL DISORDERS* (1968)

During the mid- and late 1960s, hundreds of American communities experienced racial riots. Less than two weeks after President Lyndon B. Johnson signed the Voting Rights Act into law, Watts, the ghetto area in Los Angeles, erupted into flames. In 1967 Newark and Detroit exploded into some of the worst rioting in the nation's history. President Johnson appointed the National Advisory Commission on Civil Disorders to investigate the causes of the riots and to recommend measures to guard against more disruption and loss of life and property. Headed by Illinois governor Otto Kerner—the commission became known as the Kerner Commission—and staffed by many other prominent figures, most notably Mayor John Lindsay of New York City, the body concluded that America was dividing into two separate societies, one white and one black. The commission also argued that the riots grew out of the social and economic conditions of the urban black ghetto, itself a product of white racism, and called for dramatic federal expenditures and programs to alleviate these conditions.

Most Republican politicians harshly criticized the commission's findings and recommendations, arguing that Kerner and his associates were blaming the victims—whites—for the riots, while rewarding the criminals—the black rioters. Richard Nixon and Ronald Reagan, for example, proclaimed that the federal government had spent enough money, adding that the government needed to coddle the militants less and enforce the law more. Shell-shocked by the Vietnam War, the antiwar movement, and the riots themselves, President Johnson did not attempt to rally support for the commission's findings and recommendations.

The summer of 1967 again brought racial disorders to American cities, and with them shock, fear and bewilderment to the nation.

The worst came during a two-week period in July, first in Newark and then in Detroit. Each set off a chain reaction in neighboring communities.

On July 28, 1967, the President of the United States established this Commission and directed us to answer three basic questions: What happened? Why did it happen? What can be done to prevent it from happening again?

To respond to these questions, we have undertaken a broad range of studies and investigations. We have visited the riot cities; we have heard many witnesses; we have sought counsel of experts across the country.

This is our basic conclusion: *Our nation is moving toward two societies, one black, one white—separate and unequal.*

Reaction to last summer's disorders has quickened the movement and deepened the division. Discrimination and segregation have long permeated much of American life; they now threaten the future of every American. The deepening racial division is not inevitable. The movement apart can be reversed. Choice is still possible. Our principal task is to define that choice and to press for a national resolution.

To pursue the present course will involve the continuing polarization of the American community and ultimately, the destruction of basic democratic values. The alternative is not blind repression or capitulation to lawlessness. It is the realization of common opportunities for all within a single society.

This alternative will require a commitment to national action—compassionate, massive and sustained, backed by the resources of the most powerful and the richest nation on this earth. From every American it will require new attitudes, new understanding, and, above all, new will.

The vital needs of the nation must be met; hard choices must be made, and, if necessary, new taxes enacted.

Violence cannot build a better society. Disruption and disorder nourish repression, not justice. They strike at the freedom of every citizen. The community cannot—it will not—tolerate coercion and mob rule. Violence and destruction must be ended—in the streets of the ghetto and in the lives of people.

Segregation and poverty have created in the racial ghetto a destructive environment totally unknown to most white Americans.

What white Americans have never fully understood—but what the Negro can never forget—is that the white society is deeply implicated in the ghetto. White institutions created it, white institutions maintain it, and white society condones it. . . .

It is time to make good the promises of American democracy to all citizens—urban and rural, black and white, Spanish-surname, American Indian, and every minority group.

Source: National Advisory Commission on Civil Disorders, "Report." (Washington, D.C.: GPO, 1968), p. 1–2.

Document 15
ARTHUR FLETCHER, "REMARKS ON THE PHILADELPHIA PLAN" (1969)

As the twentieth century draws to a close, the American public perceives affirmative action as the most enduring legacy of the civil rights movement. But where and how affirmative action originated remains shrouded in myth and half-truths. Affirmative action was not one of the central goals of Martin Luther King, Jr., SNCC, CORE, or for that matter the NAACP. Conservative proclamations to the contrary, neither was it the result of a liberal cabal. On the contrary, affirmative action as public policy was most fully developed in 1969 by members of the Nixon administration, most specifically via the Philadelphia Plan.

Unlike the desegregation of schools, for which a single document, the *Brown* decision, stands out, the same cannot be stated for affirmative action. No single court case, speech, law, or article enunciated the goals of this policy. Nonetheless, the following remarks, made by Assistant Secretary of Labor Arthur Fletcher in June 1969 on the signing of the Philadelphia Plan, help us understand the policy. The plan aimed at increasing the number of minority construction workers on federally funded projects in Philadelphia. It became a model for affirmative action plans in other regions and industries, both in the private and public sectors. As Fletcher's boss, Secretary of Labor George Shultz, insisted, the plan did not allow for quotas or the lowering of standards. While the particulars of the Philadelphia Plan were never reviewed by the Supreme Court, in 1978 the Court upheld,

5–4, in the case *University of California Regents* v. *Bakke*, the constitutionality of affirmative action in principle, while at the same time ruling 5–4 against the specific program implemented by the medical school at the University of California at Davis, because it had established quotas.

It is most appropriate that a plan for equal employment opportunity should bear the title "Philadelphia Plan" and should be inaugurated in this city. Philadelphia and its people have a great heritage of freedom which is rich in historical events known to every school child throughout the Nation. It was here in this city that the Declaration of Independence was signed and it was here freedom's ring was heard for the first time. It was here that the Constitution of our country guaranteeing freedom for all was drafted.

A vital freedom guaranteed by our Constitution is the right to equal participation in the economic processes of our society. This freedom has been denied to groups within our country. This denial of fundamental participation in the advantages of capitalism has even been institutionalized in our society.

The Federal Government cannot contribute to this denial of rights through blind acceptance of customs and traditions which eliminate the contributions and talents of groups of people. *The Federal Government has an obligation* to see that every citizen has an equal chance at the most basic freedom of all—*the right to succeed.*

Millions of dollars at every level of Government are being spent to correct the symptoms of the denial of this right in our society but almost no effort has been made in the past to affect this problem at its source—where Federal dollars enter the area economy.

These Federal dollars—part of which are Black, Puerto Rican, Mexican-American, and others—enter [the] local economy primarily through Federal contracts. Once these dollars pass the "Gateway" of contracting procedures—the Federal Government has no further control over them. Through the "multiplier" effect experienced by imported money in the regional economy and the existence of institutionalized segregation—the Federal Government can be pictured as contributing to the denial of the right to succeed for substantial groups of people. No amount of money spent by whatever level of Government to correct this situation can be justified after the fact.

The most fair, economical and effective point to address this problem is at the beginning—the time of contracting.

My office is dedicated to this proposition. I view this concept as being in harmony with the highest principles guaranteed by our Constitution and the sound economic cornerstones of our capitalist system. It is good business for the Government, for industry, for labor and for all the people of this country.

With this background firmly in mind, I now want to tell you about the Philadelphia Plan.

The Philadelphia Plan applies to all Federal and federally-assisted construction contracts for projects in excess of $500,000. The plan at the present time is to apply to the Philadelphia area including Bucks, Chester, Delaware, Montgomery, and Philadelphia counties, and goes into effect on July 18, 1969. It is also anticipated that the plan will be put into effect in all the major cities across the Nation as soon as possible.

The plan is aimed at increasing minority participation in designated trades. These trades are:

Iron workers

Plumbers, pipefitters

Steam fitters

Sheetmetal workers

Electrical workers

Roofers and water proofers

Elevation construction workers

The named trades have been singled out for special emphasis because in the past these trades, at least in the Philadelphia area, have been operating without significant minority participation.

Within the plan's presently established geographical boundaries, the Office of Federal Contract Compliance will, with the assistance of representatives from the Federal contracting agencies, determine definite standards for minority participation in each of the trades named and to be used on a construction project. The standard for each trade will be included in the invitation for bids or other solicitation used for every Federally-involved construction contract. The standards will specify the range of minority manpower utilization expected for each of the named trades and such standards must be maintained during the performance of the construction contract.

The standards are to be determined in each instance by applying the following major criteria:

1. The current extent of minority group participation in the trade
2. The availability of minority group persons for employment in such trade
3. The need for training programs in the area and/or the need to assure demand for those in or from existing training programs
4. The impact of the program upon the existing labor force.

When the contractor submits his bid he must include in the bid an acceptable affirmative action program. This program must contain acceptable goals for the use of minority manpower in each of the trades named within the ranges established in the invitations for bids.

The standards within the ranges established must be met by each of the named trades. There is no provision for combining trades or for obtaining an acceptable cumulative total. Failure to meet an established standard will result in the bid being rejected. In no case will there be any negotiation over provisions of the specific goals submitted by a bidder after opening of bids and prior to the award of the contract.

After the contract is awarded post-award reviews will be conducted to determine whether the goals pledged by the contractor are being met. You may rest assured that these reviews will be thorough, that they will be as frequent as is necessary, and that they will uncover any instances of non-compliance.

Perhaps I should pause at this point to discuss the concept of goals or standards for percentages of minority employees contained in the Philadelphia Plan.

Let me start by saying it would have been much better in our history if segregation had not occurred. But it has. This is a fact. None of us—white or black—like to talk about it—much less admit it. But there it remains—it won't go away.

Segregation didn't occur naturally—it was imposed. In that process quotas, limits, boundaries were set. Sometimes written—sometimes unpublished. But official or informal the effect was total, decisive, and I might add—contrary to the American sense of fair play.

Large segments of our society were oppressed by these rules and institutions until they believed it was impossible to change them. With the increasing wealth of our economic system—the gap—visible to any thinking man—between white and black—employed and unemployed—rich and poor—was growing wider and wider.

Contrary to the poet—hope does *not* spring eternal. Hope—and, therefore, the commitment to try to succeed—is directly related to the chances of success. Impossible dreams are not long sustained by anyone—white or black.

Visible, measurable goals to correct obvious imbalances are essential:

1. To provide targets or incentives for setting objectives and measuring achievements under the contracts.
2. To build the hope of the disadvantaged that the institutions that have suppressed them are willing to commit themselves to their aid and to back their pledges in definitive terms.

Fair play and definitive agreements concerning working conditions, promotional opportunities, ratios of skilled craftsmen to trainees, recognition of bargaining groups and seniority security are now an acceptable and respected tradition in our world of commerce. This was not always so. It developed in stormy times and created great feelings of anxiety, threat and insecurity.

The disadvantaged of this country are now asking that the opportunities achieved through this great movement be extended to include them. No more. No less.

It might be better, admittedly, if specific goals were not required— certainly the black people of America understand taboos—but it is imperative that we face facts and dedicate ourselves to ending discrimination in employment in this country.

What is at stake here is something more than equal employment opportunity in a specific industry or named trades. What is at stake is our basic system of Government itself. Persons in the minority communities must be assured that results can be obtained by working within the framework of the existing governmental system. The Office of Federal Contract Compliance must translate the dreams and ambitions of a large segment of our population into every day realities. This means job opportunities in at least every trade and industry which does substantial business with the Federal Government. The time for speculation has ended and the hour for action is now.

Source: Philadelphia Plan Document, U.S. Department of Labor, No. 6, Department of Labor Library, Washington, D.C.

Glossary of Selected Terms

Affirmative action: Refers to programs in the public and private sectors that seek to overcome the legacy of discrimination against minorities and women. While the courts have upheld the constitutionality of affirmative action, recently they have narrowed the scope and reach of many affirmative action plans.

Birmingham demonstrations: In the spring of 1963, Martin Luther King, Jr., and the SCLC organized massive protests against racial discrimination in Birmingham, Alabama. These protests garnered national attention and sympathy for the civil rights movement and helped convince President Kennedy to call for sweeping civil rights legislation.

Black Muslims: Name given to the Nation of Islam, the black nationalist and religious group founded by W. D. Fard in the 1930s and led by Elijah Muhammad (Elijah Poole). The Black Muslims' most famous adherent was Malcolm X. In 1964 Malcolm X resigned from the Nation of Islam, although he remained a Muslim. Another of the Nation's prominent leaders was Louis Farrakhan (born Louis Eugene Walcott). Following Elijah Muhammad's death in 1975, the Nation split into two factions, with Farrakhan taking control of one of them and Muhammad's son, Imam Warith Deen Muhammad, taking control of the other.

Black Panther Party: In October 1966, Huey P. Newton and Bobby Seale formed the Black Panther Party for Self-Defense in Oakland, California. The Panthers symbolized the rising black power movement of the late 1960s. The Panthers' "Ten Point Program" demanded decent housing and education as well as control of their own communities by African Americans. To this end, the Panthers armed themselves and monitored police activities. The Panthers also organized free breakfast programs for poor children. The Panthers quickly became involved in many confrontations with the police. By the early 1970s, nearly all of its leaders were dead, in jail, or on the run, and the organization dissipated.

Black power: This slogan, popularized in 1966 by Stokely Carmichael, the leader of the Student Nonviolent Coordinating Committee, became the rallying cry of much of the civil rights movement in the late 1960s. Advocates of black power rejected nonviolence and integration, two of the cornerstones of the early movement, in favor of self-defense, self-determination, and cultural, political, and economic unity.

Brown* v. *Board of Education of Topeka, Kansas: Historic 1954 Supreme Court decision that overturned *Plessy* v. *Ferguson* (1896) and ruled that segregation in public education was unconstitutional. The *Brown* decision paved the way for the successful challenge of many other Jim Crow laws and undergirded the civil rights movement, which henceforth argued that the law of the land was on its side.

Busing: In response to the persistence of de facto segregation for many years after the *Brown* decision, the courts ordered the busing or transportation of black and white students within school districts with the aim of achieving racial balance. The Supreme Court upheld the constitutionality of busing in the case of *Swann* v. *Charlotte-Mecklenburg* (1971). From the start, busing proved a very controversial issue, with conservative politicians arguing vociferously against it. White flight to suburban school districts often undermined the use of busing as a means of achieving integrated schools.

Civil Rights Act of 1964: Sweeping racial reform introduced by President Kennedy in 1963 and signed into law by President Johnson in 1964. The act prohibits racial or sexual discrimination against individuals by employers and in restaurants, lodgings, and other public accommodations. The act made it easier for the federal government to compel locales to desegregate public schools and other institutions, such as parks and libraries, and established federal penalties for those who deny or violate an individual's civil rights.

Congress of Racial Equality (CORE): One of the most important civil rights organizations of the 1960s. Led by James Farmer, CORE first received national attention in 1947, when it staged the Journey of Reconciliation. It regained prominence in 1961 with the freedom rides. CORE also took part in numerous nonviolent protests for racial equality throughout the early 1960s. In the mid-1960s, CORE became an advocate of black power. Its membership and influence have since waned. It is now led by Roy Innis.

Council of Federated Organizations (COFO): An umbrella organization that coordinated the efforts of CORE, SNCC, and the NAACP in Mississippi. In 1964 COFO organized Freedom Summer (see below). COFO's most prominent leaders were Robert Moses of SNCC, David Dennis of CORE, and Aaron Henry of the NAACP. COFO disbanded after Freedom Summer.

Freedom rides: Organized by CORE, the freedom rides were one of the most important civil rights protests of the 1960s. Aimed at testing the Kennedy administration's commitment to civil rights, the rides gained much attention and sympathy for the civil rights movement. Black and white riders traveled in a desegregated manner in regions where segregation was the rule. They were viciously attacked by mobs of whites outside Anniston and Birmingham, Alabama.

Freedom Summer: In 1964 close to one thousand volunteers, white and black, journeyed to Mississippi to participate in the largest civil rights campaign of the decade. In the face of death threats, bombings, and church burnings, they staffed "freedom schools" and organized the Mississippi Freedom Democratic Party (MFDP), which challenged the legitimacy of the regular state Democratic Party at the Democratic national convention in Atlantic City. Even though the party rebuffed the MFDP's challenge, the summer crusade had a considerable impact on the state and on the civil rights movement in general, marking a turning point in the history of both.

Great Migration: Between 1920 and 1970, approximately 5.5 million African Americans migrated out of the South, moving mostly to the urban North. Up until 1910, 90 percent of all African Americans lived in the South, primarily in rural areas. By 1970 nearly half lived outside the South and in urban areas. This migration, which was larger than that of any single ethnic group from Europe to the United States, transformed the racial demography and politics of the nation and paved the way for the modern civil rights movement.

Jim Crow: Taken from a character in nineteenth-century minstrel shows, the term "Jim Crow" refers specifically to the segregationist laws and practices that prevailed in the South following Reconstruction until they were done away with by the civil rights reforms of the mid-1960s. More broadly, the term encompasses all customs and laws that discriminated against blacks, from regulations that disenfranchised them in the South to racial covenants and hiring practices that limited their places of residence and the kinds of work they were allowed to do all across the nation.

Kerner Commission. See Race riots.

March on Washington: On August 28, 1963, between 200,000 and 250,000 men and women assembled in Washington, D.C., in the largest mass demonstration up to that time in the nation's history. Organized by a coalition of civil rights figures and groups, the most important of whom were A. Philip Randolph and Bayard Rustin, the march for "jobs and freedom" climaxed with Martin Luther King's "I Have a Dream" speech. While there were some tensions among the participants, the main message of the demonstration was one of unity.

Mississippi Freedom Democratic Party (MFDP). See Freedom Summer.

Montgomery bus boycott: Following the arrest of Rosa Parks for refusing to give up her bus seat to a white man, the African American community of Montgomery, Alabama, organized a boycott of the city's segregated buses. Initially planned as a one-day protest, the boycott, led by Martin Luther King, Jr., and Ralph Abernathy, lasted for 381 days. Following the Supreme Court's ruling in the case of *Browder* v. *Gayle*, which declared Montgomery's segregationist transportation ordinance unconstitutional, Montgomery's blacks returned to the buses, riding in a desegregated manner. The boycott signified the dawn of a new stage in the struggle for racial equality.

National Association for the Advancement of Colored People (NAACP): Founded in 1909 by W.E.B. Du Bois and several other black and white activists, the NAACP is the biggest and best-known civil rights organization in the United States. During the middle decades of the twentieth century, the NAACP won a series of suits, the most significant being *Brown* v. *Board of Education* (1954). It played a seminal role in getting civil rights legislation passed and pressured American presidents to implement racial reforms. Under the direction of Roy Wilkins, the NAACP tended to avoid direct-action protest, although it provided invaluable legal and financial help to those who engaged in such action in the 1960s.

National Urban League (NUL): The National Urban League, founded in 1911, is one of the most prominent civil rights organization in the nation, second only to the NAACP. Headed by Whitney Young during the 1960s, the Urban League tended to work behind the scenes, focusing especially on increasing economic opportunities for African Americans and lobbying for federal and state civil rights legislation.

Nation of Islam. See **Black Muslims.**

Open (Fair) Housing Act: The last major federal civil rights legislation of the 1960s. Legislation aimed at prohibiting racial discrimination in the renting or selling of housing failed to gain enough support in Congress in 1966 and 1967 for passage. Following the assassination of Martin Luther King, Jr., and a spate of race riots, however, the act was passed by Congress and Senate and signed into law by President Johnson in 1968.

Philadelphia Plan. See **Affirmative action**.

Plessy v. *Ferguson*. See *Brown* v. *Board of Education of Topeka, Kansas.*

Poor People's Campaign: In 1968 Martin Luther King, Jr., and the SCLC organized the Poor People's Campaign, an assemblage of protesters in Washington, D.C. Shortly before the campaign began, King was assassinated in Memphis, Tennessee. Ralph Abernathy, King's closest aide, carried on with the campaign nonetheless. Beginning in early May 1968, protesters constructed a shantytown known as Resurrection City not far from the Capitol. Beset by torrential rains and overshadowed by the tumultuous political events of 1968, however, the campaign dissipated without accomplishing much.

Race riots: From 1964 through 1969, the United States experienced the worst spate of rioting in its history. Riots erupted in Harlem in July 1964 and reached a new level of destruction in the summer of 1965, when Watts, the ghetto of Los Angeles, exploded. During the "long, hot summers" of 1966 and 1967, racial rioting occurred in many large urban areas, including Cleveland, Milwaukee, Chicago, Newark, and Detroit, the latter being the site of the most destructive riot in modern American history. In 1968, following Martin Luther King, Jr.'s assassination, more rioting took place. Often sparked by incidents or rumors of police brutality, the riots were characterized by looting, arson, and the death of innocent civilians. Black radicals often termed the riots rebellions. The Kerner Commission concluded that white racism caused the riots and called for massive federal spending to address the social and economic problems of the ghetto. Such programs, however, were not forthcoming, as the riots tended to produce white backlash rather than support for more federal intervention.

Segregation. See **Jim Crow.**

Selma protests: In 1965 Martin Luther King, Jr., and the SCLC organized massive protests in Selma, Alabama, culminating in a mass march from Selma to Montgomery. Shortly thereafter federal voting rights legislation was enacted (see below). Beginning in mid-January 1965, the Selma protests went through several stages. While the protests in Selma helped produce one of the most concrete reforms of the era, they also exacerbated tensions between black radicals and black and white moderates.

Sit-ins: On February 1, 1960, four black students from North Carolina Agricultural and Technical College sought to be served at Woolworth's in Greensboro, North Carolina. Because they were black, they were refused service. Rather than leaving, however, they continued to sit on their lunch counter stools. Hence the name sit-ins. Their action sparked a wave of sit-ins that swept across the South, involving an estimated seventy thousand individuals and over one hundred communities from Nashville, Tennessee, to Tallahassee, Florida. The sit-ins signaled the birth of a new militancy that challenged every aspect of segregation, and led to the formation of the Student Nonviolent Coordinating Committee.

Southern Christian Leadership Conference (SCLC): Following the Montgomery bus boycott, Martin Luther King, Jr., and Ralph Abernathy established the SCLC. Comprised largely of southern black ministers, most of them Baptists, and officially directed by Wyatt Walker, the SCLC was, by and large, King's organization. In 1957 it staged a Prayer Pilgrimage that drew twenty-five thousand in Washington, D.C. Following a setback in Albany, Georgia, it staged Project C in Birmingham, Alabama, which helped prompt President Kennedy to propose civil rights legislation. In 1965 it organized mass protests in Selma, which led to the enactment of the Voting Rights Act. Two years later it orchestrated anti-slum and open-housing demonstrations in Chicago,

Illinois, and, in 1968, in the wake of King's assassination, it sponsored the Poor People's Campaign in Washington, D.C. More radical than the NAACP and more moderate than SNCC or CORE, the SCLC stuck to King's goal of achieving an integrated and racially just society through nonviolent means.

Student Nonviolent Coordinating Committee (SNCC): Established by black student activists in the wake of the sit-ins, the Student Nonviolent Coordinating Committee, or SNCC (pronounced Snick), was in many ways the heart of the civil rights movement. With James Forman serving as its executive director, SNCC attracted hundreds of committed young men and women, black and white, who spread out across the South to organize a decentralized community-based movement, from McComb, Mississippi, and Albany, Georgia, to Danville, Virginia, and Cambridge, Maryland. While it had its share of differences with King and the NAACP, it initially cooperated with them. Over time, many of SNCC's members grew increasingly disillusioned with liberalism. In 1965 and 1966, SNCC purged whites from its ranks, elected Stokely Carmichael as its chair, and endorsed the goal of black power. In the late 1960s SNCC broke into rival factions and collapsed.

Voting Rights Act of 1965: The Voting Rights Act, which speedily went through Congress following the protests in Selma, Alabama, gives the federal government the power to ensure that millions of African Americans can register and vote. The act prohibits educational requirements for voting in states or districts where less than half of the voting-age population had been registered as of November 1, 1964, allows the Justice Department to send federal registrars to recalcitrant areas, and provides for oversight of voting procedures and reforms by the federal judiciary. The Supreme Court upheld the Voting Rights Act in 1966. Originally enacted with a ten-year life span, Congress has renewed the Voting Rights Act several times.

Annotated Bibliography

Abernathy, Ralph David. *And the Walls Came Tumbling Down: An Autobiography*. New York: Harper & Row, 1989. Autobiography of the civil rights years written by one of its most prominent activists and Martin Luther King, Jr.'s closest ally.

Anderson, Alan B., and George W. Pickering. *Confronting the Color Line: The Broken Promise of the Civil Rights Movement in Chicago*. Athens: University of Georgia Press, 1986. Examination of the civil rights movement in Chicago, before, during, and after King's efforts there.

Anderson, Jervis. *Bayard Rustin: Troubles I've Seen. A Biography*. New York: HarperCollins, 1997. Biography of key civil rights activist and strategist who served as one of Martin Luther King, Jr.'s advisors.

Bartley, Numan V. *The Rise of Massive Resistance: Race and Politics in the South during the 1950s*. Baton Rouge: Louisiana State University Press, 1969. Classic study of southern reaction to the civil rights movement.

Bennett, Lerone, Jr. *Before the Mayflower: A History of Black America*. 5th ed. New York: Penguin, 1982. Overview of African American history from a black historian's perspective.

Blaustein, Albert, and Robert Zangrando, eds. *Civil Rights and The American Negro: A Documentary History*. New York: Simon & Schuster, 1968. Documentary overview of civil rights law and struggle for equal rights.

Bloom, Jack M. *Class, Race, and the Civil Rights Movement*. Bloomington: Indiana University Press, 1987. Theoretical exploration of the class dimensions of the civil rights movement.

Branch, Taylor. *Parting the Waters: America in the King Years, 1954–1963*. New York: Simon & Schuster, 1988. Pulitzer Prize–winning life-and-times study of King and civil rights; first of two projected volumes.

Brauer, Carl M. *John F. Kennedy and the Second Reconstruction*. New York: Columbia University Press, 1977. Monograph on the civil rights policies of the Kennedy administration.

Brown, Elaine. *A Taste of Power: A Black Woman's Story*. New York: Doubleday, 1994. Autobiographical account of the Black Panther Party.

Burk, Robert F. *The Eisenhower Administration and Black Civil Rights*. Monograph on the civil rights policies of the Eisenhower administration. Knoxville: University of Tennessee Press, 1984.

Burner, Eric R. *And Gently He Shall Lead Them: Robert Parris Moses and Civil Rights in Mississippi*. New York: New York University Press, 1994. Brief biography of SNCC stalwart.

Carawan, Guy, and Candie Caravan. *We Shall Overcome*. New York: Oak Publishers, 1963. Collection of freedom songs compiled by Highlander Folk School musical leader.

Carson, Clayborne. *In Struggle: SNCC and the Black Awakening of the 1960s*. Cambridge, Mass.: Harvard University Press, 1981. Award-winning study of SNCC.

Chafe, William. *Civilities and Civil Rights: Greensboro, North Carolina, and the Black Struggle for Freedom*. New York: Oxford University Press, 1980. Rich case study of the civil rights movement in the birthplace of the sit-ins.

Chappell, David L. *Inside Agitators: White Southerners in the Civil Rights Movement*. Baltimore: Johns Hopkins University Press, 1994. Scholarly examination of the role played by whites on the local and national level in the civil rights movement.

Cleaver, Eldridge. *Soul on Ice*. New York: Random House, 1968. Provocative essays written by Black Panther Party's minister of culture.

Colburn, David. *Racial Change and Community Crisis: St. Augustine, Florida, 1877–1980*. New York: Columbia University Press, 1985. Exploration of race relations in a single southern community.

Crawford, Vicki L., Jacqueline Anne Rouse, and Barbara Woods, eds. *Women in the Civil Rights Movement: Trailblazers and Torchbearers, 1941–1965*. Bloomington: Indiana University Press, 1993. Wide-ranging collection of essays on women and the civil rights movement.

Dittmer, John. *Local People: The Struggle for Civil Rights in Mississippi*. Urbana: University of Illinois Press, 1994. Detailed regional study of the civil rights movement.

Eagles, Charles, ed. *The Civil Rights Movement in America*. Jackson: University Press of Mississippi, 1986. Solid collection of essays written by a number of the movement's leading scholars.

Eastland, Terry. *Ending Affirmative Action: The Case for Colorblind Justice*. New York: Basic Books, 1996. Good example of argument for ending affirmative action written by a leading conservative journalist.

Egerton, John. *Speak Now Against the Day: The Generation before the Civil Rights Movement*. New York: Alfred A. Knopf, 1994. Study of race relations and southern progressives prior to *Brown*.

Evans, Sara. *Personal Politics: The Roots of Women's Liberation in the Civil Rights Movement and the New Left*. New York: Vintage, 1980. Study of relationship between the women's and civil rights movement.

Farley, Reynolds, and Walter R. Allen. *The Color Line and the Quality of Life in America*. New York: Oxford University Press, 1987. Quantitatively oriented examination of status of black Americans since the civil rights years.

Fine, Sidney. *Violence in the Model City: The Cavanaugh Administration, Race Relations and the Detroit Race Riot of 1967*. Ann Arbor: University of Michigan Press, 1989. Case study of the worst race riot in the history of the United States.

Foner, Philip S., ed. *The Black Panthers Speak*. Philadelphia: J. B. Lippincott, 1970. Collection of significant writings and speeches by Black Panther Party members.

Forman, James. *The Making of Black Revolutionaries*. New York: Macmillan, 1972. Autobiographical account of the civil rights years written by SNCC's executive secretary.

Franklin, John Hope, and August Meier, eds. *Black Leaders of the Twentieth Century*. Urbana: University of Illinois Press, 1982. Solid collection of biographies of prominent black leaders, ranging from Booker T. Washington and W.E.B. Du Bois to Martin Luther King, Jr., and Malcolm X.

Franklin, John Hope, and Alfred A. Moss, Jr. *From Slavery to Freedom*. 7th ed. New York: Alfred A. Knopf, 1994. Classic overview of African American history.

Garrow, David J. *Bearing the Cross: Martin Luther King, Jr. and the Southern Christian Leadership Conference*. New York: William Morrow, 1986. Pulitzer Prize–winning biography of King and his civil rights activities.

————. *The FBI and Martin Luther King, Jr.* New York: W. W. Norton, 1981. Provocative exploration of FBI's vendetta against Martin Luther King, Jr.

————. *Protest at Selma: Martin Luther King, Jr. and the Voting Rights Act of 1965*. New Haven: Yale University Press, 1978. Case study of Martin Luther King, Jr.'s successful campaign to win voting rights in 1965.

————. *The Montgomery Bus Boycott and the Women Who Started It: The Memoir of Jo Ann Gibson Robinson*. Knoxville: University of Tennessee Press, 1987. Autobiographical account of the Montgomery bus boycott.

Goldman, Peter. *The Death and Life of Malcolm X.* 2nd ed. Urbana: University of Illinois Press, 1979. One of the first scholarly studies of Malcolm X's life.

Graham, Hugh Davis. *The Civil Rights Era: Origins and Development of a National Policy.* New York: Oxford University Press, 1990. Detailed examination of civil rights policy from Kennedy through Nixon.

Grant, Joanne, ed. *Black Protest: History, Documents and Analyses, 1619 to the Present.* New York: Fawcett, 1968. Contemporary collection of civil rights documents.

Haines, Herbert. *Black Radicals and the Civil Rights Mainstream, 1954–1970.* Knoxville: University of Tennessee Press, 1988. Theoretical examination of the civil rights years.

Hampton, Henry, and Steve Fayer, eds. *Voices of Freedom: An Oral History of the Civil Rights Movement from the 1950s through the 1980s.* New York: Bantam Books, 1990. Oral history compiled by the producer, Henry Hampton, and the screenwriter, Steve Fayer, of the documentary *Eyes on the Prize.*

Harris, Fred, and Roger Wilkins. *Quiet Riots: Race and Poverty in the U.S.: The Kerner Report Twenty Years Later.* New York: Pantheon, 1988. Examination of race relations in the United States twenty years after the climax of the civil rights years.

Hill, Herbert, and James E. Jones, Jr. *Race in America: The Struggle for Equality.* Madison: University of Wisconsin Press, 1993. Collection of essays on race in America, ranging from studies of the legacy of *Brown* to discussions of affirmative action.

Holt, Len. *The Summer that Didn't End.* New York: W. W. Norton, 1965. Sympathetic exploration of Freedom Summer written by a lawyer-activist.

Jaynes, Gerald D., and Robin M. Williams, eds. *Common Destiny: Blacks and American Society.* Washington, D.C.: National Academy Press, 1989. Rich overview of race relations and assessment of the achievements and limitations of the civil rights movement.

King, Martin Luther, Jr. *Stride toward Freedom.* New York: Harper & Row, 1958. King's autobiographical account of the Montgomery bus boycott and his discussion of the nature of the civil rights movement.

King, Mary. *Freedom Song: A Personal Story of the 1960s Civil Rights Movement.* New York: William Morrow, 1987. Autobiographical account of the movement written by a white female SNCC activist.

Kluger, Richard. *Simple Justice: The History of Brown v. Board of Education and Black America's Struggle for Equality.* New York: Random House, 1975. Rich study of the history of the *Brown* decision.

Lawson, Steven. *Running for Freedom: Civil Rights and Black Politics in America since 1941.* New York: McGraw-Hill, 1991. Assessment of the struggle for and the impact of black voting rights.

Lemann, Nicholas. *The Promised Land: The Great Migration and How It Changed America*. New York: Alfred A. Knopf, 1994. Sweeping and provocative exploration of race relations and politics in the twentieth century.

Levy, Peter B., ed. *Let Freedom Ring: A Documentary History of the Modern Civil Rights Movement*. Westport, Conn.: Praeger, 1992. Collection of contemporary writings, speeches, and other documents of the civil rights years.

Lewis, Anthony. *Portrait of a Decade: The Second American Revolution*. New York: Random House, 1964. Overview of early civil rights years written by one of the *New York Times* reporters who covered them.

Lewis, David L. *King: A Critical Biography*. New York: Praeger, 1970. A relatively brief biography of King written by a prominent black historian.

Malcolm X and Alex Haley. *The Autobiography of Malcolm X*. New York: Grove Press, 1966. Classic autobiography that traces the life of the leading black nationalist.

Marable, Manning. *Race, Reform and Rebellion: The Second Reconstruction in Black America, 1945–1982*. Jackson: University of Mississippi Press, 1984. Theoretically oriented survey of the civil rights years.

McAdam, Doug. *Freedom Summer*. New York: Oxford University Press, 1988. Theoretical study of Freedom Summer and its legacy.

McCoy, Donald, and Richard T. Reuten. *Quest and Response: Minority Rights and the Truman Administration*. Lawrence: University of Kansas Press, 1973. Examination of civil rights policies of the Truman administration.

McGreevy, John T. *Parish Boundaries: The Catholic Encounter with Race in the Twentieth Century Urban North*. Chicago: University of Chicago Press, 1996. Provocative examination of white backlash against the civil rights movement.

McMillen, Neil R. *The Citizens' Council: Organized Resistance to the Second Reconstruction, 1954–64*. Urbana: University of Illinois Press, 1971. Detailed study of the White Citizens' Councils that resisted desegregation in the South.

McNeil, Genna Rae. *Groundwork: Charles Hamilton Houston and the Struggle for Civil Rights*. Philadelphia: University of Pennsylvania Press, 1983. Study of the lawyer who initiated the NAACP's fight against segregation.

Meier, August, and Elliot Rudwick. *CORE: A Study in the Civil Rights Movement, 1942–1968*. Urbana: University of Illinois Press, 1975. Definitive study of CORE written by activist-scholars.

Meier, August, Elliot Rudwick, and Francis L. Broderick. *Black Protest in the Twentieth Century*. 2nd ed. Indianapolis: Bobbs-Merrill, 1971. Documentary overview of modern African American struggle for equality.

Moody, Anne. *Coming of Age in Mississippi*. Garden City, N.Y.: Doubleday, 1968. Classic autobiographical account of the movement in Mississippi.

Morris, Aldon D. *The Origins of the Civil Rights Movement: Black Communities Organizing for Change*. New York: Free Press, 1984. Best work on the roots of the modern civil rights movement.

Norrell, Robert J. *Reaping the Whirlwind: The Civil Rights Movement in Tuskegee*. New York: Alfred A. Knopf, 1985. Rich case study of the civil rights movement in Booker T. Washington's community.

Oates, Stephen B. *Let the Trumpet Sound: The Life of Martin Luther King, Jr.* New York: Harper & Row, 1982. Well-written biography of King.

O'Reilly, Kenneth. *Racial Matters: The FBI's Secret File on Black America, 1960–1972*. New York: Free Press, 1992. Disturbing examination of FBI's efforts to undermine the civil rights movement.

Parker, Frank. *Black Votes Count: Political Empowerment in Mississippi after 1965*. Chapel Hill: University of North Carolina Press, 1990. Detailed study of the political impact of the civil rights movement in the Magnolia State.

Payne, Charles M. *I've Got the Light of Freedom: The Organizing Tradition and the Mississippi Freedom Struggle*. Berkeley: University of California Press, 1995. Valuable case study of the civil rights movement.

Raines, Howell. *My Soul Is Rested: The Story of the Civil Rights Movement in the Deep South*. New York: Penguin, 1983. Oral history of civil rights years by one of the journalists who covered and sympathized with it.

Ralph, James R., Jr. *Northern Protest: Martin Luther King, Jr., Chicago, and the Civil Rights Movement*. Cambridge, Mass.: Harvard University Press, 1993. Solid case study of the civil rights movement and King's efforts in the North.

Robinson, Armstead L., and Patricia Sullivan, eds. *New Directions in Civil Rights Studies*. Charlottesville: University Press of Virginia, 1991. Collection of essays on the civil rights movement written by both scholars and former activists.

Rowan, Carl T. *Dream Makers, Dream Breakers: The World of Justice Thurgood Marshall*. Boston: Little, Brown, 1993. Biography of Marshall written by one of America's best-known black journalists.

Seale, Bobby. *Seize the Time: The Story of the Black Panther Party and Huey P. Newton*. Autobiographical account of the Black Panther Party written by one of its co-founders.

Sellers, Cleveland, with Robert Terrell. *The River of No Return: The Autobiography of a Black Militant and the Life and Death of SNCC*. New York: William Morrow, 1973. First-person examination of SNCC, written by an activist who rose to the top leadership position within the organization in the late 1960s.

Silver, James W. *Mississippi: The Closed Society*. New York: Harcourt, Brace & World, 1963. Classic examination of race relations in Mississippi written by an Ole Miss history professor.

Sitkoff, Harvard. *A New Deal for Blacks: The Emergence of Civil Rights as a National Issue*. New York: Oxford University Press, 1978. Solid monograph on government's policies and their impact on African Americans during the 1930s.

———. *The Struggle for Black Equality*. Rev. ed. New York: Hill & Wang, 1993. One of the first surveys of the civil rights movement written by a professional historian.

Taylor, Clyde, ed. *Vietnam and Black America*. Garden City, N.Y.: Doubleday, 1973. Collection of essays and documents on blacks' views of the Vietnam War.

Van Deburg, William L. *New Day in Babylon: The Black Power Movement in American Culture, 1965–1975*. Overview of the origins, development, and legacy of black power.

Watters, Pat, and Reese Cleghorn. *Climbing Jacob's Ladder: The Arrival of Negroes in Southern Politics*. New York: Harcourt, Brace, 1967. Early study of the political impact of the civil rights movement.

Weisbrot, Robert. *Freedom Bound: A History of America's Civil Rights Movement*. New York: W. W. Norton, 1990. One of more recent overviews of the civil rights movement written by a professional historian.

Weiss, Nancy J. *Whitney Young, Jr., and the Struggle for Civil Rights*. Solid biography of National Urban League's longtime leader. Princeton, N.J.: Princeton University Press, 1989.

Whalen, Charles, and Barbara Whalen. *The Longest Debate: A Legislative History of the 1964 Civil Rights Act*. New York: Mentor, 1985. Study of the fight to pass the Civil Rights Act of 1964.

Whitfield, Stephen J. *A Death in the Delta: The Story of Emmett Till*. New York: Free Press, 1988. Study of the murder of Emmett Till written with an eye toward understanding the state of racism at the dawn of the civil rights movement.

Wicker, Tom. *A Time to Die*. New York: Quadrangle, 1975. Disturbing exploration of the riots and suppression of them at Attica Prison in New York.

Williams, Juan. *Eyes on the Prize: America's Civil Rights Years, 1954–1965*. New York: Viking, 1988. Well-produced companion guide to much-heralded television documentary series on the civil rights years.

Wilson, William Julius. *The Truly Disadvantaged: The Inner City, the Underclass, and Public Policy*. Chicago: University of Chicago Press, 1987. Brief and compelling study of race relations in the aftermath of the civil rights years.

Wolter, Raymond. *The Burden of Brown: Thirty Years of School Desegregation.* Knoxville: University of Tennessee Press, 1984. Exploration of the legacy of the *Brown* decision.

Woodward, C. Vann. *The Strange Career of Jim Crow.* Rev. ed. New York: Oxford University Press, 1974. Classic study of the era prior to the modern civil rights years.

Zinn, Howard. *SNCC: The New Abolitionists.* 2nd ed. Boston: Beacon Press, 1979. Study of SNCC written by a scholar-activist.

FILMS

A. Philip Randolph: For Jobs and Freedom. 1995. Produced by Dante J. Fames, WETA-TV, Washington, D.C. 86 minutes. California Newsreel. This sympathetic documentary traces the life of the dean of the civil rights movement, from Randolph's years as an organizer of the Brotherhood of Sleeping Car Porters to his leadership of the 1963 March on Washington.

Common Ground. 1990. Produced by Lynn Raynor. 190 minutes. Morimar. Based on J. Anthony Lukas's award-winning book, this made-for-network-TV film traces the school desegregation controversy in Boston during the 1960s and 1970s.

Eyes on the Prize: America's Civil Rights Years. 1987. Produced by Henry Hampton, Blackside, Inc. 6 hours. PBS Video. Highly effective documentary history of the civil rights movement, which combines contemporary film footage with interviews. Focuses on the period 1954–1965.

Eyes on the Prize II: America at the Racial Crossroads, 1965–1985. 1989. Produced by Henry Hampton, Blackside, Inc. 8 hours. PBS Video. Sequel to initial *Eyes on the Prize* documentary series, it traces the black freedom struggle from 1965 to the mid-1980s, with especially effective episodes on Malcolm X, the repression of Fred Hampton, and the Black Panther Party and Martin Luther King, Jr., in Chicago.

Four Little Girls. 1997. Produced by 40 Acres and Mule Filmworks. Directed by Spike Lee. HBO. Documentary on 1963 bombing of Birmingham, Alabama church in which four black girls were killed.

Freedom on My Mind. 1994. Produced by Connie Field and Marilyn Mulford. 105 minutes. Clarity Films. Documentary of Freedom Summer, including MFDP challenge at the Democratic convention in Atlantic City in 1964.

Fundi: The Story of Story of Ella Baker. 1981. Produced by Joanne Grant. 63 minutes. New Day Films. Documentary on prominent but little-known civil rights activist.

George C. Wallace: The Politics of Race. 1994. A & E Television Networks. 50 minutes. New Video Group. Straightforward biography of Governor George Wallace, chief antagonist of the civil rights movement.

Ghosts of Mississippi. 1996. Produced by Charles Newrith, Jeffrey Stott, and Frank Capra III. Directed by Rob Reiner. 131 minutes. Columbia Pictures. Story of Byron de la Beckwith, the man who assassinated civil rights leader Medgar Evers in 1963.

Goin' to Chicago. 1994. Produced by George King. 70 minutes. California Newsreel. Documentary examines the "great migration" of blacks from the rural South to Chicago during the middle decades of the twentieth century.

In the Heat of the Night. 1967. Directed by Norman Jewison. 107 minutes. Mirisch Corporation. Murder mystery set in a fictional Mississippi town, starring Rod Steiger as a white southern sheriff and Sidney Poitier as the northern black detective, with music by Quincy Jones.

The Long Walk Home. 1990. Produced by Howard W. Koch, Jr., and Dave Bell. 97 minutes. Fictional film examines the Montgomery bus boycott through the eyes of a southern white woman, played by Sissy Spacek, and her black maid, played by Whoopi Goldberg.

Malcolm X. 1992. Produced by Marvin Worth. Directed by Spike Lee. 201 minutes. Warner Brothers. Based on *The Autobiography of Malcolm X*, this Hollywood film, staring Denzel Washington, effectively captures persona of famous black radical.

Mississippi Burning. 1988. 125 minutes. Orion. Fictionalized account of the murder of three civil rights activists in Mississippi in 1964. Best if used in combination with critiques of film written by professional historians.

Mrs. Fannie Lou Hamer. 1979. Reissued 1992. Produced by Gil Noble, WABC-TV, New York City. 50 minutes. Making use of contemporary film footage and interviews, the documentary traces the life of this legendary civil rights activist from Mississippi.

Panther. 1995. Produced by Tim Beven, Lisa Chassin, and Mario Van Pebbles. Directed by Mario Van Pebbles. 123 minutes. Poly Gram Entertainment. Fictionalized account of the rise and repression of the Black Panther Party.

Simple Justice. 1993. Produced by Avon Kirkland, Yanna Kroyt Brandt, and Preston Holmes. 120 minutes. New Image Productions. PBS Video. Docudrama based on Richard Kluger's account of *Brown* v. *Board of Education of Topeka, Kansas*.

Thurgood Marshall: Portrait of an American Hero. 1985. 30 minutes. Columbia Video Productions. Drawing heavily on interviews, the documentary examines the life of NAACP's chief attorney and first African American Supreme Court Justice.

To Kill a Mockingbird. 1963. Produced by Alan J. Paluka. Directed by Robert Mulligan. 129 minutes (B&W). Universal. Based on Harper Lee's best selling novel, the film focuses on the defense of a Negro on trial for allegedly raping a white girl in a southern town. Stars Gregory Peck.

We Shall Overcome. 1989. Produced by Jim Brown, Ginger Brown, Harold Leventhal, and George Stoney. 58 minutes. The Ginger Group. California Newsreel. Insightful story of the evolution and use of the anthem of the civil rights movement.

ELECTRONIC RESOURCES
(CD-ROMS AND WEB SITES)

Birmingham Civil Rights Institute. Http://www.bham.net/bcri. Contains information on institute and links to other sites.

DRUM Civil Rights Page. Http://www.drum.ncat.edu/~carter/civil.html. History of civil rights movement developed by African American history group.

Martin Luther King, Jr. Http://www.seattletimes.com/mlk/index.html. Information and links on King developed by *Seattle Times* for students.

National Civil Rights Museum. Http://www.mecca.org/~crights/ncrm. Contains information on museum and links to other similar sites.

Webcorp: Voices of the Civil Rights Era. Http://www.webcorp.com/civilrights/index.htm. Audio clips of King, Malcolm X, and other prominent civil rights figures.

Index